STORMING
THE
STATEHOUSE

ALSO BY CELIA MORRIS

Fanny Wright: Rebel in America
[Celia Morris Eckhardt]

STORMING THE STATEHOUSE

Running for Governor with ANN RICHARDS and DIANNE FEINSTEIN

Celia Morris

CHARLES SCRIBNER'S SONS
New York
MAXWELL MACMILLAN CANADA
Toronto
MAXWELL MACMILLAN INTERNATIONAL
New York   Oxford   Singapore   Sydney

Charles Scribner's Sons	Maxwell Macmillan Canada, Inc.
Macmillan Publishing Company	1200 Eglinton Avenue East
866 Third Avenue	Suite 200
New York, NY 10022	Don Mills, Ontario M3C 3N1

Macmillan Publishing Company is part of the Maxwell Communication
Group of Companies.

Library of Congress Cataloging-in-Publication Data
Morris, Celia.
Storming the statehouse: running for governor with Ann Richards
and Dianne Feinstein/Celia Morris.
p.   cm.
Includes bibliographical references and index.
ISBN 0–684–19328–0
1. Richards, Ann, 1933–   . 2. Feinstein, Dianne, 1933–   .
3. Governors—Texas—Election. 4. Governors—California—Election.
5. Texas—Politics and government—1951–   6. California—Politics
and government—1951–   I. Title.
F391.4.R53M67 1992
976.4'063'092—dc20   91–25644
                                                                  CIP

Macmillan Books are available at special discounts for bulk purchases
for sales promotions, premiums, fund-raising, or educational use.
For details, contact:

Special Sales Director
Macmillan Publishing Company
866 Third Avenue
New York, NY 10022

10 9 8 7 6 5 4 3 2 1

Designed by Jack Meserole

Printed in the United States of America

THE SERENITY PRAYER*

God
Grant me
The serenity
To accept the things I cannot change,
The courage
To change the things I can,
And the wisdom
To know the difference.

*adapted from Reinhold Niebuhr, "Prayer," 1934

ACKNOWLEDGMENTS

I am happily indebted to the following people, who turned their friendship into a cornucopia of giving:

Mary Edsall, who came up with an idea and then pushed ferociously, and Tom Edsall, who offered piles of information; Betty Dooley, executive director of the Women's Research and Education Institute, who believed so quickly in the book that she took it on as an official project of WREI when it was little more than a paragraph; Mildred Wurf, who raises listening to the level of art and who was there from beginning to end—suggesting, challenging, encouraging; Heather Booth, Norman Dorsen, and Peter Edelman, who knew so many of those I needed to interview; my reporter friends Peggy Simpson, Margie Freivogel, Christy Bulkeley, and Kay Mills, who gave me lists of people to call, who insisted, and who were usually right; Tom Wicker, who picked up his telephone and opened some doors; Ray Farabee, who found the answers to unlikely questions, loaned me a car, and gave me a computer; Atelia Clarkson, without whose patience and computer genius my research might never have been translated into usable form; Thelma Hamrick, my beloved second mother, who sheltered me in Austin while enjoying the adventure and ignoring the mess; Bill and Diana Hobby, who gave me the key and loaned me the top floor of my favorite home in Houston; Ruth and Bill Bowers, who threw open my favorite home in San Antonio to me and to my friends; Virginia Whitten, who squirreled away a wealth of information; Congressman Henry Waxman, whose thoughtful letters introduced me to California politics; Catherine and Mario Pascale, my hosts in Santa Monica, whose wit, sense of wonder, and amazing cooking grounded my stay on the West Coast; Pat Nagle, who made her home in San Francisco into my refuge; John, Billie, and Mary Maguire, who pointed me in directions I needed to go; Pat Krause and J. Edward Weems, who faithfully clipped the newspapers; John Sullivan and Judy Godfrey, who gathered their friends to shed the necessary light; Shirley Schneider, who meticulously transcribed some of my most important tapes; Claire Foudraine, Shirley Garner, Sally Leach, and Roberta Weiner, who jollied me along while bringing their editorial judgment to bear on the manuscript; Dave McNeely, Joe Holley, and Judith Michaelson, who combed it for mistakes; Ellen Levine, my agent, who was steady and tenacious when it counted; Ave Bonar, who opened her treasure trove of photographs to me, and her agent, Ted Siff, who held my hand through the hard choices; Joy Smith at Scribners, who juggled her dual roles as booster and custodian to the manuscript with exemplary skill and grace; Barbara Grossman, my editor at Scribners, who is gifted with an infectious enthusiasm and a keen editorial eye; Martha Carroll, who spent four days looking for the right moment, and found it; and finally, my thanks go to the almost two hundred people, most of whom are listed in the Sources section, who gave me their time and their perspectives on two of the most important and exciting political races in the United States in 1990.

STORMING
THE
STATEHOUSE

CHAPTER 1

There is an energy that is a fusion of people who are focused and working together ... we worked with our hearts and not just with our heads.

—ANN RICHARDS

In midafternoon on November 7, 1990, Ann Richards stood in the middle of a big room in her campaign headquarters pinning an orchid corsage on consultant George Shipley. Looking as he does rather like Charles Laughton, Shipley is an unlikely candidate for orchids, but it was that kind of day. A big sign on butcher paper hanging from the ceiling carried the legend "Ann Richards Is Head of the Class," with childlike handprints in red and blue surrounding the words. Like the high-spirited *grande dame* she is, Liz Carpenter was waving her arms and calling to the fifty-odd people slowly assembling for a staff picture: "I'm going to tell you how to do it!"

Many in the room had scarcely been to bed since the night before, when Richards had faced a packed ballroom at the Hyatt Regency Hotel and, with thumbs triumphantly pointing upward and a grin the size of the state she comes from, acknowledged the roar that pronounced her governor-elect of Texas. Six months after her own polls had shown her twenty-four points behind Republican Clayton Williams and six weeks after every self-respecting analyst in Texas and the nation at large had written her off as dead in the political water, she stood exultant before a riotous crowd. Ann Richards was the first woman elected in her own right to be governor of the state that set the American standard for macho. Her triumph was not only a tribute to her courage, shrewdness, tenacity, and luck, but a cultural phenomenon tantamount to revolution.

The mood at Richards' headquarters ranged from high to manic as Liz Carpenter orchestrated the picture taking. "Focus on one person so you're not all looking off in different directions!" she wheedled

impatiently, while people whistled and called for the missing: "Juan!"
"Bill Cryer!" "Chula!" Finally, when the stragglers had been roped
in and the mix was right, Carpenter cried joyfully: "Smile now, and
don't wipe it off for eight years!" After the shutters clicked for the
last time and Carpenter headed toward the door and a long-deferred
rest, she threw over her shoulder a teasing comment to Richards: "I
heard about a woman who said she didn't have to go to the polls
because she'd heard you say he'd bought the election."

In the laughter that followed, Mary Beth Rogers, Richards' campaign manager, unobtrusively took the floor. Her capacity for stillness
and understatement is reminiscent of a Buddhist monk's, and her
face that day wore a disconcerting smile. "The last few weeks have
been fun," she began, though six weeks earlier she had confessed,
"I'd forgotten how awful campaigns can be." In fact, this one *had*
been awful for those who supported Ann Richards until two or
possibly three weeks before, but victory provides its own amnesia.

"If you all don't know it," Rogers said, "you did a fantastic job!
Not only the staff, but all the volunteers. It's been a hard campaign,
but we had a lot of fun. And the best thing about it is that we never
gave up, we never stopped pushing. We did everything we were
supposed to do, and we did it well!" The cheers began for Rogers,
and they went on a long, long time, until she controlled her emotion
long enough to say, "I don't think I've ever worked with a group of
people who've given more of their heart and soul" and called on Ann
Richards.

As the woman in the cerise suit and the now-famous halo of white
hair made her way forward, she wailed hoarsely and with mock self-
pity: "Am I supposed to talk? Oh, I've talked so much!" Someone
yelled, "Keep it short!" and the laughter ricocheted off the walls and
rattled the windows. But by the time she reached the front and turned
to face the people who had had her political life in their keeping for
so long, the room was once more still.

"Last night before I went to the hotel," she began, "I went to an
AA meeting. Most of you don't know that the reason those twelve-
step programs work is that they not only teach you how *not* to indulge
in whatever your addiction is, but they teach you a way of life. And
that way of life is to live one day at a time.

"I truly did that in this campaign. Every day, when I was really tired, and I got up and thought, 'My bones are weary and I can't go again!' I thought, 'But I don't have to go more than a day!' And I did that, and then it was done.

"But the other thing that this program teaches us is that we must let go and let God. . . . And in a sense. . . ." For a few seconds, while all attention in the room was riveted on her, she fought back tears until she could continue: "In a sense, *you are God to me.*"

She leaned forward, speaking urgently: "Do you understand that? That the dynamics put together by a group of people working intensely and cohesively together—there is nothing more omnipotent or powerful than that. So despite the times when I might crawl your back—and I know there were some of those. . . ." The tension in the room released in cascading laughter. "The truth of the matter is that for me, I *did* let go and let God! We won this race because of you, not because of me. We were a part of the whole."

Virginia Whitten called out truculently, "I dispute that!" and laughter lightened the air as Richards continued: "I make these jokes at roasts, and I talk about a fifty-cent word called 'synergism,' which means 'greater than the sum of its parts.' . . . But it is a very good word—synergism—for you to remember. Because that's what transpired here: the force of this campaign became greater than each of us could ever have been individually. There is an energy that is a fusion of people who are focused and working together, and the reason, I think, that it all worked so well is that we worked with our hearts and not just with our heads.

"And we had a truly fantastic person who kept us on course. That is because Mary Beth had a little chart, and some days I wanted to *strangle* her with it because my priority was not on her list that day. But that's what kept us on course. . . . We couldn't panic her. . . .

"What transpired here in this campaign will transpire in the governor's office with the same energy and the same dynamic and the same focus and the same planning and the same success. And the recipients of all that energy and work will be the people of Texas, who need us. *Who need us very badly.*"

She paused dramatically. By this time almost everyone in the room was in tears. Dan Richards and his sister Ellen, who were sitting on the floor, were crying together. Snuffles and little gasps came from all around as their mother took a few steps backward, crossed her arms, bent her head, and began again in a lower voice:

"I am—for me—humbled. As you know, humility has not always been my long suit." Again laughter rose and fell and rose again. "But I know how I got here." She repeated and underscored it: "*I know how I got here*, [and] you dance with them that brung you! . . .

"I've been thrilled that we had a lot of young people involved in this campaign. Because what you learned here you cannot buy. You cannot buy it with money. You cannot get it in college. You can only learn it through experience. . . .

"And I know that what we began here will not end with me, or my life, or the governorship, because your lives will go on, and you will do great things, and you will nurture other young people along to do great things. And in doing so, our having lived and done this campaign is even more important than the winning of it. . . .

"It's been a really thrilling time. It's been hard. It's been really hard. But I think none of us would have traded it for anything. I love you all."

As the applause rose and the tears fell shamelessly, she bent and fished around in a big cardboard crate behind her and then, with that big grin, she turned back sharply to hold up the first of many shiny blue jackets with "Ann Richards/Governor" printed boldly across the back.

Half a continent away, at San Francisco's Fairmont Hotel, Dianne Feinstein was bidding her campaign staff farewell after conceding the nation's first-ranked political prize: she had fallen short in the grueling race for governor of California by 3.46 percent of the vote. With a hoofer's resilience, she told her husband, Richard Blum, "The good news is we raised the money; the bad news is we lost!"

To her public she reflected on the "dramatic change in California from the primary to November." In the primary, most propositions and ballot measures had passed: "There was a kind of enthusiasm to move the state on. In November, you saw virtually everything lose." Perhaps, she added, this result indicated "people's concern about the economy." Whatever the cause, she was undaunted: "My life has been public service. It is what I want to do [and] what I intend to do, one way or another."

Her campaign organization had been far more experienced and professional than Ann Richards'. Its manager, Bill Carrick, had worked in seventeen campaigns and had run Richard Gephardt's ambitious 1988 race for the presidency. Carrick estimated that he, John Plaxco, her primary fund-raiser, and Hank Morris, who handled the media, had eighty years' worth of campaign experience between them. Carrick took over in the fall of 1989, when Feinstein was so far down in the polls in her Democratic primary race against Attorney General John Van de Kamp that she had considered withdrawing. After that, the crises that had plagued her staff ended and the campaign team worked with enviable ease and cohesiveness. For all that, as *New York Times* columnist Tom Wicker says, politics is about winning, and Feinstein had lost.

Nevertheless, from a political base of one medium-sized city, in her first statewide campaign, Dianne Feinstein had come within 266,700 votes out of 7.3 million cast of beating an incumbent United States senator who was running his fourth statewide campaign and who had learned from a disastrous 1978 try for governor not to make mistakes. Beverly Thomas, who ran Kathleen Brown's winning race for state treasurer, put Feinstein's central problem succinctly: "Every time Pete Wilson runs, he has more money than God, and he's running in '90 because the stakes were so incredibly high. They picked their strongest, best Republican candidate who's been collecting people and constituencies for twenty-five years! He's got all the money in the Republican party behind him and a sitting president." Furthermore, since the Roosevelt era, California had given its electoral votes to only one Democratic presidential candidate—Lyndon Johnson in 1964—and in the entire twentieth century has had only three Democratic governors—two of them Edmund G. Browns—Pat and Jerry.

Feinstein had been given scant chance to win even the Democratic nomination for governor. As they say in California, the water is in the north and the votes are in the south. Feinstein is from the north, and her primary opponent, John Van de Kamp, is from Los Angeles. Although in 1984 Walter Mondale had considered Feinstein seriously

as his vice-presidential running mate, she had no statewide network
of support, while Van de Kamp was a longtime fixture in the Democratic political establishment and 1990 was conceded to be his year.
The state convention had endorsed him for governor and booed
Feinstein when she spoke from the podium in favor of capital punishment. Still, she beat him in the Democratic primary with a 13
percent margin.

The day after losing the 1990 gubernatorial election, then, Dianne
Feinstein, however disappointed, had reason to be both proud and
optimistic. She had built a network of support throughout the state.
She had assembled a first-rate campaign team that had performed
with finesse. She had come close to winning in one of the most
merciless ordeals in American politics.

Two days later, Senator Alan Cranston made his long-awaited
announcement that he would not run for reelection. This meant that
in 1992, for the first time since 1849, both of California's United
States Senate seats would be up for grabs. And no one who had paid
attention to Dianne Feinstein's political career can have been surprised when, on January 13, 1991, she announced that she was
seriously considering running for the Senate seat Pete Wilson had
vacated.

In 1990, Ann Richards and Dianne Feinstein were both fifty-
seven years old, and though that bald fact made them women of a
certain generation, the similarities might seem to end there. One was
born to wealth in a city so bright and cosmopolitan it ranks third
after Paris and London as the city tourists most want to visit. The
other was born poor near Waco, Texas—a place so drab that Willie
Nelson, who was brought up close by, said that when he got too old
to have any fun, he thought he might move back to Waco. The former
had a grandfather who was a Polish Jew and a Christian grandmother
who fled Russia in 1917 at the onset of the revolution. The latter
has a daddy born in the town of Bugtussle and a mama who comes,
she swears, from a community called Hogjaw. For those who believe
that places shape people, it would seem unlikely that Ann Richards
and Dianne Feinstein could even speak the same language.

For generations of Americans, the city of St. Francis has defined
the romantic, tumbling from its hills down to a bay as heart-stirring

as the Bay of Naples—Alcatraz notwithstanding. In the 1950s, the makers of a pricey champagne ran a multi-million-dollar advertising campaign featuring a sparkling night view of the city taken from above, along with the single line, "Tonight may be the night!" Eighteen different languages are spoken in San Francisco. Golden Gate Park, like the Tuileries, is known throughout the world. The city's cultural life runs the gamut from rambling North Beach bookstores and Chinese parades to periodic visits by the Bolshoi and the New York City Ballet. And the San Francisco Opera House is the grandest on the North American continent.

So dismal is Waco, by contrast, that it is known primarily as the biggest city on Route 35 between Austin and Dallas and the home of Baylor University, the largest Baptist institution of its kind in the country. Perhaps the most notable event in its history occurred in 1898, when a feisty newspaper editor known as Brann the Iconoclast, who had attacked small-mindedness and hypocrisy, along with the manifold sins of the church in general and Baylor University in particular, was shot in the back. As recently as fifteen years ago, a Baylor honor student was "asked to leave" for organizing a successful boycott against mandatory chapel attendance. Midnight curfew is still in effect on week nights in the dorms. A leading citizen told a speaker in Austin who quoted a line from Larry McMurtry with the word "cunnilingus" that she could never give that speech in Waco. And a well-known political organizer insists on pronouncing the city's name to sound like "wacky" and "tacky."

Their divergent origins, of course, shaped both Ann Richards and Dianne Feinstein. An admirer said of Richards that she has some Elvis in her: she is a cutup, a show-off—she had "a great time" at the 1988 Democratic National Convention mocking the incumbent vice-president before the eyes of the world and says that for all the grief it caused her, she would love to do it again. Another confidant, however, observed shrewdly that despite her flamboyant public image, she remains an anxious only child, born to demanding parents, who grew up during the Depression.

Richards' fervent liberalism has been publicly tempered by the conservative realities of Texas in the 1990s, and she learned very early not to take on battles she could not win: Don Quixote has never been her model. Although she endorsed capital punishment with what many felt to be marked reluctance, she was invariably in top form among plain people, and she lambasted her Republican opponent, Clayton Williams, on the grounds that a man who could write a $6 million personal check to his own campaign could not possibly understand the real folks of Texas. All through the fall, she ended her speeches with a ringing promise: "In January, we are all gonna gather on the Congress Avenue bridge, and we are going to link arms, and we're gonna march up Congress Avenue, and we're gonna take back the Capitol for the People of Texas!"

Dianne Feinstein, by contrast, is a lady who wears elegantly tailored suits and silk blouses with a trademark bow and lives in the Presidio Terrace mansion she admired when growing up in a spacious home across the street. Her bearing is regal—she is almost six feet tall in high-heeled pumps—and she makes no apologies for the fact that in 1989, she and her husband, Richard Blum, had a combined income of over $7 million. Her style is not wholly free from noblesse oblige, and she has often been put down as a "goody-goody" or a League of Women Voters politician. In her early years on San Francisco's Board of Supervisors, she led a campaign against porno theaters and adult bookstores, and though she gamely donned jeans during the 1990 gubernatorial race to tour the Central Valley, she looked faintly ridiculous.

Feinstein's political instincts are moderate, and when she endorsed capital punishment, she convinced most people that she meant it. A canny observer called her a police groupie, and she insisted throughout her campaign that she would be tougher on crime and criminals than her Republican opponent, Senator Pete Wilson. Since she and her husband had loaned her campaign $3 million, her populist rhetoric did not ring quite true, even to those who did not believe she used it cynically.

But for all their differences, Ann Richards and Dianne Feinstein have a great deal in common, largely because both are women breaking barriers in a world designed and ruled by men. In the 1990 elections, when people all over the country were convinced that those responsible for government had made a mess of things, they had a special opportunity.

Until late October, Congress remained in session wrangling over the budget, and many disgusted voters found it incredible that elected officials should do their jobs so ineptly. Anti-government sentiment took the form of term-limitation propositions in several states, most notably in California, and this gave Richards and Feinstein a chance to present themselves as obviously different from the norm and there-fore a bright hope in a drab world.

The news for women candidates was mixed, of course, as it in-variably is: to be a woman is to be in a whole passel of double binds. Women are convinced they have to be twice as smart and hard-working as men to compete successfully. Two decades ago, Gloria Steinem remarked that women will have "made it" when a mediocre woman moves up in her chosen profession as quickly and effortlessly as a mediocre man.

Ann Richards and Dianne Feinstein had both achieved firsts—Richards, the first woman to be elected statewide in Texas in fifty years, and Feinstein, the first woman mayor of San Francisco. As Feinstein put it, "The first anything in a situation is put through a whole host of litmus tests. . . . Once you get there, your back is always against the wall. . . . There's always, I feel, this testing of me, this testing, testing, testing." Men with their drive and talent would surely have long since gone on to higher office, but the public often expected more of these two women than of their opponents.

The good news, then, for women candidates in 1990 was that since women had been historically excluded from a process that seemed to be unraveling, they could offer themselves as uniquely qualified to clean up the mess. Poll results show that voters perceive women as more honest and caring than men, and when the foremost issues in the minds of the electorate are education and health care, they are more likely to trust women to choose the right solutions.

The bad news for women candidates was that they could not run convincingly against government, even if they wanted to, because they had to have experience to get where they were in the first place. No matter how rich and flamboyant she was, no woman as ignorant of government as Clayton Williams, the Republican nominee for governor of Texas, could have been taken seriously as a candidate.

Most women did not want to run against government, however—certainly Ann Richards and Dianne Feinstein did not—because they had seen the unique power that government has to solve problems people cannot solve on their own. Reverend Cecil Williams of San Francisco's Glide Memorial Church tells a story about Feinstein that might as easily be about Richards: "One night she said to us: 'Do you know that this is a very powerful state? And do you know that if the right person with the right goals and the right commitment were to serve as governor, it can really touch people from all walks of life like they're not being touched?' She knows now that she can take the structures of society and make something happen. She wants to be able to say, 'I'm going to do this, and you can't stop me!' "

For many politicians, such language can be blinding, even to themselves. What they really mean is: "I want the power. I want to get it, and keep it, and make sure nobody else gets it." Whether some women candidates mean something different altogether remains to be seen, and even when they win the necessary power, they may not be able to use it as they want.

But more and more often, the electorate is turning to women candidates to "give us," as Reverend Williams puts it, "a whole new understanding of justice, and righteousness, and mercy." This, in fact, is at the core of their appeal, and if such a hope seems akin to the hope that springs eternal in the human breast, it is no less powerful for all that.

According to pollsters like Harrison Hickman, who worked for Richards, the typical woman candidate does better with suburban voters and with women—particularly those who work outside the home. Her biggest problem is likely to lie with older women. For candidates like Ann Richards and Dianne Feinstein, "older women" are those of their own generation and beyond who were brought up to believe that women should stay at home. Even older women who like a candidate may be dubious about voting for her for governor. On top of that, since suburban voters are more likely than not to be Republicans, Richards and Feinstein, as Democrats, have to mute or moderate their partisan identification in order to win them.

Hickman says the other group that resists a woman candidate is made up of younger men. After two decades during which the rigid stereotypes that prescribed who men and women should be have been assaulted more relentlessly than ever before in world history, today's young men remain more macho than their elders. Hickman puts the blame on hormones, which is to say, on young men's place in the life cycle. They turn their backs on their mothers to prove they are grown-up men. They compete with women for jobs, for attention, for advancement. Sexuality leaves them wary and baffled. But as the life cycle progresses, many come to like women more and to appreciate their mates and sisters—and even their mothers. They develop higher ambitions for their daughters than their wives, whom most want to be devoted solely to their own well-being.

Conservative attitudes that look dimly on women in high office are stronger in rural areas and towns. They are also stronger among minority groups who live for the most part to themselves, and they diminish as those minorities blend into mainstream American society. Most data about the way Hispanics vote, for instance, come from Hispanic precincts, rather than from Hispanics generically.

But since women candidates have been excluded from politics dominated by white men, Richards and Feinstein had a special appeal to minorities—especially minority women. Both had been drawn to the cause of civil rights and knew that private solutions are inadequate: public policy alone could determine whether large numbers of people would acquire the education and skills they needed to live decently. Contempt for government is a luxury neither women nor minorities can afford.

Both Richards and Feinstein ran as leaders who could resolve conflicts more effectively than they had been resolved in the past. Richards talked about how important it was not to draw lines in the sand that pitted people against each other. Feinstein spoke of getting quarreling groups together in the same room, knocking some heads, and working through to agreement. Both focused on process and believed that when the time came to master substance, they would be ready. Although both are commonly described as quick studies, both were nevertheless accused of not knowing enough.

And even in a state with a celebrated history of political brawling, Ann Richards was held to a higher standard than her opponents. As Lieutenant Governor Bill Hobby pointed out, "Everybody has much higher expectations of Ann. Nobody, particularly the press, held [her primary opponent, Attorney General Jim] Mattox to the same stan-

dards. She's a better person than Mattox. Certainly Claytie Williams'
most ardent advocate wouldn't accuse him of knowing anything
about the issues in the campaign, but they expect Ann to."

Although neither Richards nor Feinstein attacked her opponent
until he attacked her, both were then accused of acting like mere
politicians. And because they had chosen to run for two of the most
important offices in the country, they would be subjected to more
sustained scrutiny than any political woman since Geraldine Ferraro
ran as the vice-presidential nominee on the 1984 Democratic ticket.

The offices they sought were unusually important because their
states are huge and 1990 marked the end of one decade and the
beginning of another. Every ten years the census is taken and then
used to determine how representation in the United States Congress
must be readjusted. Since the number of members in the House of
Representatives remains constant at 435, each ten years, on the basis
of population shifts, the census figures mandate which states will lose
and which will gain power in the nation's most democratic legislative
body. The state legislatures and the governors then redraw the lines
for both congressional and state legislative districts, and these can
determine which party will dominate during the next decade.

Over the course of the 1980s, the United States population continued to shift significantly from the industrial Northeast to the Sun-
belt, and the states that would gain the most new seats in Congress
were California, Florida, and Texas. The last had grown by more
than 18 percent to over 17 million people and therefore would gain
three new congressional seats. California had grown by almost 24
percent to nearly 30 million people and would gain seven new seats,
giving its fifty-two-member delegation almost 12 percent of the House
of Representatives.

During that decade, furthermore, the acrimony between the two
political parties ballooned, the advent of Ronald Reagan accentuating
their ideological differences more sharply than at any time since the
Great Depression. The Republican party had been dominated by its
conservative wing, while repeated electoral defeat on the presidential
level had thrown the Democratic party into even more than its usual
disarray. The two parties were primed for battle royal over the coming rearrangements of power.

The genius who had demonstrated to an astonished audience how the drawing of district lines could shape the political future was a California congressman, a radical named Phillip Burton of San Francisco. Largely because of Burton and his "Philmandering" of legislative district lines during the 1960, 1970, and 1980 reapportionments, the California delegation to Congress, like the state senate and the state assembly, remained overwhelmingly Democratic even though the state has almost as many registered Republican voters.

In 1981, for instance, Phil Burton increased the Democratic edge in the California delegation from 22–21 to 28–17, gerrymandering a district for his brother John that snaked through the Democratic portions of four counties and creating boundary lines so improbable that Phil called it "my contribution to modern art." The Republicans had spent years in court fighting his wizardry but to little avail because the law had been followed to the letter, districts were more nearly equal than in the past, and minorities had been given a greater voice.

At Phil Burton's memorial service in Golden Gate Park in 1983, Willie Brown, the powerful Speaker of the California assembly and a protégé of Burton's, celebrated the flair of the master by remembering a particular district in southern California. "There was no way to make that into a Democratic district," Brown said emphatically. "But Phil Burton did it. And that's when I found out you could count ships at sea."

If Burton was Machiavellian, he was also incorruptible: a protector of the environment, a crusader for workers' rights, a defender of the aging, a man who raged at a reporter, *I like people whose balls roar when they see injustice!"* Along with using his legerdemain to win liberal battles that nobody else thought had a chance, in 1974 he had spearheaded the most important House reforms of the twentieth century. To his admirers, Phil Burton was an avenging angel; to his critics, the devil incarnate. To anyone who cared about politics, he set an example that practitioners ignored at their peril. And in 1990, his disciples fixed hawklike eyes on California and Texas to discover the material they would have to work with.

Neither Ann Richards nor Dianne Feinstein ran, like Phil Burton, as a tribune of the people, and if they had, they almost surely would have doomed themselves to defeat. Instead, their goals were more understated—some would say obscured. They ran as women who stood for change, competence, and a more inclusive society.

As Richards says in the preface to her autobiography, *Straight from the Heart*, civil rights is the thread that has run through her political life since 1958, when Henry Gonzalez ran for governor and the only place that would welcome the racially and ethnically mixed group she joined to work on his campaign was the local NAACP headquarters. At Scholz's Beer Garden in Austin in the middle 1970s, she left a racist east Texas judge slack-jawed when, after he visibly shuddered while shaking hands with a black man named Charlie Miles, she smiled and introduced herself as Mrs. Miles.

Dianne Feinstein was often at her most engaging and most natural with blacks. In the early 1960s, she had caught the attention of Willie Brown, who would become a crucial ally in her first race for supervisor, when she strapped her baby daughter, Katherine, into a stroller and joined a demonstration protesting his exclusion as a black man from a fashionable residential area in San Francisco.

But women like Ann Richards and Dianne Feinstein had come of age in a culture that expected them to be wives, mothers, and, at most, civic volunteers. They were brought up with an ethic of service to others, and as they transformed the old volunteer approach into a highly professional commitment, they and women like them extended that ethic outward to the larger community. When Richards said to her campaign workers the day after her victory that the people of Texas needed them—indeed, needed them "very badly"—she was speaking the language of her generation of women.

Both were pro-choice, and in 1990, the political energies of the organized women's movement, as well as hundreds of thousands of women who did not formally identify with it, were focused on legal abortion. Until 1973 and the United States Supreme Court's decision in *Roe* v. *Wade*, abortion had remained illegal in most states. After *Roe*, women had taken freedom of choice for granted until 1989, when the Supreme Court had handed down a decision in the *Webster* case that seemed to threaten it. Women who had seldom bothered to vote before were swept up in a wave of political enthusiasm, and women in Texas and California rallied to the cause of a woman running for governor with a zeal unprecedented in American politics.

*   *   *

It takes a hardy soul, male or female, to run for office. Not only is politics commonly a brutal and brutalizing affair, but the higher the office, the more likely this is to be true. And by the end of the twentieth century, most of the problems a politician faces are real and intractable because there is simply too little money at every level of government to deal adequately with too many problems.

By 1990, the problems were arguably worst at the state level because, beginning with Jimmy Carter and accelerating through the Reagan administration, the federal government had shifted a heavy financial burden to states and cities by cutting or eliminating federal grants for housing, education, mass transit, and public works. At the same time, a growing body of federal rules and regulations had imposed burdens on states that cost a great deal of money. Since every state but Vermont is legally bound to operate with a balanced budget, the governors and legislatures found themselves hemmed in by rocks and hard places. Henry Aaron, director of economic studies at the Brookings Institution in Washington, D.C., said that not since the Great Depression had there been such anguish in states "facing an unprecedented cutback in service or significant increases in taxes."

But the terms of the political dialogue remained confusing. During the 1980s, while the United States went from being the world's largest creditor nation to the world's largest debtor nation, the word commonly used to describe the decade's movement was "progress." By 1990, the poorest 20 percent of the American people had lost 11 percent of their real income, while the top 20 percent made 19 percent more than they had ten years earlier, the top 10 percent made 29 percent more, and the top 2 percent made 41 percent more still. The top fifth of the American population now has more than twelve times the income of the bottom fifth. As populist historian Lawrence Goodwyn puts it, the sanctioned term to describe the decade that witnessed the most massive transfer of income in American history from the poorest citizens to the richest is "a time of prosperity."

A politician's money was likely to come from people who had grown richer; a Democrat's votes were likely to come from people who had gotten poorer. So the problem of framing the issues was even tougher than usual.

Framing the issues, in fact, is part of a process as demanding as governing itself—and one that requires very different gifts and skills. The great irony of life in an age dominated by television is that those who might be superb at governing are often inept at running for office, and those who are fine media candidates are too often facile and ignorant. And for women brought up in an era when the culture expected them to stand slightly behind and to one side of a man, the psychological feats involved are complex and formidable. They have to wheel and deal in a world of big-time campaign operatives dominated by men who talk like jocks and whose style is combative. "The consultants use that 'ya gotta take 'em out' vocabulary," says former Sacramento staffer Jane V. Wellman. "I think of one woman associated with [Lieutenant Governor] Leo McCarthy who talks that talk and walks that walk, but she's the only one."

In 1988, for instance, when Richard Gephardt took on Senator Albert Gore in the fight for the Democratic presidential nomination, the St. Louis Post-Dispatch reported that Gephardt's campaign manager, Bill Carrick, had been so abrasive and confrontational that he'd told a reporter that he hated Gore: "I hate all of them! I think they're the phoniest two-bit bastards that ever came down the pike." Carrick, who would later run Dianne Feinstein's campaign for governor, had also targeted Michael Dukakis by using an ad implying that Dukakis was an effete snob—an ad he thought was "a killer." In a 1990 campaign postmortem, he said of the opposing campaign, "They had to throw the bomb, they had to go long."

Not only is the style abrasive, but the process itself is alienating in the clinical sense. As Wellman says, "In order to participate in big-time politics, you have to separate yourself from your ego . . . to be a public persona and to watch yourself as a caricature, as an object." Especially in huge states like Texas and California, where candidates running statewide have to condense themselves into sound bites and thirty-second television spots, each has to "devolve from a complex, centered individual into something one- or two-dimensional." Apart from anything else, that ability to separate oneself from a public persona is a necessary protective device. Ann Richards, for instance, warned her children that by the time her opponents got through with her, they would not recognize their mother.

The electoral process also puts a premium on short-term solutions. Voters, for instance, do not cotton to politicians who might raise taxes, and any politician who really believes that our current set of problems can be solved without raising taxes is likely also to believe in the tooth fairy. So the process tends to reward people who can either lie to themselves or persuade voters that fantasy is reality.

The extravagant cost of modern campaigns leaves a politician in another double bind, inescapably indebted to contributors who do not give her money merely because they like the style of her hair or the lilt in her voice. Referring to lobbyists, Jesse Unruh, Speaker of the California assembly in the 1960s, described a good politician as a guy who could take their money, drink their whiskey, eat their steaks, fuck their women, and vote against them. His quip inadvertently reveals the place of women in traditional politics, and therefore the psychic obstacles women politicians have to scale. But the problem for anyone is even worse now than in Unruh's time because running for office and staying there costs more. By 1990, big-time politicians were always running and campaigns never ended.

Those who ignore the big donors run the risk of losing their jobs; those who pay attention risk being corrupted; and most politicians are more likely to run the latter risk. Former California Governor Edmund G. (Pat) Brown admits: "If a person gave me $10,000, he'd have a greater opportunity to talk to me on the telephone than somebody who just voted for me."

Finally, in big states like Texas and California, a politician has to meet hundreds of thousands of people, many of whom will expect her to remember not only their names and faces but a mother who has Alzheimer's and a mate who lost his job at the refinery six months earlier. The better she is at it, the more they will expect of her. Ann Richards, for instance, is very good at it, and people repeatedly called her headquarters with hurt feelings, saying, "Ann is one of my best friends, and she didn't notice me."

So big-time politics means spending months and even years tired, hurt, and hungry—rocketing between adulation and enmity—with a face that freezes and feet that swell and hands that crack from thousands of receiving lines and millions of greetings. And the higher the office, the more likely a candidate is to be narcissistic, thin-skinned, and impossible. "All politicians are alligators," said the political director of a major union who has worked with candidates for more than thirty years. Then he added wistfully, "Of course, I hold their coats while they go out and do the fighting."

Bill Zimmerman, a campaign consultant who lives in California but has worked in Texas, explained why he would never run for office: "Eighty percent of the time you spend asking people for money. The rest of the time you're asking people to vote for you because you're the best candidate in the field. If you're not a megalomaniac, you don't make it in either arena. A career politician *has* to be a megalomaniac: most sane, normal people aren't willing to do the kinds of things you have to do to get elected to a statewide office in a place like Texas." A man close to the Richards campaign said: "All candidates are crazy! They wouldn't be candidates unless they were crazy!" Hadley Roff, Feinstein's longtime chief of staff, suggested a less pejorative phrase: "very determined."

Furthermore, people with powerful egos who are playing for high stakes under the intense pressures of a campaign are sometimes at their worst. Willie Brown called Dianne Feinstein the most decent person he knew, and Ann Richards' former husband used the same word for her. Nevertheless, in the course of the 1990 campaign, both were described as abusive, and many women politicians *are* abusive. The assumption that women are more sensitive and caring to the people around them than the typical male politician has been shattered too often to leave any grounds for illusion. (A woman who worked for Bella Abzug subsequently got a job with the Capitol Police and claimed it was a better and safer job than working for Abzug.)

Richards and Feinstein could also be unusually thoughtful. And at least in part because the people working for them thought they demanded at least as much of themselves as they did of others, most stuck it out, no matter how wounded.

For reasons that have to do with class, temperament, and personal history, Dianne Feinstein lived the first twenty years of her adult life more unconventionally, for a woman of her generation, than Ann Richards did. More than anything, this may be why women found it harder to identify with her.

After graduating from Stanford University, Dianne Goldman got a Coro fellowship to study public policy and for a year worked in the district attorney's office.* Governor Pat Brown subsequently appointed her to the state board that deals with prison terms and paroles for women—she had been in school with one of Brown's daughters and had caught his eye—and over a period of more than five years she sat on five thousand parole hearings. Both assignments taught her about the criminal justice system, and her ability to convince voters that she was by no means "soft on crime" kept her in the governor's race.

When Goldman was twenty-two, she eloped with Jack Berman, now a superior court judge in San Francisco, but ended that marriage after less than three years and, with her nine-month-old daughter, Katherine, started over. Claiming that Berman wanted to keep her barefoot and pregnant, she lets it be known that she does not want to be in the same room with her former husband, and since their circles of friends and acquaintances overlap, this unresolved bitterness on her part has caused more than one awkward moment. A friend of Berman's reported that she refused to come to her daughter Katherine's wedding if her father were invited, and the force of her anger after more than three decades suggests that Berman represents a trap she found terrifying.

By Feinstein's own account, that trap was marriage. When she says of her first husband's expectations, "I could not be that kind of wife," she dismisses the kind of marriage that Ann Richards and most women of their generation had.

In 1962, Feinstein married the man whose name she has kept, Bertram Feinstein, who was a top neurosurgeon, a colleague of her father's, and twenty years older than she. He adopted her daughter, reestablished her in the world from which she had come, provided for her very comfortably, and, according to Henry Berman, her campaign treasurer, left her alone: "Doctors are busy seven days a week.

---

*Coro is a nonprofit, nonpartisan educational foundation that was founded in 1942 in San Francisco and now has centers in Los Angeles, New York City, and St. Louis as well. Its primary purpose is to train the public policy leaders of the future. Joyce Ream, who has run Coro programs and serves on the board of directors, explains its importance in the state where it began: "For a number of California people, Coro is a common element of political experience. When [Speaker] Jesse Unruh decided to professionalize the California assembly and provide for full-time committee consultants, he hired something like thirty-five Coro graduates." In its influence within California, Coro resembles the Berkeley School of Public Policy.

That was great because Dianne was never cut out to be a house-wife. . . . She can't even boil water. So she created a life for herself in politics."

For several years after she left the women's parole board, Feinstein stayed at home to be a wife and mother, but in 1969, ten years after her divorce, she won election to San Francisco's Board of Supervisors. By garnering more votes than any other candidate, she automatically became president of the board, and it was as president that she succeeded Mayor George Moscone when he was murdered nine years later.

For all her temporary setbacks, then, Dianne Feinstein has pro-ceeded steadily from intern to appointee to elected officeholder and finally, in 1990, to the most ambitious campaign in the country. Her second and third husbands have been wholly supportive, and her daughter, Katherine, has had to trim her own hopes and needs to the rigors of her mother's life. Doing so has not always been easy.

Katherine Feinstein told a reporter she had hated the fact that her mother didn't pick her up after school like other mothers and was embarrassed that hers seemed to be the only parents who were divorced. Nevertheless, she is appealing and capable enough to belie the common fears for children of working mothers.

A lawyer in her early thirties who looks like Dianne, she took a leave of absence to work in the campaign, and onlookers commented on the ease with which she spoke and the good cheer she radiated. A woman who has known Katherine since childhood noticed that she has begun to dress like her mother and to use the same gestures, and during the campaign, while they traveled together and shared hotel rooms, they became real friends.

Feinstein's experience, then, is fundamentally different from Rich-ards': when she was in her middle twenties, she established herself irrevocably as the person at the center of her own life. David Richards and their four children were at the center of Ann Richards' life until she was well into her forties.

Richards' experience was as full as Feinstein's but much more unconventional for a politician. "I did what you do," she says. "I cleaned and cooked and sewed and took care of my family." Still, her training for politics began early, when Ann Willis represented Waco High School at Girls' State, the annual gathering of talented high school students who role-play state government. There she met Lieutenant Governor Allan Shivers, and when she graduated to the peak experience of Girls' Nation in Washington, D.C., she got to walk through the Rose Garden and shake hands with President Harry Truman.

Not only did she learn on those occasions how to run elections and pass bills, but she met vibrant new people who made the standard hopes of Waco girls seem pallid. Ann Willis not only loved to talk, but she delighted in being rewarded for it, and early in her teens she had learned to work a room. With "so much energy that sitting still was painful," she began unconsciously to create the network of people who would become her political mainstays. As Virginia Whitten, who has known her for more than thirty years, puts it, people do not forget Ann, and she seldom forgets them.

David Richards, whom she married when they were both nineteen, was intensely interested in politics, and when he was in law school at the University of Texas, they began to learn its lessons the way most people of their generation in Austin did: by sitting around the tables at Scholz's Beer Garden and talking until somebody turned out the lights. David became the president and Ann the parliamentarian of the University of Texas branch of the Young Democrats, which was dead earnest about itself, and they went to its state conventions and fought there for what they believed in as hard as if the outcome might affect the welfare of the polity. Ann joined the group that called itself the Law Wives, which met at the Driskill Hotel to play bridge "like crazy, for such prizes as corn-on-the-cob holders," and she became, in due time, the group's president.

After the first of their four children was born in 1957, and for more than two decades, the pattern was set: Ann would follow David, but the pair would rapidly become the center of whatever world they lived in, with Ann invariably starting some group or project on her own. Though 90 percent of her time went to her family, she "learned more about management from running a household" than from any other single occupation, and she later wrote, "I was involved in whatever political opportunities I could find, [within] the constraints of raising a family."

In 1962 in Dallas, for instance, where David joined the principal labor law firm in the state, Ann and her friends discovered that the party organization was controlled by men who looked upon women "as little more than machine parts," and so they created the North Dallas Democratic Women to do "something substantive." Since the party apparatus was in the hands of men who not only voted but campaigned for Republican presidential candidates, the North Dallas Democratic Women took it upon themselves to identify loyalist Democrats. "We kept a card file upstairs in my house," she says, "where we were literally trying to get the names of every Democrat on three-by-five cards because we did not have access to any lists or files or organization."

They focused on strengthening party loyalists by persuading like-minded people to run for precinct chair as well as for public office. "While we were all pretty strong personalities," Richards says now, "in the North Dallas Democratic Women our focus was not feminism. We certainly wouldn't have called it that, [but] it may have been feminism and we didn't know it."

She also helped form a group called the Dallas Committee for Peaceful Integration. J. Edgar Hoover looked on such activities with a skeptical eye, and the committee was "exposed" in the papers by an FBI agent who claimed to have infiltrated its ranks. White people who believed in the equality of blacks and browns had a hard time of it in the early 1960s in Texas, though not nearly so hard a time as blacks and browns did, and their neighbors' hostility created a bond among them that would prove enduring. Many of Ann Richards' most reliable supporters a quarter-century later were people who met at her house for coffee or beer in the 1960s, and when, in the 1990 Democratic primary, her commitment to civil rights was questioned, she could point to a history of dogged work for equality that few white people in Texas could match.

Dallas was a bastion of conservatism: in 1962, United Nations Ambassador Adlai Stevenson was booed off a stage, and Vice-President Lyndon Johnson and his wife, Lady Bird, were spat on and jostled by pickets outside the Adolphus Hotel. Living there required Ann Richards to master the indirect approach and the ironic style that would serve her well. She and David stayed for six years after President John F. Kennedy was assassinated, but when they left, they moved to Austin, the most progressive city in Texas.

In 1971, when Richards was in her late thirties, she agreed to help run Sarah Weddington's campaign for the Texas House of Representatives. (She now sees it as the first action in her adult life that she did on her own.) At twenty-five, Weddington, who had already argued *Roe* v. *Wade* before the Supreme Court, was the first "out-and-out feminist activist" Richards had met. Like many women of her generation, Richards learned from someone almost fifteen years younger to begin to see the world differently.

That year Frances ("Sissy") Farenthold was running for governor in a crusade against corruption in the state legislature that had finally become so blatant it was making the front pages of newspapers that for decades had largely ignored it. Women were coming out of the creekbeds and the cupboards to help in Farenthold's race and in Weddington's, and for the first time, Ann Richards was involved with a group of people who would talk through problems and decide jointly how to deal with them. "We encouraged cooperation in that organization," she would write, "and, being women, we were more apt to give and get than the people in other Democratic campaigns in which I had worked." Never again would she fully respect the hierarchical structures or strategies of conventional politics.

Along with Mary Beth Rogers, the daughter of a friend from Dallas, she created a unique mailing list for Weddington by identifying the largest single body of employees in Austin, the nonteaching staff at the University of Texas. Sending a postcard to each saying they had been treated unfairly by way of stagnant wages, they implied that Sarah Weddington could improve their situation. After they designed a Get-Out-the-Vote strategy that threw Weddington into a runoff she subsequently won, Richards went home to what she still considered her "real" life.

If one incalculable issue for political women is children, the other is men. In 1990, Ann Richards was in trouble because she was not married and Dianne Feinstein was in trouble because she was—or at least because of her particular husband. On the question of husbands and politics, Richards' experience provides a cautionary tale.

Not long after Ann Willis married David Richards, her high school sweetheart, they became what they remained for more than a quarter-century: not only man and wife but an institution. In her autobiography, she describes David as a handsome man with very

dark eyes and a commanding presence even when young. He had a
fine sense of humor, and by the time they met, he was well read,
articulate, and principled—in short, an interesting man.

They raised four children in a series of homes full of gaiety, action,
purpose, and music. For almost three decades they shared the laughter
and tears of hundreds of friends and colleagues. They camped and
canoed. They plotted, schemed, struggled, and experienced everything from exhilaration to near despair in each other's company.

In 1975, David was approached about running for Travis County
commissioner, and because he had neither the patience nor the ability
to suffer fools gladly, he declined. When Ann was approached in his
stead, she hesitated, afraid that officeholding might destroy her marriage, and finally she too declined.

David told her she was making a mistake: she had the "dogged-
ness at doing mundane things" that a candidate needs and far more
patience than he. Ann reconsidered, and after they spent a month
poring over precinct statistics from a woman's city council race in
the previous election and mulling over every angle, Ann agreed to
run. By this time, they had been married for twenty-two years.

Nine years later, they were divorced.

David Richards is now married to a younger woman, with whom
he has two children approximately the ages of his oldest grandchildren. He remains an extraordinarily attractive man: vital, sharp, sexy,
and fun. In her autobiography Ann admits that she thought she would
die if she could no longer be Mrs. David Richards and that she loves
him still. Two months before the 1990 election, her longtime friend
and colleague Jane Hickie confessed: "I've always thought that if
David came back on October 31, 1990, and said, 'I've changed my
mind: I made a big mistake. Can't we go off to the Peace Corps and
work in Nigeria?' she'd be gone."

It is a truism of American culture that a middle-aged woman is
far less likely than a middle-aged man to find a new mate. Although
a handful of women marry younger men, a large majority of men
take younger wives the second or third time around. As novelist Mary
Gordon puts it, a middle-aged woman has a better chance of being
hijacked on an airplane than of making a happy marriage after the
age of forty-five or fifty.

Heavily influenced by its Puritan beginnings, American culture has historically been suspicious of sexuality, and an attractive single woman is commonly perceived as a threat. An unmarried woman politician can therefore count on having her sexuality questioned if she runs for an office others want. To the charge that she was lesbian, Barbara Roberts, for instance, some months before she was elected governor of Oregon, responded dryly by asking: "Who has time?"

According to a number of accounts which he denies, Jim Mattox, one of Richards' Democratic primary opponents, repeatedly badgered reporters with queries like "Why don't you write about Ann Richards and Lily Tomlin in the hot tub?" Even honors graduates of the finest liberal arts program at the University of Texas at Austin took these charges of lesbianism seriously and, because of them, would not vote for Ann Richards.

Dianne Feinstein did not have this problem, and on one level, her experience might seem aberrant. A woman who performs on the high wires of big-time politics cannot count on having a wealthy, attractive husband to stand behind her—a man who confesses to the media: "What Dianne does is more important than what I do."

Feinstein was unusually lucky to find a third husband two years after Bertram Feinstein's death in 1978 who not only supported her political ambitions but was eager to share the burdens. Richard Blum advised her; he stood behind her on platforms; he helped raise money and gave it in abundance. In the primary, he provided the $600,000 to pay for the commercial that was widely credited with turning the election around, and by October 1990, he had become her largest contributor: the two of them had loaned her campaign $3 million. And therein lies yet another tale of double binds.

Blum is a wealthy investment banker. Shortly after the 1984 election, people on the inside of the Mondale campaign claimed that it was largely because they were suspicious of Blum's financial dealings that Mondale did not ask Feinstein to be his vice-presidential running mate. (Mondale apparently now denies this.) Given what happened to the woman he did ask, and the catastrophe the Ferraro/Zaccaro finances brought on them and in some measure on the Democratic party, rumors that Blum's finances might be even more suspect were bound to surface in a gubernatorial campaign.

Bill Boyarsky, columnist and longtime political reporter for the

Los Angeles Times, recognizes the handicap many husbands present to women candidates by virtue of their work. "There's very little a person can do in the world," Boyarsky admits, "that can stand the scrutiny of another campaign or a clever reporter." A lawyer, for instance, is almost bound to have dubious clients: "If they're honest, why do they need a lawyer?" A doctor or dentist or schoolteacher might bear up under investigation. But an entrepreneur, much less a financier whose business involves playing close to the edge, is problematic.

Kevin Phillips' book *The Politics of Rich and Poor* has helped to focus public attention on how people make money, as well as on who gets it and who does not. In a period when candidates are rigorously analyzed, Richard Zeiger and A. G. Block, editors of the *California Journal*, believe that Blum's potential conflict of interest is serious and inescapable. "His is a business that operates best in the shadows," Block points out, "and not because it's a shady business, but because in order to maximize your effectiveness, you have to do things out of the spotlight."

"He takes large sums of money and invests them in things that will pay off for him," Zeiger explains, "and in his line of work, I can't think of anything that would pay off for him better than having a wife who's governor of California."

Virtually every California company of any size does business with the state, and in Blum's work inside information is the stock in trade: he gets paid to put important people together and to know what is likely to happen in the future. The argument that shows the Feinstein/Blum problem at its most elemental goes something like this:

Blum can put together a deal with three people leveraging stock out of a company that sells widgets. Somewhere in the Department of General Services, California is buying widgets. If you are the company, would you think that having Richard Blum as your financier when his wife is governor would give you a leg up in getting the widget contract?

Who knows?

Is somebody in the Department of General Services going to think it might?

Maybe.

Is it going to help you?

It may give you a little goodwill.

A little goodwill may be all you need. And you may be willing to lose this widget contract, or the next, as long as you get the third widget contract.

As Zeiger puts it: "These things can be so convoluted that you never know the answer. The evidence is always going to be ambivalent enough so that Feinstein and Blum can make the argument that nothing wrong's going on here. And that may be the case—but you're never going to know. The perception that Blum is somehow advantaged may be damaging to Feinstein's credibility as a politician and a leader."

Opinions on Blum range from those who call him a crass operator to those who consider him not only honest but sensitive to the slightest hint of impropriety. Boyarsky describes him as "delightful and sophisticated" and claims that "they've been investigating this guy for years. . . . They're only letting up now because it's a dry hole."

No doubt the Ferraro debacle showed Blum the scrutiny to which the press and a tough opponent subject a candidate for any major office, and since his wife was determined to stay in politics, he would surely have cleaned up as much of his act as possible. Specific questions remained, however, only to emerge from time to time during the 1990 gubernatorial campaign, and the perception that he was a wheeler-dealer businessman who worked with blue smoke and mirrors was inherently impossible to destroy.

The other major question about women candidates that the 1990 campaigns in Texas and California raised revolved around negative campaigning, and the question was, Can women do it?

Here was another classic double bind. Women candidates were thought to have an advantage because voters perceived them to be more nurturing and more honest than men. If a woman aggressively attacked her opponent, she risked destroying that advantage by "lowering" herself to his level. But if she did not attack, the available evidence suggested that she would lose, and Michael Dukakis' recent example was cited ad nauseam.

The dilemma women candidates faced came out of the splintering of the whole human self that arose with industrialism in the early nineteenth century, when men left the farms to take on paid work in factories and shops, and women remained doing unpaid work at home. The male world was expected to be cruel and unprincipled. Men "got their hands dirty"; those who didn't were either sissies or stupid. Women were expected to have finer moral natures so that the homes they created would be a refuge for the admirable virtues.

Politics was a creation of the male world, and therefore, in order to be players, women had to "get their hands dirty." Women's hands, in fact, had always been dirty with the blood and muck and debris of life. There was nothing wrong or alien to women about a little honest dirt. But the rules of politics really meant something else: they meant that to win, people had to attack, to be sure, but if necessary, to cheat, lie, and possibly steal as well.

Neither Ann Richards nor Dianne Feinstein wanted to resort to negative campaigning. Both had objected to it in the past. Both continued to dislike it. But when Feinstein protested, Bill Carrick would say, "Dianne, do you want me to show you the numbers? Your friends who are objecting to your attack commercials are still going to vote for you. But the public's saying, 'Is that right about Pete Wilson?' "

Richards and Feinstein would never have become credible candidates for governor by relying on rosy promises to the electorate or burnished self-images. The question for them was, To what lengths were they willing to go to win? The question for the public was, Would it allow these women to use the same political tools men are allowed to use? The election answered the former question, but the answer to the latter would remain murky.

CHAPTER 2

> *I have seen in the faces of our citizens a vision of The New Texas. It is a vision that grows out of our Texas spirit, our traditions and our common belief in a Texas where hard work and honesty are rewarded.*
> —ANN RICHARDS, *The New Texas*
> (campaign brochure)

Her 1988 keynote address to the Democratic National Convention at once turned Ann Richards into a celebrity and presented her with a new set of problems. First, she had to decide which statewide office she would run for. Second, when she mocked George Bush for being born with a silver foot in his mouth, she infuriated Republicans and lost support on which her political future was expected to hinge.

In 1982, when Richards won her race for state treasurer, she was the first woman in fifty years to be elected statewide. Her mold-shattering political strength derived in part from her appeal across party lines—principally to women, but also to men. Molly Ivins, the *Dallas Times Herald* columnist, attributed this to her "hard hair." In her elegant suits and with her proud carriage, she looked like a Republican.

She attracted voters in the rapidly multiplying suburbs—voters who tend to be young and Republican—by being smart, articulate, immaculately groomed, and exquisitely in control. Their support had been expected to counter the defection of older Democrats, male and female, who are culturally conservative and loath to vote for a woman for high executive office. (A Texas Poll taken after the 1990 election found that four Texans out of ten who are sixty-two or older believe that "women should stay home and take care of the house, and leave running the government to men." Fewer than one-tenth of Texans under thirty agree.)

The backlash, therefore, to her "silver foot in his mouth" quip was no joking matter. *New York Times* columnist Anna Quindlen had taken the Richards speech in the spirit in which it was given: "She was nobody's fool; she made them listen and she made them listen good, with precisely those qualities that we often try to iron out of politicians in general and female politicians in particular: a sense of fun, irreverence and general cussedness."

Such delight was by no means confined to New York, but Texas newspapers were deluged with letters flailing Richards for embarrassing their state before the world. More important, Republican pro-choice women who might have crossed party lines were so irate it seemed certain that many of their votes would go to Richards' opponent, even if he were anti-choice. As Lieutenant Governor Bill Hobby pointed out, George Bush had become the most popular president since Dwight Eisenhower, and unlike the British, Texans do not laugh at heroes.

The uproar revealed a curious fact about Texas culture: in a state that prides itself on individualism, there is a deep strain of reverence for authority. To the fundamentally conservative American mind, anyone critical of authority is suspect; someone who makes fun of it is unnerving; and if that someone is a woman, she can be frightening. Richards had ridiculed an incumbent vice-president who was, furthermore, one of Texas' own. Barbara Bush began referring to her as "that woman," and other Republican women were not so kind.

The episode threw a bold public spotlight on Ann Richards' dilemma: as a wisecracking, tart-tongued woman, she offended one large constituency for each she won. Now she could only hope that time would heal, as it sometimes does, and meanwhile she had to decide her political future.

For years Richards had argued that in Texas the lieutenant governor is more powerful than the governor, and her friend Bill Hobby seemed inclined to relinquish that office, which he had held for four terms. If she ran a campaign to succeed him, she would not attract the attention she would if she ran for governor, and, therefore, her vulnerabilities would be less likely to metamorphose into serious political problems. As Hobby says: "There's all the difference in the world between a top-of-the-ballot race and those for lieutenant governor on down. The focus on them is one-tenth what it is on the governor's race." The lieutenant governor gets an annual salary of only $7,200, however, and Hobby, who is one of the richest men in America, could afford to work for coffee and doughnut money. Ann Richards, who had to support herself, could not.

Furthermore, attracting attention was part of the point. As uninspiring as most Texas governors have been, the glamour inherent in that office is a powerful inducement, and Richards would obviously cut a bolder figure on the political landscape if she captured the Mansion. Still, to win, she would have to defeat Attorney General Jim Mattox, who had made it known at least two years earlier that he aimed to be governor and for even longer had been amassing funds for the race. And Mattox's reputation as a ruthless campaigner could not be wished away.

She could count on invaluable help. Even before the Democratic convention, Richards had talked over her next big campaign with her children, and three of the four, as well as her son-in-law, had agreed to play a role whenever she decided to run. Her elder daughter, Cecile, and her husband, Kirk Adams, were willing to leave their jobs in California as organizers for the Service Employees International Union and move to Austin with their daughter Lily to work as field directors. Her son Dan, who had given her nine months of his life in 1982, when she ran for treasurer and needed a man to travel with her, agreed to do it again. Ellen, her youngest, was game to be her surrogate and travel through the state giving speeches and riding in parades. (Clark, who lives with his wife and daughter near Kerrville in the Hill Country and works as a drug and alcohol counselor, would be the least engaged in the campaign's daily workings.)

In the spring of 1988, at least three months before the Democratic National Convention, Richards had hired pollster Harrison Hickman to find out as best he could how Texans might respond to the idea of a woman governor. That Texas had already had a woman governor, Miriam ("Ma") Ferguson, was not particularly germane because Ma had been a surrogate for Pa—Jim Ferguson—who resigned in 1917 to avoid being impeached and was barred from ever running for office again. Although Ma Ferguson was governor of Texas from 1924 to 1926 and 1932 to 1934 and was the first Texas governor to be voted out of office and then back in, she was considered a figurehead. Her slogan was "Two Governors for the Price of One," and she and her husband kept their offices side by side. Her most memorable position may have been the one she took against bilingual education, when she purportedly said, "If the English language was good enough for Jesus Christ, it's good enough for the children of Texas," a line Ann Richards never tired of quoting. (Texas historian David G. McComb suspects that the story is apocryphal.)

In his polls and focus groups, Hickman found that men in Texas were more likely to disdain women openly than in most parts of the country—even the South. He believed, nevertheless, that if Richards' appeal were pitched in exactly the right key, she had a chance to win. "She's a great motivator in speeches," Hickman says. "When she walks into a room, she's electric. She has presence. She carries herself very well, and she has a very distinctive personality. People respond to that."

After twenty years of analyzing electoral polls, Hickman had become convinced that when people vote for governor they vote from their hearts, making a statement of values, rather than a statement about party preference or the direction of the state as a whole. "Elites believe that people are in office to perform public policy goals," Hickman says. "My impression is that people get into office for a whole variety of reasons, and they vote for a whole variety of reasons. They don't just think: 'Is he in my party and do I agree with his positions?' They ask: 'Is this a special kind of person?' " To stir the heart—to convince voters that she is "a special kind of person"— Hickman was convinced that a candidate needed to tap into the myths that underlie a culture.

For Ann Richards, the need to engage with a deep stratum of belief presented a stunning problem because the myth of the cowboy, which is so nearly all-pervasive, glorifies not only a man, but a loner who is strong, silent, and brave. The fact that Ann Richards is a woman put her inescapably at odds with the principal Texas myth. Glenn Smith, her campaign manager in the primary, described her position precisely: "Because she's a woman, she's essentially a challenger: she's challenging the status quo. So it's as though she were running against an incumbent for the highest office in Texas."

To help Richards decide how viable she might be as a gubernatorial candidate, Hickman began to look for some part of the Texas myth that a woman could use to engage the electorate. His quest took him to a lot of movies, especially Westerns about the frontier, where he discovered a Barbara Stanwyck sort of character—a very strong woman who is the conscience of the community. If Ann Richards decided to run for governor, Hickman saw his challenge in helping the media people connect Ann Richards with that part of the Texas myth.

Since she first ran for Travis County commissioner in 1975, Richards, of course, had been gradually shaping her own public persona, and she was acutely aware of the power of image. But the qualities people found acceptable and even charming in a state treasurer were not necessarily transferable to the office of governor, and Richards knew that. As Hickman discovered, she not only "had a much truer sense of the voters in the rest of Texas than many people in the campaign [but] also a more accurate understanding of the way stereotypes of women work. She understood that there were *advantages* to being a woman—certainly better than her male consultants did. They always saw Ann's sex more as an impediment to the campaign than as a reality that had plusses and minuses associated with it."

Jane Hickie, Martha Smiley, and the core of women who had been at the center of Richards' political rise from Travis County commissioner to state treasurer had already begun to test her strengths as a major-league candidate. At central places outside the state where Richards' support was concentrated, they had begun planning as early as July 1988 for fund-raisers in the fall. In Washington, D.C., that September, for instance, a packed Woman's National Democratic Club heard Richards make a spirited foray into big-time fund-raising, and the audience had gone away both poorer and impressed. (When Richards spied Mayor Marion Barry entering the room, however, she welcomed him from the podium by saying, "When I grow up, I want to be like Marion Barry." Since Washington was rife with rumors that Barry was using drugs and heading deliriously for a spectacular fall, one guest turned to another and said, "I hope her advance work improves!")

At about the same time, Richards had written her Texas supporters to say, "I may enter the toughest political campaign of my career for just about the toughest political job in the country: gov-

ernor of Texas." Then in early December, she had held a successful
$1,000-a-plate fund-raiser in Houston which she repeated in other
big Texas cities. By the end of 1988, Richards had about eleven
thousand contributors—more than either Senator Lloyd Bentsen or
former Governor Mark White had ever had—and she had not even
officially decided to enter the race.

Such dramatic evidence of support tightened the screws on Richards to run for governor, but still she wavered. No one knew better
than she how hard it would be to elect a woman governor of Texas,
or how grueling a campaign she could expect if she undertook it.
And it was obvious that if she decided against it, her life could be
both pleasant and easy. Consultant Jack Martin, who ran Lloyd
Bentsen's reelection campaigns in 1982 and 1988, recalls that after
the Atlanta speech, Richards was "a hot property on the speaking
tour," pulling in $10,000 and $15,000 a speech in one-night stands
throughout the country. Had she decided not to run for governor,
had she "either run for reelection as treasurer or gone on to do
something else, she could have made an absolute fortune."

In January and February of 1989, Martin remembers, Richards
was in such a bad mood most of the time that he wondered whether
she would take on so formidable a challenge. He thinks she did it
finally because "Ann genuinely believes that this is part of her destiny,
and she knows full well this will advance the cause of women being
elected to high office."

According to Martin, Bill Hobby would also "enjoy tremen-
dously" being governor of Texas, but Hobby "had the personal serenity to be able to say 'No.' " Richards did not have that serenity,
and if she were inclined to use religious language, she might have
said she had been "called." She felt an obligation both to other
women and to herself, and her friends said they would do their best
to sustain her in whatever she decided.

In early 1989, as the probability that Ann Richards would run
was sliding into certainty, she had to look hard at her strengths and
weaknesses as a gubernatorial candidate. No one could afford to take
on such a challenge without a cold-blooded understanding of what
might work for and what might work against her, and Richards'
careful planning was legendary.

As for the plusses, she had held office continuously since 1976, and her record ranged from respectable to excellent, depending on the observer. Her stewardship of the treasury, in management terms, had been both imaginative and frugal, and by the end of her tenure, she would have made $2 billion in non-tax revenue for the state.

She had learned how to be an exacting boss—she wanted everything right—and so she could present herself to the electorate as a woman who knew how to get what she wanted. She managed people in large organizations superbly.

Although she had been unopposed for reelection to the treasury in 1986, Richards had nonetheless run two statewide campaigns and proved her ability to raise big money. When she was asked originally to run for the treasury, in fact, she had told her friends in midmorning that she would consider it if they could raise $200,000 by sundown, and they did. Whether she could raise the $10 million and more that she would need to be a viable gubernatorial candidate was another matter, and she recognized fund-raising as perhaps the central problem from the start.

Though the campaign itself was likely to be nasty, Richards was convinced that after her first treasury race she knew exactly what running for governor would be like. "I could have called almost every one of the most difficult situations," she said later. "I'm pretty realistic, and I know the tough sides of this business. I had to accept the absolute worst before I could decide to make the race."

As for Richards' personal qualities—those that could woo a vast audience of supporters—Bill Hobby puts first her "warmth and caring." She hugs and holds, and when she is talking to someone she looks her straight in the eye. She is the mistress of the winning personal touch, and her formal thank-you messages are often accompanied by a note scrawled on the bottom in her bold, distinctive hand. To an out-of-state woman who could neither vote for her nor give her money, but had sent a postcard with Queen Victoria on the front and a message on the back that read: "She was a tough old broad—hang in there!" Richards took the time to reply, "Loved your card of Queen Vic. I feel more like Rambo."

She is smart and learns fast, and she has a first-rate memory for names and faces. Trained as a high school debater, she has an orderly mind accustomed to the give-and-take of political argument.

For the most part she had an excellent rapport with journalists, especially the Austin press corps. And her wit and skill at clever repartee had helped her transcend the stereotypes of women and politicians that might have worked against her.

On top of all that, she is a great performer. When she is on, nobody can be more fun than Ann Richards, and the fun is infectious. Remembering their early days in Dallas, Virginia Whitten said, "You didn't dare sleep late or take naps, because you'd miss something." High spirits translate into political gold. As Jack Martin puts it, "You let Ann get on that airplane out there on the stump and get her in a real good mood and let her get fired up, and I mean she could charm. . . ." He didn't need to finish his sentence.

With so much that was fine, it would be no wonder if even Richards, much less most people around her, underestimated the obstacles. They were considerable.

First, over the last two decades Texas has grown increasingly Republican in "big-ticket" races. The sitting governor, Bill Clements, was the only Republican to hold the Mansion since Reconstruction, but except for Richard Nixon in 1968, Republican presidential candidates had carried the state every time they won nationally since the days of Harry Truman. No liberal Democrat had been elected governor or lieutenant governor since 1939, and only one, Ralph Yarborough, had been elected to the United States Senate.

The president of the United States calls himself a Texan, and the main street in College Station is named George Bush Avenue. In 1990, the formidably popular Senator Phil Gramm would be leading the Republican ticket. And when both the president and an ambitious junior senator have their self-interest engaged and their prestige on the line, the Republican party machinery is certain to be working at top form. Comparing that apparatus to its Democratic equivalent is like comparing a 1990 Ferrari to a 1978 Chevrolet that a family of six with three dogs has camped in.

To this underlying Republican strength, one would have to add a substantial bias against women—hard to measure accurately, but there nevertheless—which manifests itself for the most part in hard-held notions of "a woman's place." Over the past two decades that place has been extended to include municipal office: more than one hundred Texas cities, including some of the biggest, now have women mayors, and more than a thousand women hold elective office in the state. But Elizabeth Fox-Genovese, director of Women's Studies at Emory University in Atlanta, Georgia, observes that although there is more than one Texas, "all of them are resolutely and defiantly male." No other state has "so successfully and unabashedly identified itself with male individualism," and Genovese suspects "that the primary point of agreement among East and West, Anglo and Hispanic, white and black Texas men is male dominance." It is a state where even the road signs—"Don't Mess with Texas"—are macho.

As consultant George Shipley puts it, Texas, unlike California, "is a right-wing, conservative state," which means that traditional values that locate woman's place in the home are dominant. Exit polls in the 1990 election, for instance, would show that 32 percent of the Texans who voted believed that abortion should always be legal, compared to 54 percent of Californians; 6 percent of Texans called themselves feminists, compared to 11 percent of Californians; 52 percent of the voters in Texas attended church, compared to 31 percent of those in California. In Texas, then, the challenge of transforming a heroine of the women's movement into a candidate with wide bipartisan appeal was not to be taken lightly.

One exaggerates only slightly in saying that Ann Richards can terrify men—a fact her inner circle understood when they scoured their closets for incriminating videotapes of her performances as Mr. Harry Porko. At the 1983 biennial convention of the National Women's Political Caucus, for instance, she put on a rubber pig's nose before a riotously appreciative audience and, in a pronounced drawl, parodied the owner of an electronics factory:

> My girls are happy. My girls are happy because I know how to treat 'em. A smile of appreciation, a little pat, that means more to a girl than any amount of money.
>
> I do a lot for my girls. I put the horoscope on the bulletin board every day. I started the Yellow Rose award for girls who've worked five years without being absent. And I put up lights in the parking lot to cut down on rapes. But I still say to my girls, "Honey, you watch how you dress."
>
> 'Cause you know, some of 'em are just asking for it.

A man did not have to hear this takeoff to sense that Richards could go at it with gusto, and it was scarcely less threatening to women who had built their lives on the premise that men are sacrosanct.

The problem was arguably exacerbated in the minority communities, although no white woman of Richards' generation could be more genuinely without prejudice than she, or more committed to civil rights. Her formative experience had come during World War II, when she and her mother joined her father in San Diego, where he was stationed, and she went to school with blacks, Greeks, Hispanics, and Italians—an experience that white girls growing up outside Waco, Texas, do not, even now, have as a matter of course.

Still, her off-the-top-of-the-head, sometimes bawdy humor did not always sit well, especially with black and Hispanic men. A woman who can take Texas' primary myth and cut it down to size by describing a cowboy as the guy who kisses the horse instead of the girl before he rides off into the sunset is a dangerous woman.

The question of her style was reflected in the backlash to her quip about George Bush. As consultant George Shipley says, "She has a tart tongue, a natural instinct for ridicule and invective." Before a certain audience, this style works superbly. To another, she comes off as "a smart-ass white woman." Taken out of context or in print, she can appear cute or sassy—qualities most people do not associate with leaders.

Still another problem had to do, simply, with the part of Texas where Richards lives. In the rest of the state, and especially in rural areas, Austin is as suspect as New York or San Francisco. According to Shipley, "Austin is held in complete contempt: it is a little bastion of socialism, 'The People's Republic of Travis County.' " Hickman agrees: "The voters who live in the Austin media market . . . are different from any other voters in the state. So anyone who imagines the common wisdom in Austin to reflect the state is wrong."

Richards was not only tainted by association with Austin, but she had learned her politics in an atypical school. "Ann did not have the kind of political experience that you get working a black church in east Texas or organizing," Shipley insists. "*I mean really organizing!* I don't mean walking the streets with Henry Gonzalez, *I mean winning elections in hotly contested environments.*"

Some even argued that Richards' Atlanta speech had catapulted her over a developmental stage, politically speaking. Except for her years as county commissioner, she had not had to spend her energies reconciling powerful warring factions, and with all due respect to Travis County, it is not the major leagues.

The fact that Richards was a recovering alcoholic had been public knowledge since 1982, when Lane Denton, her primary opponent in the race for the treasury, brandished the information as though it were the original scarlet letter. Since she not only whipped him but went on to win the general election and even to frighten off all opposition to her reelection in 1986, it seemed likely, though not certain, that she had laid that specter to rest.

That Richards had allegedly taken drugs on a handful of occasions was a fact that lay wrapped in secrecy, where it remains. A man who would play a key campaign role discovered a week after he was hired that a crucial part of his job would be containing that keg of political dynamite. Harrison Hickman had apparently done focus groups on the drug issue in December 1988 and concluded only that it would be a problem. Long after the dynamite had exploded, the campaign insider speculated that Richards had simply practiced denial: had she allowed herself to imagine clearly how her opponents would use the drug issue, he thought she would never have run.

Finally, there were rumors that Richards spent a suspicious amount of time in the company of lesbians, and in late-twentieth-century Texas that term triggers fears even more elemental than "communist" did in the 1950s. Of course there were gays in the Richards entourage: lesbians have made up the shock troops of virtually every battle that has to do with women. And since Richards was going up against an opponent Shipley could describe as "one of the most politically violent characters in America today . . . [whose] mind is such that he would almost rather see her go down if he couldn't win himself," her gay friends meant sure trouble.

Insiders' accounts of the process by which Richards decided at last to run for governor are fundamentally at odds. One claims that her friends were opposed and she overruled them. Another insists that she was pushed into it by her admirers. Mary Beth Rogers puts the truth somewhere in between, but the persistence of the controversy suggests not only how tough the decision was but also how many different sides there are to Ann Richards.

She had written that getting a divorce was the hardest thing she had ever done. Now she approached a gubernatorial race that promised to be harder still. As the spring of 1989 began to green the soft hills of Austin, she knew she could count on her family, her Alcoholics Anonymous support system, and a group of men and women—but mainly women—she had known and worked with for years, some of them for decades. They had sustained her through her confrontation with alcoholism and then through a protracted divorce. They were lovingly adept at symptoms and remedies.

Her children were crucial. "I would never have made the decision," Richards says, "without their being a part of it." And when she speaks of that decision in the plural—"we decided!"—she is using the familial "we." "There is no way to overemphasize the significance of having my son travel with me," Richards could say when the ordeal was over; "not only does he know me very well, but he was stabilizing, he was reassuring. He has a good sense of humor. I think having someone with you whom you know very well and love very much makes things more tolerable."

She could count on many friends to contribute significantly to her campaign, but three at least deserve to be singled out. One, Virginia Whitten, whom she had known since Cecile and Dan were in diapers, not only turned up at headquarters daily to collect and register the checks sent to the campaign, but acted as a custodian of health: whenever Richards was in town and her schedule allowed, Whitten would pick her up in the mornings to take her walking around the lake, and every night for almost two years she would leave nourishing food waiting in the kitchen.

In addition, Whitten has a temperament so soothing that her very presence is a balm. In her autobiography, Richards remembers bursting into Whitten's house when they were in their twenties and finding her surrounded by "snotty-nosed children crawling, banging, screaming," while their mother quietly folded diapers. When Richards cried, "Virginia, I am just losing my mind!" Whitten would say, "I know. Why don't you sit down and have a cup of coffee." As Ann put it, Virginia knew "that all of this madness didn't last forever."

The second of Richards' friends whose role was crucial is Jane

Hickie, the shrewd lawyer and political tactician in her early forties who became what Jack Martin calls "the chief cheerleader." Both strong-willed and strong-minded, she had become Richards' administrative assistant when she was elected Travis County commissioner in 1976, had brought Richards into the Texas Women's Political Caucus, and had run her first campaign for treasurer. The wit of the one plays off the wit of the other, and women in Washington still remember national caucus meetings, when they would sit long into the night, laughing at the pair until they were almost literally hysterical. Perhaps the greatest service Hickie ever did Richards was to organize the intervention of friends and family to confront her over her drinking—an intervention that may well have saved her life.

For years, Jane Hickie had focused with almost tunnel vision on Ann Richards' political future, and though a dispute that swirled around campaign manager Glenn Smith's salary took her out of the gubernatorial campaign for some nine months, she was there during the critical periods. She always found ways to be optimistic, however devastating the news, and Jack Martin claims that "she psyched herself up to keep Ann up better than anybody I've ever seen."

The third is Mary Beth Rogers, an organizational genius whose serenity approaches Virginia Whitten's. After signing on to help with the transition after Richards was elected treasurer, Rogers had discovered that she was enjoying it. "It was great fun to get involved in transforming that agency," she says. "I didn't know anything about money, but I knew something about management. It was a great adventure." Ultimately she became Richards' second in command.

But Rogers was not only a political junkie and a superb administrator, she was a woman who needed to understand analytically the things that absorbed her. As Richards puts it, Rogers "is the one of us who deals in systems. She figures out why things happen, and then she translates that into language that anyone can understand." As a young wife and mother, she had helped conduct voter registration and Get-Out-the-Vote drives on San Antonio's West Side, and in the mid-1980s, she decided to write a book about Ernesto Cortes, a Hispanic organizer trained by Saul Alinsky whose profound "commitment to make 'unimportant' people important in the public life of their communities" had inspired new political institutions throughout Texas and the Southwest that seemed to be "developing a new kind of political participant." After Rogers' husband died suddenly in the fall of 1987, she brought "new emotions and new insights" to bear on the book, which became an expression of "the renewal of [her] own political hope."

Rogers did not finish her book, *Cold Anger: A Story of Faith and Power Politics*, until the spring of 1990, and when she came into the Richards campaign after the primary runoff, she intended to stay only until someone could be found to take over as campaign manager. Since no one appropriate would take on that awesome challenge, Rogers remained.

Her connections to the Democratic party were first-rate: Jack Martin, who is central to Senator Lloyd Bentsen's operations in Texas and a consultant to the Democratic National Committee, claims, "If Mary Beth were running the University of Texas Library and called me five times a week, I'd try to help her find rare books." At the same time, Rogers' immersion in "people's politics" suggested to Ernie Cortes' network of organizations all through Texas, which had a membership base of almost half a million, along with several hundred well-trained leaders, that her friend Ann Richards must not be your ordinary politician.

Rogers also had perspective. Quoting an Ernie Cortes line she uses in her book, "Politics is not war. Politics is not life or death," she observes, "It's only politics. I've had life and death decisions, and I've had political decisions, and I know the difference." Her presence at the center of the Richards campaign brought calm and at the same time had political resonance.

When Richards looked over the political demography of Texas, she could gloat over the fact that women made up a disproportionate share of the electorate. Between 56 and 58 percent of the Democratic primary voters would be female, compared to 54 percent of the electorate as a whole. And Richards' connections with women across the state were probably better than any candidate's in history.

Over the course of almost twenty years, she had been a major force in organizing Texas women. Different groups had come together for a wide range of reasons: they wanted to discover and explore their past; they wanted to help each other see the present realistically; they needed to band together to work for political and social change. Most important, they had organized more highly than ever, and Ann Richards was connected to every remotely progressive women's political network in the state. The power of this dedicated following was something no one could measure accurately.

Although the Foundation for Women's Resources was one of the least explicitly political groups Richards helped to form, she locates the burgeoning "hard core" of women crucial to her campaigns in its board. Cathy Bonner, whom she had met during Sarah Weddington's campaign and who would work for her in 1989 and 1990 as a key media consultant, had come up with the idea of a foundation that would be, as Richards puts it, "a conduit to do projects we wanted to do. [It would] have a 501C3 [IRS] designation so we could raise [tax-deductible] money."

Through one of the foundation's projects, Leadership Texas, Richards and her cohorts tapped promising women all over the state and introduced them both to each other and, through a series of seminars and trips, to the realities of modern-day Texas. Leaders in their communities and masterful organizers, they would eventually add their political support to that of Richards' personal friends such as Claire Korioth, and although their individual contributions to Ann Richards' campaign could fill these pages, for reasons of time and space, they must remain for the most part anonymous.

It was these women who were largely responsible for what Nancy Clack, an itinerant political craftswoman, called "the enormous people resources"—the grass-roots support—that Ann Richards had. Clack, who had already worked in forty statewide races before she arrived in Austin in February 1990, was amazed to discover that the Richards campaign had pulled in people who had never been involved before. "We had volunteer organizations in almost every one of the 254 counties," Clack says. "We had phone banks in about 150 counties, which is phenomenal in a state this size. And they were really working. People were walking their blocks, and they were having teas for Ann."

The core of this network had been a lifetime in the building. Richards had lived in two of the major cities in Texas—Austin and Dallas—and her roots were in a third of no inconsiderable size. From her earliest days in both cities, she had been active in progressive and Democratic party politics, and her friendships were vital and lasting.

After 1972, when Sarah Weddington was elected to the Texas legislature, many of the women who had worked in her campaign and in Sissy Farenthold's had banded together to form the Texas Women's Political Caucus. Most people assume that Richards was an important part of that group from the beginning, and many who wanted her to be governor considered her feminism a liability: they worried that she would be taken to be merely a feminist candidate, which in Texas means shrill, narrow, and off center.

According to Jane Hickie, however, who was the caucus's first state chair, Richards' membership was merely formal for the first few years. Hickie, in fact, remembers when Richards would advise women to read the sports page every day so they could talk to their husbands: "She gave speeches about how to have it all, how to have a perfect husband and a perfect family, and a perfect career . . . how to look good and be smart and have friends, and so on."

Richards' first major public declaration that might be described as feminist came in 1977, at the International Women's Year Convention in Houston, when Bella Abzug looked down from the podium to see her standing at one of the floor mikes and called on her to introduce the Equal Rights Amendment (ERA) plank. When she met Abzug, who called her "Texas" and told her she was spunky, she was impressed by a woman who spoke out so strongly and minced no words.

But with her roots strong in Texas, Richards resisted the Bella Abzug line. She was a member of President Jimmy Carter's Commission on Women when he fired Abzug as chair—an act most commission members took as an insult they resigned to protest. Richards, however, refused to resign because of her loyalty to Sarah Weddington, whom Carter appointed in Abzug's stead.

A good many women were outraged. "They said, 'How dare she not do that?' " according to Jane Hickie, "and she dared not do it because when you peel back all the layers, Ann Richards is a very hardheaded politician. She is smart and capable and never confused." A woman who wanted to rise in Texas politics could not afford to be linked too closely to Bella Abzug.

Richards' growing feminist awareness would feed into her ability to organize statewide. A key experience that ultimately produced a crucial organizing tool, for instance, sprang from a family outing to the Institute of Texan Cultures in San Antonio. As they were leaving that capacious exhibit of the Texas past, Richards' daughter Ellen asked, "Where were all the women?"

Dumbfounded to realize that the historical accounts were lop-sided at best, Richards instigated what turned into a four-year project on Texas women. She persuaded Mary Beth Rogers to take primary responsibility for putting together a collection of artifacts. (They got Betty Graham's Mixmaster, for instance, which she had used in making the first formula for Liquid Paper, a product that simplified secretaries' lives.) When the exhibition opened at the Institute of Texan Cultures in 1981, Richards could say, "I started this project for my daughters and discovered along the way that it was for me."

This confession was true in ways her audience did not fully appreciate. After the collection had been displayed with appropriate fanfare and drama in San Antonio, the core of it became a traveling exhibit. Richards introduced that exhibit all over Texas, and it provided an enormously effective platform for her to meet women who would subsequently become involved in her statewide campaigns.

The other vehicle Richards used to get to know women across the state was a political slide show Rogers put together in the late 1970s on a grant from the National Women's Education Fund. The fund had published a book to teach women how to get elected to office, and, as Richards put it, "they wanted a slide show to go with it . . . a graphic way of making women understand the principles of what they were trying to do." For years, Richards and Rogers, along with Jane Hickie, would take that slide show and go wherever they were invited to teach women the fundamentals of politics and the basics of running for office. They talked to PTAs, garden clubs, community groups, and political caucuses.

The trio was always hardheaded about Texas politics. As Hickie tells it: "These women would want to run for office because they cared about the ERA, and we would say, 'But the things the people care about are the sewer lines. So why don't you shut up about the ERA and talk about whether you can get the sewer line built?' "

Richards always knew that she could do something about the sewers. "She's not an idealist," Hickie insists, "she's extremely practical." And she was being practical about her own career: every trip added a strand to the network of support that she and her friends were weaving for a statewide Richards candidacy.

Finally, in the late 1970s, the transforming spirit of feminism began to infuse Ann Richards. It was a trip to Colorado, according to Hickie, that prompted Richards to cast her own experience into a feminist political perspective. She went there for a conference of women elected officials sponsored by the National Women's Education Fund, and she came back saying, "You know, I've been talking to some of these women, and there are some things going on that aren't right!"

Hickie says mischievously that in Austin, "because she had run Sarah Weddington's campaign and Wilhelmina Delco's campaign—and because she didn't really know Barbara Jordan or Sissy—she thought she knew everything. She thought there wasn't anybody like her. But as soon as she started meeting women from other parts of the country who were *exactly* like her—who had a bunch of common experiences—then feminism began to work for her."*

And so, from the late 1970s on, Richards was a crucial member of the Texas Women's Political Caucus, which meant that she was at the center of the most politically active women's network in the state. Through that group, she met women in the National Women's Political Caucus, who became her advocates to the political community at large.

When Ann Richards announced that she would run for governor, enormous amounts of money began to pour into Texas, and the single largest contributing group was the Democratic women's political action committee called EMILY's List. (EMILY is an acronym for Early Money Is Like Yeast: it makes the dough rise.) Ellen Malcolm, its founder, had worked at the national caucus in the late 1970s, when Richards was becoming most active, and many of EMILY's contributors owe their political awakening to it.

---

*In 1974, Wilhelmina Delco, a black woman who had served on the Austin school board, asked Richards to help in her race for the state legislature. As Richards put it: "Wilhelmina didn't know about raising money . . . [and] that was one thing I was able to help her do. . . . Not everyone in the black community and in the headquarters was going to open their arms and say, 'Oh hurrah! Here's this white woman from the west side come over to tell us what to do!' . . . My job was to fit in and to help Wilhelmina where she needed me." Delco won and has become a figure of considerable importance in the legislature.

The other source of Richards' potential statewide strength derived from her wit. During her years as treasurer, she had built up a loyal following as a favorite on the political roast circuit. As Hickie says: "She's a performer. She feeds off an audience: she gets all these endorphins. And she's not going to leave an audience disappointed." She seldom did. By the mid-1980s, she was out of Austin two or three nights every week speaking to gatherings as small as fifty as well as to crowds in the thousands. Nor was her following confined to Texas. According to Congressman Jake Pickle, she even upstaged movie stars and the best orators in the Democratic party at a roast in Washington, D.C., for Walter Cronkite. The keynote address transformed support she had been building for almost a decade into an incipient grass-roots organization.

Richards already had what amounted to a campaign organization among her close friends and family. Now she was in the market for experts, and she wanted the best résumés that money could buy. Her goal was to run a Democratic primary campaign that not only would win but would put her well on the way to being elected governor in November. She and everyone around her assumed this to mean that she needed to appear both less liberal and less feminist than she was commonly taken to be. It meant, among other things, that she needed experts who were male.

In November 1988, shortly after the presidential election, Jane Hickie had asked Jack Martin if he would consider running Ann Richards' campaign for governor. In 1986, Martin had been her campaign treasurer, though merely as a figurehead, and had heard her think out loud about running for at least a year. The day after Hickie approached him, Richards herself called, and he told her he'd like to keep the discussion going.

He loved Ann Richards. He was excited about a woman running for governor. And he liked the idea of changing his own image from "one of the boys" to someone complex enough to be politically astute in the interests of a wider range of candidates than just white men.

But by January, he had decided against it—primarily for personal reasons, but also because it seemed to him "that they didn't want me to *run* the campaign as much as they wanted me to *say* that I was running the campaign." Lloyd Bentsen had taught Martin that the manager was the executive director behind the scenes—not someone conspicuous. But he had begun to believe that the people around Richards wanted him as "a high-profile fixture," and he doubted seriously "whether any one person was going to be able to run that campaign."

From then on, he served as an informal adviser, and it worried him that "the more I pulled away, the more effort there was to draw me in." A local political newsletter quoted one of Richards' friends calling him their Jim Baker, and in meetings, Richards herself would "generally allude to the fact that I was 'running the show.'" What she said would be "vague enough to be technically correct, but it left the clear impression that I was running the campaign." To the contrary, he never signed on even as a consultant.

In February 1989, Richards hired consultant George Shipley to do "opposition research": to find her opponents' weaknesses, sins, misdemeanors, and, if possible, felonies. Known alternately as Dr. Dirt and Dr. Doom by both admirers and detractors, Shipley was the bane of many Texas liberals because he had fought the Texas Trial Lawyers Association, a key element in the liberal coalition and a group he was convinced had bought the Texas Supreme Court. Some advised Richards to hire him to make sure he did not work for the other side.

In fact, Shipley saw Richards as a vehicle for reform, and however improbable it may seem to his detractors, he has a wide streak of idealism and a tough-minded determination to be honest with himself. Shipley thought too many Texans had their hands in the cookie jar. "We are in the nineteenth century when it comes to campaign finance," he says with matter-of-fact disgust. "We have no limits and we permit third-party interventions. The bribery laws are not enforceable, and lobbyists are glorified as heroes."

The Texas mental health system was under court order to provide better service for its patients. The prison system was under court order to reduce endemic overcrowding. And the courts had recently thrown out a school finance plan. Shipley thought that Ann Richards had the bent and ambition not only to change all that but to accomplish as much in the governor's office as anyone in history, and so he signed on for the duration.

On several weekends in March, Kirk Adams, Richards' son-in-law, flew in from southern California to talk strategy, mainly with Jane Hickie, and just in time for the headquarters opening on May 8, he and Cecile Richards moved to Austin. Adams was to be field director, a position that was a natural for him. Field people are the ones who do the precinct work, who telephone their neighbors, who knock on doors and pass out leaflets, and, most important, who get voters to the polls on election day. A native of Massachusetts, Adams had worked in campaigns for Ted Kennedy, Michael Dukakis, and Congressman Ed Markey and for the past ten years had been a union organizer. A self-described "phone bank maven," he and Cecile together had done union organizing for four years in east and southeast Texas, learning every back road and hamlet from Beaumont to Dallas while they conducted twenty-five nursing-home campaigns.

This core group set up a finance council of effective fund-raisers around the state who planned to meet once a month. Martha Smiley, a lawyer in her forties and one of the original members of the Texas Women's Political Caucus, took a leave of absence from her firm to become state chair of the Richards finance committee. "My husband and I sat down," Smiley says, "and we thought about our kids who were five and seven, and we decided there wasn't any better investment we could make in their education and in the future of Texas than to work for Ann Richards." George Bristol, who had been Lloyd Bentsen's finance chairman since 1976, when he also ran Bentsen's reelection campaign, was hired to put Richards in touch with some of the big-money people who give to Democratic candidates in Texas.

At a time in early 1989 when Jim Mattox had already raised and squirreled away over $3 million, Martin and Shipley were dismayed to find that Richards' early strategists had already raised and spent more than half a million dollars. The money raised in the fall of 1988 in Washington and the big Texas cities seemed to have vanished.

According to sources who asked not to be identified, the Richards people had spent the money hiring a direct mail house that targeted too broad an audience and then had to start over with a different vendor. As Shipley says, "You don't do that: with campaigns, you husband your money." The disappearing half million plus was the first instance of what became a persistent dispute between people like Shipley and Martin on one hand and Richards' personal entourage on the other.

Raising the amount of money needed to run a viable gubernatorial campaign in a state as big as Texas takes uncommon brass and tenacity. As Bristol puts in, "All fund-raising is tough unless you're an incumbent like Bentsen with a long track record." So all through the summer of 1989 and well into the fall, he and Richards concentrated on "one-on-ones": "We'd go from one law office to the next, from one corporate office to the next, one big giver's office to the next. I'd take her around. Somebody in Houston would take her around." Next would be Dallas, then El Paso or San Antonio, seemingly ad infinitum. Richards had to give donors a sense of who she was. As Bristol says: "There's a lot of difference between being treasurer and being governor of the state. People needed to feel her and touch her and ask her questions and get to know her. . . . It doesn't matter whether somebody has $25 or $25,000—they don't want to back a fool."

Meanwhile, the rest of the campaign work went on, and to fill a crucial spot, Jack Martin recommended Glenn Smith as press secretary—a recommendation Lieutenant Governor Bill Hobby was quick to endorse. Smith turned out to be very interested. Now in his mid-thirties, he was a reporter who had begun in Houston on the *Chronicle* and then moved to Austin, where he headed the *Houston Post*'s capitol bureau. As a former colleague, Darla Morgan, put it: "He got along with the male leadership of the House and the Senate. He got stories nobody else could get, and not by plowing through the documents. He'd meet [the politicians] at the watering hole and hear their stories."

From the *Post*, Smith had gone to work for the paper's owner, Bill Hobby, as press secretary and then had served as Hobby's liaison with the Bentsen reelection campaign in 1988 as issues and research director. Of the Democrats up for election in 1990, Richards was the one he most wanted to work for: he had covered her, though never in a crisis, and she struck him as "warm and wonderful."

Within three weeks after Smith started as press secretary, Jane Hickie had talked him into being Richards' campaign manager. Shipley considered Smith a "first-rate political operative," but he had never managed a statewide campaign, much less one as tough as this was likely to be. Still, Shipley thought it would be virtually impossible to snare anyone who did have experience because "once you run a big one, you never want to do it again." As Smith sees it now, "They wanted good, competent, high-profile men involved in the campaign. . . . It was just a public relations thing on their part: Ann was sensitive to being the feminist candidate always surrounded by capable, competent women."

Despite her anxiety over being identified as a woman's candidate, Richards added Lena Guerrero to her staff as political director. A Hispanic state representative from Austin who had been state chair of the Texas Women's Political Caucus in 1983 when she was only twenty-five, Guerrero had won her seat in the legislature in 1984 against a field of five male candidates. Referred to invariably as a political "comer," Guerrero, in the jargon of the trade, is a "three-fer": a woman, a minority, and young. A campaign insider described her as a force of nature—aggressive, even abrasive—and a woman who does exactly what she wants. In 1989, what she wanted more than anything was to see Ann Richards elected governor of Texas.

Early in the spring, Richards and Glenn Smith together persuaded Mark McKinnon to speed up his planned return to Texas from New York to set up the Richards press operation, design her announcement for governor, and act as communications director through Labor Day. McKinnon had first come to Texas in the mid-1970s as a musician and later went to the University of Texas at Austin, where he became a crusading editor of the newspaper, the *Daily Texan*—taking his place in an outstanding tradition that goes back at least to World War II. His *Texan* notoriety had caught the attention of Lloyd Doggett, the Democratic nominee for the U.S. Senate, whose press work he did in 1984. He was Governor Mark White's press secretary before leaving in 1986 to finish learning his craft on a national and then international basis with the Sawyer Miller Group in New York City.

McKinnon had become convinced that regional media firms were doing better jobs for candidates than "these institutional media people" brought in from New York and Washington, and so he had decided to move back to Austin and set up his own consulting firm with Dean Rindy, who was doing outstanding work with candidates throughout the South and Southwest. They would use Texas as their base and work regionally.

As it turned out, McKinnon would remain part of the campaign team until after the primary. He had a strong commitment to Ann Richards: he thought she had fine leadership qualities and a powerful message to communicate to voters. But his advice would be ignored in the councils of the Richards campaign.

Shipley explodes at the idea of hiring regional talent: he believes the best people in media work out of New York and Washington. And so he set up meetings for Richards and her advisers to interview consultants Frank Greer, Ray Strother, and Bob Squier. Richards tentatively decided on one of the first two, and then she met Squier.

McKinnon sat in on her initial interview with Squier, whose firm, Squier-Eskew-Knapp, had helped elect and reelect eighteen Democrats now serving in the United States Senate—more than any other consultant in the business. He also had the best win/lose record: in the 1984 election he had won five out of six races; in 1986, six out of seven; and in 1988, eight out of ten. One of Squier's triumphs had been Frank Lautenberg's victory in the U.S. Senate race in New Jersey over General Pete Dawkins, a former All-American football hero and Rhodes Scholar.

Jane Hickie was impressed. "He can tell you, with the resources you have, how many moves you have to make and what moves are likely to come from the other side." He had also spent several years in central Texas, had a reputation for doing his own work, and was so tenacious Shipley could say, "Bob never quits—never, ever, ever!"

No doubt the Richards team also knew that both Republicans and Democrats had accused Squier of playing fast and loose with facts and of winning by savaging his opponents. He had designed a series of ads for New Jersey gubernatorial candidate Jim Florio that characterized his opponent as a polluter and a liar and showed him with a foot-long nose. The media campaign had pushed Florio dramatically ahead in a race that had been a tossup and carried him on to a 63 percent victory. Frank Luntz, a GOP pollster who credits Squier with "almost warlike strategies," says he is tough to beat because he plays every game differently: "You can't pin him down to a consistent course of action." Hiring him would be tantamount to a declaration of war with the nuclear option held in reserve.

Squier knows how to put on a top-of-the-line performance. He looks a little like Robert Redford, though with neither the sensuality nor the ironic wit, and even sitting down, he is a torrent of energy. In that first interview, he was captivated by Ann Richards: "Boy, she looked like a governor to me! She sounded like a governor. She knew what she wanted to do. She understood her campaign, and she was performing in a way that was wonderful!"

Squier then did something highly unusual. His firm had already been negotiating with Mattox, and he went back to Washington, told his partners about Richards, said how much he wanted to do her media, got them to agree, and called Mattox to withdraw their presentation.

Since he had sat in on the show, Mark McKinnon was not surprised when Richards hired Squier, even though bringing someone in from Washington went against the theory he had touted that regional media firms were more effective for regional candidates. But if McKinnon might be understandably biased, Bill Hobby was not, and he took the same position: "There's no way in a few weeks, or a few months, or even a few years," Hobby says emphatically, "to pick up the political insight and instinct about the dynamics in a state that somebody who's been involved in that state's politics for a long time would have. You wouldn't know how to gauge the unforgivable political slight."

Richards' decision to sign Squier on also sent shudders through a sizable slice of the feminist political community in Washington that considered him not only a throat-cutter—as a competitor put it, when Squier is in the game, the question becomes who will be left standing at the finish line—but insensitive to the special strengths and liabilities of women candidates. Because Richards was running against Jim Mattox, however, Shipley, among others, thought she needed "the meanest media guy she could hire." And the final decision was hers.

On June 10, 1989, Richards announced on the capitol grounds that she was officially in the race for governor of Texas. Her energy and commitment came through as she said, "When I'm governor, one of the things you won't hear anybody saying is, 'That's not my job!' " Underlining a new concern for ethics, she announced that she would make her income tax returns public and called on her opponents to do the same. Her campaign literature envisaged "A New Texas" where children would "learn to think and develop their full human capacity in good schools and caring families," where "drug dealers are punished and treatment is available to any individual who desires to rid his or her life of its scourge," where "quality health care is available to all."

By July 1, the bulk of the campaign team was together, and in August, they mapped out the strategy of the entire campaign. A dozen people were involved, and with Hickman's polling data in hand, they met for two days. They calculated how much money they thought they could raise and decided how to spend it. As it would turn out, they never deviated from that plan.

Squier's view was simple, if demanding. He said that for the primary they would need $700,000 or $800,000 for television ads, and they would hold the ads until the last three weeks. That meant they would have to suffer through a long period when it would look to the outside world as though the Richards campaign was falling to pieces. Jim Mattox, as Shipley put it, would be as implacable as the Soviet army: "He'll come up [on television] and stay up." People would be calling in panic and dismay with unsolicited advice because it would look as though Mattox was walking all over Richards and she was doing nothing about it.

The triumph of this strategy meant that Harrison Hickman had lost an internal power struggle: by waiting until the last weeks to respond to their opponents, the planners had decided to disregard Hickman's hopes of connecting Ann Richards with Texas myth in order to engage some deep stratum of trust and belief. They had decided to lean in a negative rather than a positive direction. But Squier had won after a protracted debate by saying, "Let them open the argument and we'll close it!" He thought it was their only hope against Mattox, who had almost three times the money they did.

Until after Valentine's Day 1990, then, the campaign would have to be sustained on free media. This meant holding press conferences and talking about issues, and everyone knew it would be hard to capture the public's attention, much less keep it.

Richards would make even more than her usual quota of speeches and trips around Texas, though the facts, if read literally, seemed to say that all her work made no difference whatever. She had spent the preceding year giving substantive speeches all over the state. But when Hickman compared his polls from the end of 1988 with those in the late summer of 1989, neither her name identification nor her positive/negative ratings had changed appreciably. As Glenn Smith put it, "She was busting her butt on her own every day. She was all over the place. And it made no difference."

If Richards averaged twenty speeches a week, and spoke on occasion to three or four hundred people, she could reach at most several thousand people. One major television buy in the Dallas market would reach 2 million. Free media, then, was relatively insignificant. As Hickman put it, especially in big states, "unless you set yourself on fire on the capitol steps, or get indicted, or make a real nuisance of yourself, you don't get the kind of media coverage that people remember."

So speeches were not the way for Richards to introduce herself to the public. Still, they had the virtue of strengthening support she already had: they were crucial to sustaining and fanning the enthusiasm people had for Ann Richards, and that enthusiasm was ultimately what made her different from her opponents.

Jim Mattox not only had much more money for television, he had a large paid field operation that he had been building for years. Richards' field staff of four included Cecile and Kirk Adams. But when Adams began to fashion the Richards organization, he discovered people all over the state who were keen to work, and to work for nothing.

In Fort Worth, for instance, a man named Gary Lipe volunteered to set up a Richards phone bank. Lipe's banker wife had been impressed with Richards' work at the treasury, and after hearing her effusive praise, Lipe walked into the Democratic headquarters and asked for a list of Democratic voters and their phone numbers so that he and a group of volunteers could work for Richards. The people behind the desk guffawed and allowed as how they too would like to have such a list!

So Lipe took it upon himself to develop a computerized data base by purchasing the Tarrant County voter rolls, compiling a list of everyone who had voted since 1986, and breaking it down, where possible, into categories. He found approximately 85,000 Republicans, 75,000 Democrats, and 170,000 Independents. The Independents were therefore targeted for the Lipe efforts at persuasion, which included both phone banks and block walking.*

For the 1990s, the Richards organization would be unusual in that it harkened back to the days of voluntarism. But if Richards' pool of enthusiastic volunteers staffed the phone banks and Get-Out-the-Vote efforts, the campaign could then spend most of its money for media.

From his years as a union organizer, Kirk Adams had learned to find money in the bark of a tree and squirrel it away. He created programs the rest of the staff did not know existed and prevailed on local communities to fund them. The campaign work he did required even more patience than regular union work because his job was not to persuade people to vote for Ann Richards but to organize them once they had been persuaded.

Several key insiders thought that having Richards' family involved in her campaign spelled disaster. Her children threw off the tenuous equilibrium a campaign needs by swelling the ratio of chiefs to Indians. No matter how self-effacing they might try to be, their tie to the candidate gave them more weight than could be good either for them or for other people.

But Ann Richards is very close to her children, and what they gave her, no one could buy. They did a phenomenal amount of work, extending her reach far beyond what any one candidate, however energetic and driven, could accomplish. When people shook hands with Cecile or Ellen, they came away feeling they had virtually touched the candidate herself. And almost every day for nine months, Dan Richards gave his mother an arm and a shoulder for balance and an ear wholly discreet. Most important, as Ann Richards would put it later, they kept her in touch with who she really was.

At the same time, in the words of Kirk Adams, it was a very rough ride for everybody.

---

*In 1990, of the hundred thousand people who would vote in the Tarrant County Democratic primary, 40 percent were apparently Republican crossovers or Independents, and so efforts like Lipe's seemed to make a significant difference. In the runoff, he would give each volunteer fifty names of female Independents to call and ask to vote for Richards. Lipe predicted that she would get 72 percent of the Tarrant County vote in the primary runoff, and that is exactly what she got.

CHAPTER 3

She had to look into the heart of darkness.
It had a name, and the name was Mattox.
—GEORGE SHIPLEY

Everything's fair in politics.
—JIM MATTOX

The woman who performed with such aplomb before the Democrats gathered in Atlanta for their quadrennial tribal rituals was to be subjected to an attack so vicious and sustained that it shocked even the national press. Journalists found the 1990 Democratic primary in Texas among the nastiest in American history, and if that said more about their sense of decency than their knowledge of history, it nevertheless registered the disgust the spectacle aroused in many observers.

But the level of vitriol was nothing new for Texas. Robert Caro's books on Lyndon Johnson have made the state's politics a synonym for chicanery. And some of the most notorious campaigns in the last four decades have been waged by conservative Democrats against liberals—mainly against Ralph Yarborough. When United States Senator Lloyd Bentsen, for instance, described Texas politics as a contact sport, few people, even among the national press that quoted him so widely, realized that the courtly, silver-haired gentleman was adept at the double-knee in the groin tactic of playing the game.

Few campaigns have been uglier than the one Bentsen won against Yarborough in 1970 for his seat in the United States Senate. Using photographs of street demonstrations at the 1968 Democratic convention in Chicago, Bentsen implied that Yarborough, who had indignantly protested the police brutality, had inspired and even spurred on the kids with the rocks. He insinuated that a man who would vote, as Yarborough did, against a constitutional amendment allowing prayer in the schools was a man whose Christian faith was suspect. And he lambasted the senator for his votes against confirming

Judges Clement F. Haynsworth, Jr., and G. Harrold Carswell, Nixon
nominees to the United States Supreme Court who had so embarrassed many members of the president's own party that they joined
with Democrats to deny Senate confirmation to Supreme Court nominees for the first time since one of Herbert Hoover's in 1930. Haynsworth and Carswell both had histories that were interpreted as racist,
and Texas Democrats understood Bentsen to be saying that folks
had the right to their own prejudices.

Allan Shivers had used much the same tactics when he ran against
Yarborough in 1954 for governor. He had sent a camera crew to
film at 6 A.M. on a Sunday in downtown Port Arthur, a Gulf port
that labor was trying to organize, and then had called on its deserted
streets to witness what union terrorism was doing to a fine Texas
city. The Shivers forces had made a hit road show of their film *The
Port Arthur Story*, taking it all over the state with an accompanying
handful of local citizens testifying to the forces of darkness and evil
ready to descend over Texas if the powers of right and justice failed
to stand up to the "Nigras" and the union goons. Larry L. King
wrote of their performance, "I never saw anything to approach it
for sheer chutzpah, corn, or effectiveness—though I would later
spend ten years in the political major leagues, some in the company
of LBJ." After coming within twenty thousand votes of Shivers in
the primary, Yarborough had been swamped in the runoff, and King
argued that the election determined "the course of race relations in
Texas for years."

Racism doesn't invite plain speaking; on the contrary, it lends
itself to code words and innuendo. So out of debacles like the Yarborough defeats had grown a conventionally accepted response: instead of answering an opponent's charge directly, you counterattack.
Unless you do that, you allow your opponent to choose the weapons
and write the rules of the game. You will be forced to play defense,
rather than offense. One of the best instances of this strategy, and
Ann Richards' pre-1990 attitude toward it, comes from the 1984
Texas Democratic primary campaign for the United States Senate,
which featured three politically distinct competitors: Lloyd Doggett
on the left, Kent Hance on the right, and Bob Krueger in the middle.

Doggett was a state senator from Austin, a liberal with a circle
of informal advisers that included Richards and Commissioner of

Agriculture Jim Hightower. Krueger, who had been a promising member of Congress from New Braunfels, had a statewide base of support built up from a run for the United States Senate six years earlier against John Tower, whom he very nearly defeated. Hance had been a member of Congress with a financial base in west Texas when there was still a good deal of money to be found there.

For obvious reasons, in any campaign, each side has to focus its advertising on those people who have not yet made up their minds. And as Bill Zimmerman of California, who designed Doggett's media strategy, puts it, the "good" citizens, who are moved by positive messages, have already made up their minds. They read; they talk with their friends; they are not influenced by TV advertising. Early on, they become the "decideds," as opposed to the "undecideds."

In a hotly contested election, therefore, a built-in dynamic pushes a candidate in a negative direction. The candidate has to use his or her advertising budget to talk to the undecideds, which is to say the people in the middle. They are in the middle because they are either uninformed, uninterested, or cynical, and in Zimmerman's experience, "you can't move them as easily with positive messages as you can with negative messages."

In a few seconds, there is not much a candidate can say that is snappy and memorable to distinguish himself from someone else. So in 1984, when Krueger and Hance discovered that Doggett was gaining on them in the polls, the easiest and most effective course for them to take was to attack. It was easy to say: He's against the death penalty! He's for gay rights! And it was effective because majority opinion in the state takes the opposite side.

"Once someone attacks you," Zimmerman explains, "as they did us in the Doggett campaign, you can't respond by being defensive about the charges. *You have to be negative. You have to counterattack in an entirely different area.* And that dynamic creates a downward spiral into very negative campaigning."

When Zimmerman insisted that Doggett's problem required a negative response, Ann Richards repeatedly objected, arguing that Doggett should be running a positive campaign because otherwise they would split the party and lose to the Republicans in November. She took her position forcefully, and Zimmerman had to take the offense on behalf of the opposing strategy.

The 1984 Texas Democratic primary was one of the closest three-way elections in American history: the candidates finished within 0.07 percent of each other. Each got 31 percent of the vote, but Krueger got the smallest fraction above that and so was eliminated.

Hance immediately went on the air attacking Doggett's stand against the death penalty and for the next four weeks outspent him two to one ramming that message home. Doggett's own polls showed that 59 percent of the Democrats likely to vote in the runoff election would vote against a candidate who opposed the death penalty—even if they agreed with him on every other issue. Therefore, Doggett had to figure out a way to get around an extraordinary liability.

"Given those poll results," as Zimmerman says, "you can't go out and talk about some positive attribute Mr. Doggett has. So we had to open a line of attack against Hance that meant more to people than the death penalty. We created probably the most vicious spot that's ever been used in politics: it's won all kinds of awards. It's called 'the butler spot': it shows an actor playing a butler, and the voice-over tries to indicate that this figure is Kent Hance. He's wearing a tux and white gloves, and he's carrying a silver tray. On the tray is a book titled *Tax Breaks for the Rich*. The narrator describes how Hance was the author of the 1981 Hance-Conable tax revision, which was a series of tax breaks for the rich. And he concludes by saying Kent Hance isn't a congressman: he's a butler!" That ad won the election for Doggett "by a squeaker."

Critical from the beginning, Richards was adamantly opposed to running the butler ad. Her counsel was overridden. What she had predicted then proceeded to happen, though not for the reasons she anticipated. Republican nominee Phil Gramm beat Doggett by doing a ranker version of the same thing Hance had done and doing it more effectively because he had more money.

The week after the Democratic primary runoff in June, Gramm began spending $200,000 a week attacking Doggett for accepting money he said came from a male strip show put on by a gay rights group in San Antonio. Doggett had taken money from the gay rights group, though the strip show had been a fund-raiser for the gay organization. The cry "Lloyd Doggett takes money from male strippers," however, drowned out the nuances, and after spending $11 million in the 1984 general election to win the seat, Phil Gramm will be United States senator from Texas for the foreseeable future.

A good many unhappy Democrats subsequently wailed that unlike Lloyd Doggett, Bob Krueger, who would be elected in 1990 to the Texas Railroad Commission, could have beaten Phil Gramm in the 1984 general election, and that may well be the case. Democrats have not yet solved a characteristic problem: the people who vote in the Democratic primary appear to be significantly more liberal than those who vote in the general election. Therefore, the Democrats have a tendency to nominate candidates who may not be strong enough to defeat their Republican opponents in November.

Doggett, however, could hardly be faulted for winning an election he set out to win, and when Richards looked to the 1984 primary for lessons, she would have found at least two. One was that supporting the death penalty is part of the dues one pays to be elected in Texas. The other was that negative campaigning works.

The 1990 Democratic primary differed from the one six years earlier by engaging people who had fought more nearly on the same side: Ann Richards and Attorney General Jim Mattox were liberals, and former Governor Mark White was a moderate. Mattox had been David Richards' boss, and all of them had been friends and colleagues for years.

By 1990, the rules of relevance in political attack had changed dramatically from the days of John F. Kennedy, a relentless womanizer whose "indiscretions" were protected by a predominantly male press who not only for the most part found him enchanting but who considered a candidate's private life off-limits. The Gary Hart scandal of 1987, however, seemed to open up personal life as the legitimate grounds for political poaching, and it was this territory that Jim Mattox was determined to exploit.

As a candidate, Mattox was known to be cruel and vengeful. *Dallas Times Herald* columnist Molly Ivins described him as "a man so mean he wouldn't spit in your ear if your brains were on fire." And because reporters knew his bent, at the 1988 Democratic National Convention in Atlanta, Dallas television station WFAA trained a camera on him as Ann Richards gave her keynote address. According to reporter Robert Riggs, it caught him swelling and darkening with rage: convinced he was entitled to be governor, Mattox saw on the podium a spoiler the Democratic National Committee and the media were creating.

As an officeholder, he had harnessed his awesome capacity for rage to fight for "the downtrodden of society." A three-term member of Congress from Dallas with a fine record in support of labor and liberal issues, he had been attorney general since 1983, and he thought the minorities and women he had fought for owed him their support. On women's rights, he believed he had "a stronger record than virtually any candidate in the United States, male or female," while he considered his opponent "a media darling" who "had never done anything," had "no record of accomplishment," and therefore no scars. His scars, his reputation as a "pit bull" had come from fighting "a tremendous number of battles" for women and consumers.

Mary Beth Rogers, who would run the Richards campaign in the general election, said Mattox "may have been one of the best attorneys general Texas has ever had." He had many Democratic party activists on his side, and his political director, an impressive black woman named Hazel Falke-Obey, was vice-chair of the Texas Democratic party. Like Richards, he had a committed following. So for Rogers, "Even if I hadn't known either candidate, that race would have been a sad and distressing development." Others were not so charitable, and by the end of the primary, Mattox was openly referred to as the junkyard dog of Texas politics.

It was generally assumed that Mattox's threats of personal exposure had discouraged Lieutenant Governor Bill Hobby from trying for the office his father had held sixty years earlier. Almost two years after the fact, David Richards recalled the last time he had had a substantive conversation with his former boss: "He asked me how he was doing attacking Hobby. And I told him, 'Jim, my guess is that Hobby's not much interested in running for governor. If you end up pushing him out of the race, you'll get Cisneros or Ann for an opponent, and you'll wish you had [Hobby] back!' "

After Mattox threatened San Antonio Mayor Henry Cisneros with leaking lurid tales to the press of an extramarital affair, Cisneros preempted the initiative and announced it himself, finally declaring a moratorium on politics for the nonce. Their abdication left only Richards standing in the way of Mattox's long-standing ambition to be governor.

In Mattox's eyes, Richards had an unfair advantage he was called upon to destroy. She had "no negatives to speak of . . . because she had a job that caused her to have absolutely no enemies and [she] had not done anything to create any," whereas he had had a high-profile job "that carried [him] from one battle to the next for many years and generated a lot of enemies."

According to Jane Hickie, Richards knew, at least theoretically, what was coming. Mattox had called her in 1988 and said, "If you get into this race, this is what I'm going to say about you." Theoretical knowledge, however, is different from emotional understanding. The latter, as Ann Richards would discover once again, one learns only from experience. As George Shipley says, "It's one thing to think a baseball bat hurts, and another to get hit by one in the head." Hickie describes the horror of waiting for the scandal to break: "I think it was almost a relief when it started happening. You'd wake up every day and think, 'God, what's he going to do today?'"

No doubt Richards wanted to believe that the trauma would be no worse than in 1982, when Lane Denton, her primary opponent in the treasurer's race, not only told the press she was alcoholic but, according to Jane Hickie, said she was an abusive mother. For a week he had preceded her to every town on her itinerary and left a host of questions for her to answer. She had stood up to that trial nicely: she had said that indeed she had been treated for alcoholism, was in recovery, and looked to the future. Denton's electoral support had proved negligible, and the whole experience seemed to suggest that Texans did not cotton to mean-spirited attacks on women—and that she could deflect the blows by refusing to run and hide.

At the 1989 AFL-CIO convention, Sam Dawson, political director of the Steelworkers Union, which endorsed Mattox, warned him against slamming Richards. He said that before he attacked her on alcoholism or anything else he ought to talk with Denton. He cautioned: the day Denton started attacking her alcoholism, his campaign went down the toilet, and he never got it out. Dawson also told Mattox he had watched campaigns around the country, and men could not attack a woman the way they could a man. Mattox replied that they just didn't know how to do it and he did.

Even a battle-scarred pro like Harrison Hickman, who had been warned about Mattox, was dumbfounded when he proved so venomous. One of Mattox's staff members called after Hickman had signed on with Richards and ostensibly tried to hire him. When Hickman said he had a contract with Richards, the man said, "You're gonna be sorry because she's gonna lose." Hickman said, "If you're trying to intimidate me, you're dealing with the wrong guy." But when he hung up, he realized that the Mattox people had known about his contract all along and wanted to send a message back to her. It was just one brief note in a terrorist campaign. Even with that warning, Hickman was astonished at Mattox's relentless nastiness.

Had Mattox ignored Richards and run a positive campaign, Dawson is convinced he would have been the Democratic nominee, and he believes that if John Rogers, Mary Beth's late husband, had been alive, Rogers could have talked Mattox out of it. "There's no question in the mind of any political professional in the state of Texas," Dawson says: Mattox had the money; he had the organization; he had the record. "When he votes, he votes right down the line with women, with labor, with the folks." But he does not listen.

In August 1989, while Richards took a week-long cruise up the Texas coast to catch the public's attention by way of some free media that would give her a chance to talk about the environment, former Governor Mark White began to speak publicly about a comeback. The incumbent governor, Bill Clements, had beaten him in 1986, after having lost to him in 1982, and White had both a hankering for an office he had enjoyed and a lust for vindication.

A smooth performer, White had once commanded a substantial network of wealthy, influential supporters, and the voters had forgotten some of the reasons they had turned him out of office. By early fall, White was in the race, and if Mattox and Richards got into a poisonous fight, it seemed likely that White could emerge the cleanest of the three candidates.

The polls Harrison Hickman took around that time, however,

showed Richards in a clearly dominant position: whatever the nig-
gling criticisms, her convention speech had catapulted her into the
lead—at least with the Democratic electorate. But Mattox was much
stronger than public polls suggested. Many Democrats liked his populism, and he was well positioned to win the nomination.

To the core of women around Richards, the most astonishing of
Hickman's findings was that for all her national reputation, she was
comparatively unknown among Democrats in Texas. Still, she could
expect strong support in the places women candidates typically found
it: in the suburbs and among other women, especially those who
worked.

Although political parties in the United States are far less ideological than their European counterparts, there are essential differences between them, and party primaries offer a rare chance for their
members to decide among themselves what they stand for. Issues are
more likely to be discussed in some depth in primary campaigns than
in the general election, where candidates commonly fuzz their positions and party affiliations to reach out to Independents and even
to the other side. It behooved the three Democratic candidates for
governor, then, to look hard at Texas and decide what they could
and should do about it.

For all its flamboyant image, the state they proposed to run was
now in very deep trouble. By 1995, Texas is expected to become the
nation's second most populous state. But with a gross national product equal to that of 95 percent of the richest countries in the world,
in 1990 it ranked fiftieth among the states in per capita spending on
public welfare, forty-fifth in mental health funding, fiftieth in benefits
for poor people, forty-eighth in spending on prenatal care for pregnant women, forty-seventh in health care in general, forty-fifth in
spending on Medicaid, and thirty-seventh in per pupil expenditures
in the schools.

An estimated 2.7 million Texans had no health insurance.
Roughly one-third of Texas students dropped out before receiving a
high school diploma, and 575,000 adults were illiterate. By the year
2000, the majority of the school population will be made up of
minority groups, while 90 percent of the teachers will be white. There

is only one evening law school in the whole state, so it is very unlikely that women with children or people from the barrios will be able to go to law school.

Near the beginning of the primary campaign, newspaper head-lines called attention once more to one of Texas' most serious prob-lems. In October 1989, the Texas Supreme Court unanimously ruled against the state's method of financing public education and ordered that an alternate plan be submitted by the following May. For the third time in ten years, the courts had imposed fundamental changes—a clear sign that the legislature was failing to deal with basic questions of equity and public policy.*

About the same time, Dave McNeely of the *Austin American-Statesman* recorded the fact that Texas led the nation in the number of births to children fifteen years and younger—a clear indicator of social dysfunction. Pointing to overwhelming evidence indicating that children's performance in school depends primarily on their parents' wealth and level of education, in addition to whether they live with one parent or both, he cataloged several other alarming statistics: almost one-fourth of American children are born to single mothers and brought up by them, and single-parent families are four times poorer than two-parent families.

The heaviest burden of poverty and social dysfunction falls on the minority communities, so that in 1986, 61 percent of all black children in Texas were born to single mothers. One out of every twelve young black males was in jail or prison; 47 percent of Texas' prison population was black; 13 percent was Hispanic. Nine out of ten prison inmates did not graduate from high school.

Here was a wealth of material for the people who asked to lead Texas to reflect upon and debate. State Representative Dan Morales, a candidate for the Democratic nomination for attorney general, for instance, made some important connections. He noticed that the state was making projections for prison beds that would not be available for ten years, while at the same time it was insisting that it had no money to provide for equal educational opportunity. He concluded

---

*During the 1980s, Federal District Judge William Wayne Justice had issued a series of rulings that mandated changes to end overcrowding in the state prison system. A series of other decisions—also handed down from the federal bench—required far more money to be spent on the state's mental health and mental retardation system.

that the state was saying, "We don't have enough money to educate you now, but we're reserving a $70,000 room for you in the future, where you can live at the taxpayers' expense for more than $15,000 a year."

Ann Richards had exactly the background to understand these problems. In the 1970s, she had served on the special committee on the delivery of human services that Bill Hobby appointed to hold hearings all over Texas—a committee that amassed volumes of information. Hobby had chosen Richards' friend Helen Farabee of Wichita Falls, Texas' preeminent volunteer, to chair the committee, and Farabee in turn had assigned Richards the special responsibility of studying the young: the segment of the population from birth to seventeen years of age. This is how a commissioner from a county in central Texas learned about matters far beyond her normal purview so that by the time Richards was elected treasurer, she knew from the local level to the federal all about the problems of families in crisis and something about how to confront them realistically.

Both Farabee and Richards believed, in Hubert Humphrey's phrase, that "the moral test of government is how it treats those in the dawn of life—the children; those in the twilight of life—the aged; and those in the shadows of life—the sick, the needy, and the disadvantaged." As Richards said in a film celebrating Farabee's life, people connected with government needed to see "the people beyond the policies, the people affected beyond the laws," and by the late 1970s, she herself had also learned how to use the instruments of government for humanitarian ends.

The 1990 campaign posed the question: Would the political system encourage or even allow a gubernatorial candidate to deal straightforwardly with issues like child poverty that would profoundly affect the lives of Texans for generations to come?

The answer was no. The consensus in Texas was that no candidate could discuss issues that might raise the specter of taxes if he or she expected to remain viable.

In response to a projected state deficit of over $2.5 billion, Jim Mattox came out early for a lottery, which apparently strikes voters as the least disagreeable way to raise money for state government, and both Richards and White quickly said, "me too." Bill Hobby had gone around the state arguing that Texas had to have an income tax, but as a lame duck lieutenant governor, Hobby could suffer no political consequences. To stay in the gubernatorial race, Ann Richards had to play to voters' fears and soft-pedal subjects about which she cared passionately.

As a result, the issues that surround child poverty and teenage delinquency were not joined in the first months of the Democratic primary campaign—nor were many others. Matters of public policy seemed buried under questions about who would raise how much money for a media blitz and by what means.

Mattox had gone into the second half of 1989 with $3.7 million, compared to Richards' $1 million. In the first half of the year, he had raised about $650,000 to her $410,000, and he had raised it by receiving larger contributions from mainstream Texas sources. As *Fort Worth Star-Telegram* columnist Kaye Northcott wrote, "He has such power as attorney general that many politically active establishment types dare not slight him." Richards, on the other hand, had three times the number of donors he did and, by now, a superbly functioning direct mail operation. Since White had entered the race late, his fund-raising capability remained an open question.

For once, however, it seemed unlikely that big money would have its way with Texas. In September, political scientist Richard Murray of the University of Houston released a poll showing Richards with 35 percent of the Democratic vote, followed by White at 23 percent and Mattox with only 8 percent. Four months later, in January, another Murray poll gave Richards 35 percent, White 29 percent, and Mattox 10 percent. The most remarkable fact about her commanding lead was that Richards, following the plan her team had put together in June, had spent nothing as yet on television. White would make the first television buys, and Mattox would precede Richards on television by many weeks.

Northcott shed crocodile tears for "Poor Jim": "The years of brash hustling, of strong-arming his way into other people's reception lines, of always being in the camera shot, of unseemly pressure on people to give him campaign contributions and endorsements, of inevitably tacky remarks about his opponents, seem to have eclipsed his significant achievements as attorney general." Richards' opponents remained better known than she, but her positive ratings were

55 percent, compared to 49 percent for White and 43 percent for Mattox.

Of course, polls are easier for the press to report than issues, and they can also mislead the public and the politicians themselves into taking them for something other than the snapshots of a process in constant motion that they are. But the fact that the public polls put Richards ahead of Mattox by more than three to one over a period of four months clearly meant something, and Mattox did not like it.

His poor showing in the polls was capped with a tactical victory by Richards' supporters, who managed to block, if only by a fraction of a vote, an endorsement he coveted by the Mexican-American Democrats. In late January, they did it again with the state AFL-CIO endorsement. On the latter occasion, he fought so hard and his forces were so exercised that at one point, Richards' people were pushing her toward a door in Austin's municipal auditorium when Mattox's troops broke into a chant and came after them. Blood did not flow, however, and the warfare was conducted primarily by means of parliamentary maneuver.

Mattox had a majority of delegates, but not the two-thirds necessary for an endorsement, and the issue over which the convention wrangled all day was whether labor would skip the top office and endorse candidates for the remainder of the slate. At midevening, the convention deadlocked, and the day ended with Mattox taking the entire slate down with him and labor making no endorsements whatever. After this debacle, McNeely described Mattox as "a self-centered bully who won't play unless he gets to set the rules," but Mattox blinded himself to criticism: the press was unfair and columnists like McNeely and Molly Ivins "might as well be on the Richards payroll."

He was acutely frustrated. Although he had "probably the strongest consumer record in the nation," consumer groups would not endorse him. Despite his "far superior record on women's issues," women's groups would not endorse him, and "the women within organized labor" had disregarded his "impeccable record" and blocked the labor endorsement. The same had happened with gay, black, and Hispanic groups. "The people I had fought the battles for for so many years," he said later, "did not respond in kind." Convinced that "everything's fair in politics," and discovering that the "record makes absolutely no difference in these races," he would bring his opponent down to his own level.

While her opponents seemed to be catching up to her in the polls, Ann Richards and her family were busy doing the job they had set out in August of 1989 to do. No matter what the day's news or the latest poll results, they had to keep doggedly at their business as though impervious to pain or exhilaration.

From February 1990, when he joined the campaign, until November 7, when it was over, Dan Richards would pick up his mother in the morning and drive her to the airport to board sleek private planes. They would spend the day climbing in and out of a small plane and a good many big cars, while Dan tried to make sure Ann got where she was expected to be on time and without any unnecessary hassle.

If Dan got to his mother's house just in time to leave, they generally left late. And if they left late, they usually ran late all day. He therefore put a high premium on getting to her house early. If that meant they didn't have time for breakfast, they would patronize the vending machines in airports. As Dan remembers, "We didn't eat much of anything good the whole time."

For nine months, they averaged five or six days out of the week on the road, with as many as five stops a day. A typical schedule might include an hour-long session with, say, the *Houston Chronicle* editorial board, a luncheon speech to six hundred at the convention center half a mile away, a midafternoon meeting with a potential contributor in Beaumont, a late afternoon reception in Port Arthur, followed by dinner with the local volunteers, and finally an appearance at some function back in Austin before the chance came to go home at last and to bed. At even unpretentious gatherings the candidate would make at least a five-minute talk.

The closer they were to election day, the more likely Ann Richards was to face, at almost every stop, a barrage from reporters. Some were polite, but many were not. They would get right up in her face with their notebooks, asking staccato questions, while the television cameramen hoisted massive black cameras onto their shoulders and pushed people aside to get their footage from the best angle. Dan had to judge when it was more politic to let a particularly aggressive reporter get a story and when his mother was not ready to take on someone abrasive.

He also had to keep her moving when supporters wanted her to listen, and he had to try to keep them from burdening her with tales of campaign foul-ups in their districts. At almost every stop, people wanted more money from headquarters and more of the candidate's time, and he had to deflect them without leaving a trail of hurt feelings.

Dan's job combined stress and tedium in almost equal measure. To relieve them, he read gory murder mysteries and played soccer when he had a free day on the weekends. He knew it was harder still on his mother, and when it was all over, he admired her even more than he had when they started. "She's tough as nails, man!" he would say with hard-edged laughter.

With each audience, Richards faced the challenge of having to repeat herself but tailor the message to the particular group she was addressing. Smart candidates typically get bored fast, but as Hickman says, "You want to be saying something consistent, so that everybody hears roughly the same thing. About the time a candidate gets bored with saying something, that's about the time the first voter has heard it." The people on the road were as interested in gossip and good stories as they were in issues, and those too come in finite quantities.

In the movie *The Candidate*, there is a scene of Robert Redford, playing the title role, in the back seat of a car going slightly berserk from the tedium of repeating himself. He begins by making fun of his own set speech—mocking his own patter—and then he goes into a television studio where he blows his precious moments of free media time because he can't stop laughing. These two scenes perfectly capture both the inanity and insanity of campaigning. Perhaps the greatest testament to the bond between Dan Richards and his mother is that he listened to her six days a week for almost nine months without bolting from boredom or despair.

While Ann and Dan were on the road—or on the wing, as the case might be—Kirk Adams could be in Houston, working with coordinators there to set up their phone bank operation, and Cecile was most likely on the telephone in Austin talking with supporters in Fort Worth or El Paso. Their daughter Lily would be running around the headquarters helping people do their work. Ellen might be at a fiesta in San Antonio or a convention in Dallas.

Much of the work they did was repetitive, tedious, and boring. All of it involved tender, clamorous egos, tight schedules, a limited budget, and a wealth of minute detail. None of it could be put off. Every bit was important.

Although the public polls showed Jim Mattox's support at a negligible 8 or 9 percent because he was disliked by the public at large, his substantial following among the Democratic primary electorate meant that in Hickman's polls he was never below 22 percent. In January, Mattox's own polls must have been showing the same things Hickman's were: that he was near to closing the gap with Richards. Her positive ratings had been essentially stable until he had gone on television to say, "They will raise taxes, and I'm for a lottery," and then her negatives began to rise. Mattox's first ads appeared roughly four weeks before hers did, and he could see that with a little luck he might overtake her.*

The first televised debate offered Mattox the perfect opportunity to drag Ann Richards down. He had begun his campaign of insinuations months earlier, and by January everyone knew it was only a matter of time before the drug question surfaced publicly. Clayton Williams, who was leading in the race for the Republican gubernatorial nomination, was making drugs the key issue in his campaign. The panel of reporters covering the debate had agreed on a range of questions, among which drugs seemed an obvious choice. Richards had rehearsed several different answers, and when Dallas reporter Cinny Kennard asked if she had used illegal substances, she responded by saying she had taken no mind-altering chemicals for ten years.

---

*Harrison Hickman explains the discrepancy between Mattox's standing in his polls on one hand, and public polls like Richard Murray's at the University of Houston, or the Texas Poll, which comes out of Texas A&M, on the other. Hickman is careful to restrict his calling to people who are likely to vote in the Democratic primary, and his questions have to do primarily with personality and character traits. Public polls are less narrowly focused, and their questions are more likely to deal with public policy. As Hickman puts it, "We are to public pollsters like psychiatrists are to Ann Landers. We do a totally different level of analysis." Ed Reilly's polls for Dianne Feinstein in California also told a somewhat different story from the one the public polls were telling.

No one, least of all Ann Richards, believed that the matter would end there. In the days after that first debate, her evasion gave Mattox and White just the chance they needed to begin hammering at her publicly, and they did that with all the sanctimoniousness they could muster. They led the chorus demanding, "Answer the question! Answer the question!" until the uproar blotted out every other issue.

As Kirk Adams says, the downside of Ann's children being involved in her campaign was that "it was a really rough ride! For everybody! It's real hard to pick up a paper and read things about your mom that you don't want to read about anybody." They had to watch their mother, confronted inescapably with the drug question, deciding between only three possible answers: "Yes," "No," and "I refuse to answer."

Her staff was split. Her friends were split. And the voting public was full of unsolicited advice.*

Jane Hickie wanted her to say, "That's a lie! Don't be ridiculous, and stay out of my life!" As Hickie sees it, if Richards had had an addiction to Valium or prescription drugs—an addiction common to women of her generation—"she would have been talking about that for years. She would have said, 'I had a multiple addiction.' But it's nowhere written that you talk about anything but the drugs you abused." The charge, however, had not been framed in terms of addiction, which is why it was so insidious.

"No" was impossible, if for no other reason than that members of the press had apparently been included in the parties on those late nights when drugs were passed around. David Richards put her dilemma clearly: "The program for recovering alcoholics says you have to be truthful, and so it wasn't emotionally available for Ann to lie. She was trapped: once you admit something, you are fair game. If she wasn't going to lie, she was right [in the answer she gave]."

Many sided with David Richards in believing that if Ann said "Yes," Mattox would never let her rest. The next questions would

---

*In retrospect it would seem clear that Richards should have dealt with the drug issue earlier. A candidate for office is well advised to reveal anything potentially damaging long before the electoral cycle begins: two years of airing can dissipate the stench of almost any scandal short of incest or murder with malice aforethought. And Ann Richards was so advised. Her autobiography had given her a chance she passed up to slip the revelation in almost casually, in a sentence or two.

be: "When?" "Where?" "How many times?" "Were your children there?" He would badger her constantly, and members of the media would pursue the issue to exploit its sensationalism and to prove that they were not playing favorites.

Uncounted numbers of people disagreed and wanted her to admit she had smoked a joint or two and get it over with. According to Hickie, between three and four hundred people called headquarters: "They wanted to tell her what to do. They were sure she was doing it wrong. . . . Her friends, her children, her parents! There was not a person around who did not beat on that woman with every weapon at their disposal: financial, intellectual, emotional. 'Answer the question!' 'Answer the question!' She could not make a telephone call without someone telling her she was doing the wrong thing."

All through February, the pressure intensified and the advice flowed abundantly. George Bristol, the chair of Richards' fund-raising committee, remembers a ten-day period when things were really tough: "It was heavy on so many levels. . . . Her family and grandchildren were hearing that crap. Her friends were hearing that crap. The mental stress alone was terrific. I've seen people go away and hide and suck their thumbs. But she just reached down into herself. . . . I was on the phone for four days. I almost never left. All her friends were crying with her, crying for her, and there wasn't a goddamn thing we could do about it. The monster was in the street. And rather than duck in the first door and nail it shut, she just stayed in the street. And she finally ate the monster." Hickie says about the period through February and into March: "People would drive up to the campaign headquarters, come in and bring a TV spot they'd written. The spots were awful, absolutely worthless. But the love was just wonderful."

Richards knew that whatever she did had to be consistent with her sobriety, and she made an intensely personal decision. Whatever the deep psychological reasons that led up to it, as Rogers put it, Richards handled it in keeping "with her own philosophy, her own sense of personal integrity. She handled it the way she *had* to handle it for herself." Reflecting her own sense of perspective, Rogers added: "I don't think every decision in a campaign is based on what the polls say. She had some need for privacy."

Glenn Smith, Lena Guerrero, George Shipley, Jane Hickie, and two or three others were in the room with Richards when she announced her final decision. She said, "This election is not that important to me—to say yes or no. I have fought to get where I am today, and I will not go back." Perhaps the most important thing about that decision was that she was willing to stand by it and lose, and the self-respect she gained by making it had to be invaluable.

Then she began to convince the people closest to her. Bristol remembers: "Ann truly believed—and it took me a little while to understand this—that the answer she gave was the right answer. She was not going to open up any other aspect of her life because she felt it might affect other people's ability to get over their addiction."

Dan Richards recalls psyching himself up for the ordeal of the second debate in Dallas on March 2, which would seem even in retrospect the lowest point in a long campaign. He told himself that he could endure the tension because he knew almost exactly how long it would last: the debate itself was one hour, and the questioning afterward would take a maximum of thirty minutes.

Everyone who cared about Ann Richards was anxious, and even a veteran debate-watcher like Harrison Hickman, who was sitting in the waiting area, had never clutched up as much as he did when reporter Cinny Kennard, expecting Richards to resolve the confusion, returned to the drug question and was bluntly insistent: "Have you used illegal drugs?"

Richards dug in: "I have revealed more about my personal life, including my alcoholism and my recovery—for ten years—than any person who has ever run for governor before. I have told my story again and again. And now by continuing to raise these questions, I think we are sending a very sad message to a lot of people who think that if they seek treatment they will forever bear the stigma of their addiction."

Kennard interrupted: "Is that a yes or no?"

Richards ignored her question and addressed herself to the audience at large, insisting that those who needed help ought to seek it because they could, in fact, get well.

When it came their turn, White and Mattox each said briefly that he had never used illegal drugs. And then Mattox addressed himself to Richards: "Ann, Mark and I have known you a long time, *and*

we understand why you don't want to answer the question! At least
eight times reporters have asked you to respond—and that's only
the Democratic primary. If you were to be the nominee of this party,
the Republicans will not be as gentle. Clayton Williams will do more
than just bust rocks. He'll bust our party. Regardless of how much
you think it will hurt you, you need to respond and answer this
question in the primary. Because it has become the biggest question
in this campaign."

Richards remained silent.

After the debate, she was mobbed by reporters and cameramen,
as many as fifty in all, shouting, "Answer the question! Answer the
question!" One drunk woman reporter was shouting louder than
anyone else and breathing alcohol fumes in Richards' face, though
she could barely stand. The crowd pressed in with a ferocity that
stunned bystanders.

Former Land Commissioner Bob Armstrong had never seen anything like it: "It was almost a wave of people. A reporter from
California was shouting, 'You cannot *not* answer me!' And she said,
'I have given my answer.' And he got closer to her and said, *'I want
to know: have you taken drugs?'* Finally someone got him away from
her."

Dan Richards cut through the crowd to stand by his mother to
try to keep either a reporter or one of the giant cameras from crashing
into her. Lena Guerrero tried to pull her away, but Richards waved
her back and stood her ground. She is not a big woman, and Armstrong remembers: "It was almost like a physical weight pressing in
on her—the compression of their shouting and screaming, 'Answer!
Answer this question!' "

Harrison Hickman stood on the fringes of the melee thinking that
most male candidates would burst into tears under the pressure, but
not Richards: "I have never seen someone as cool under such fire as
she was." Nevertheless, that night Bob Armstrong says she was convinced she had lost the primary.*

---

*Bob Bullock, the candidate for lieutenant governor, had handled the question of an
altogether more lurid past differently. He had confessed openly that he had been married five
times (twice to the same woman) and had been a terrible drunk. He said he had no doubt
taken whatever drugs were around when he was drinking, and they had made him throw up.
Now he was reformed, and all that was over. End of confession, and end, too, of the issue

"I've never seen that much anger in the press corps," Glenn Smith remembers grimly; "it was unbelievable. And Ann just stood there and took it." To compound the irony, "some of the reporters there that night had been with her when she was allegedly doing drugs," Smith says. "In their minds and hearts they knew it was really irrelevant, because Ann is recovered. They tried to make it relevant when it isn't, and then they felt bad about it."

The drug question hounded Ann Richards all through the primary and runoff, and her response to her opponents' charges and the press's insistence that she "answer the question" compounded the problem. Her negatives skyrocketed, her standing in the polls plummeted, and her confidence was shaken by the brutality. Jan Jarboe, senior editor of the *Texas Monthly*, put it succinctly: "She was afraid. She was like a punch-drunk fighter. Everywhere she went, she knew she was going to get hit with the question. So she stopped going places, and for a while, she was nowhere to be found."

Beneath the tension and crises, of course, was the unresolved question of whether Ann Richards could run as the woman she was and win. The drug business aside, Harrison Hickman thought that "Ann's internal compass" told her she was going for a job "where a different style of behavior is expected." In the midst of the campaign, when the press began to cry, "Let Ann be Ann!" and people all over the state shook their heads—bewildered at the apparent disappearance of the irrepressible Ann Richards they had loved— this was the source of her dilemma: scores of earnest people had told her she could not be elected unless she tamped down her style.

Just as important, she had evolved into a strong feminist, and the problematic nature of that issue is best seen in the diametrically opposed views of two good friends deeply committed to her campaign. Bill Hobby believed that "her campaign started out more as a feminist crusade than as a campaign for governor, and it never entirely lost that character." Although Hobby conceded that Richards, like all politicians, had to draw on her natural political base, he thought she risked alienating the bulk of Texas voters: "Well into

for Bullock. Texas has different standards, however, for women, toward whom it is far less forgiving.

the primary campaign, Ann couldn't resist including in her speech some sort of joke that was mildly derogatory to men. That's a hangover from the days when she was purely a feminist. She couldn't get that out of her system quickly enough."

Glenn Smith, by contrast, worried about Richards' tendency to shy away from her outstanding record in opening doors for women in a state where that has not been easy. He thought she saw a large potential vote that she would lose unless she underplayed that part of her life and politics.

Even so, when the pressures grew most intense, she would set up a "boys versus girls" rhetorical contest. Toward the end of the primary campaign, she said repeatedly, "The only time that this [drug] question was raised is when I got in the way of these boys who want to be governor." Although she knew she needed to run a campaign aimed at all Texans, she could say things that betrayed her anger at what she rightly felt to be the extra burden she carried as a woman running against men in a game that men had always ruled. For Hobby, such rhetoric was anathema, and he thought that "even before the primary, she developed a circle-the-wagons philosophy."

Nor could Hobby see how Richards' being a woman held to an unfairly high standard could explain the sheer ineptness of her campaign. "There were horror stories about scheduling," he said. "A number of her appointments with the editorial board of the *Austin American-Statesman* were broken, for instance, and when she finally did see them, she had only about half an hour before she had to catch a plane."

Calls from constituents and press went unanswered. Longtime Democratic party activist Kathleen Voigt of San Antonio remembers the day she placed three calls: one to Garry Mauro, who was running for land commissioner; one to Bob Bullock, the Democratic candidate for lieutenant governor; and one to Ann Richards. The next morning at 9 A.M., Bullock returned her call; at 9:15, Mauro telephoned. Three weeks later, she still had not heard from Ann Richards.

Vanity Fair was turned down on a request for a feature article, and after many weeks the candidate herself reversed that decision. Judd Rose of ABC's "Prime Time" was told no and then yes, and then no, and then yes again. Joe Cutbirth of the *Fort Worth Star-Telegram* was baffled: "Glenn Smith knows the constraints reporters

are working under. If we're on deadline and call to ask what percentage Ann won by in 1982, we don't need to know how many
counties she carried or hear a puff piece about her. Once I called at
three on Friday afternoon, and the call was returned Monday about
four. We're the fourth biggest paper in the state. That leaves the
possibility that we'll run a story saying Ann Richards refused to
respond to some scurrilous charge." Cutbirth's was a common complaint.

Kaye Northcott, who had once been Richards' press secretary
and had described her the year before as "funny, eloquent, gracious,
and genuinely likable," wrote in the Star-Telegram that her campaign
had neither a clear message nor a clear direction. "Richards has a
self-defeating tendency to lecture the media," Northcott wrote. The
candidate tried to limit the topics to be covered at a news conference
and frequently either ignored issue-oriented questions or answered
vaguely. "Feature writers, both local and national," Northcott continued, "express disappointment that they can't get interviews with
Richards. Some who do get time with her complain that she is aloof
and impatient with their questions."

A Richards volunteer said she and others in the press office were
instructed that Richards was so popular that their job was to keep
people away from her. One journalist wondered, however, if they
had been so instructed because the candidate was in such a bad temper
that it would be wise to keep the press off-limits. Hobby thought the
Richards campaign had the flavor of Jimmy Carter's second one—
wary of the press, defensive, exclusive.

After spending years cultivating excellent relations with journalists, Richards seemed bent on offending them. Reporters were
bumped off her plane far from home with no warning and no apologies from the candidate. Like many others, Jane Ely of the Houston
Chronicle said, "I don't think Ann's terribly comfortable with questioning—about anything." She stormed out of one press conference
and railed at the press for not covering her substantive positions—
but failed to reiterate those positions until they did.

Richards-watchers began to wonder if she simply could not apologize or admit mistakes, one of the most hurtful of which had come
in the first televised debate. Intending to say the state had no business
deciding "whether or why a woman can get an abortion," she seemed

to say "whether a white woman can get an abortion." Confronted immediately afterward by Bob Squier and Lena Guerrero, who warned her that this slip of the tongue could bring her grief, Richards insisted she could never have said anything so ridiculous.

Guerrero, who had to confront the political fallout, admits that "a lot of things were wrong with the way we dealt with that issue, and the hardest thing was to get Ann to deal with whether or not people *thought* she'd said it. She just couldn't believe [that she'd said it], and as a consequence it was hard to get her to react to it in any way. We lost almost forty-eight hours on it because I couldn't really get her to make calls to people who might have been offended."

Barbara Jordan responded to Guerrero's propitiatory call by saying, "This is *not* the time to panic!" (Guerrero says she'd hate to hear Jordan say, "This *is* the time to panic!") Jordan, however, whose enunciation is superb, went on to remark that if Richards only spoke clearly, there could be no question because there was a significant difference in sound between "whether or why a woman" and "whether a white woman." The comment was played over and over on both radio and television, and most people are convinced that she said "white woman."

Guerrero quickly made out a list of NAACP leaders and black ministers who could offer explanations to their constituencies, but "it was very hard to get Ann on the phone." In the second debate, when Richards was challenged on the subject, she said, "I am sorry there was some confusion about what I said," and then cited her long history in support of civil rights. Dallas state senator Eddie Bernice Johnson declared repeatedly that Richards had not only said "white woman" but meant to say it. According to Houston city councilwoman Sheila Jackson Lee, the remark caused great pain, and subsequent apologies did not reach deep into the black community.

Bill Hobby summed it up best: "Her warmth and caring have tended to get lost in this campaign, much to Ann's detriment." Nobody had been psychologically prepared for the harsh attacks. Her family in particular, who were fiercely dedicated to Ann Richards' emotional health, hunkered down around her. Along with her friends, they were accused of being groupies and she of running an unprofessional campaign. No one was happy.

*   *   *

About this time, Nancy Clack, the peripatetic political journey-woman, arrived in Austin to work her fix on the Richards campaign. Clack is a genius at working the margins: she identifies swing precincts, discovers what will move the people who live in them to vote—and to vote for her candidate—and mobilizes all the campaign machinery to focus on those voters and deliver them on election day. Swing precincts are ones that could go either way—or could sit out the election. The people who live in them are neither predictably Democratic nor predictably Republican. They may be ticket-splitters or "Reagan Democrats"—those who may be wooed back to the Democratic party now that the magic of Ronald Reagan has faded and the master magician is off the stage.

George Shipley had invited Clack to join the Richards entourage because he remembered her work in Annette Strauss's campaign for mayor of Dallas. She had been held responsible for getting the black and Hispanic communities to the polls, and the turnout of blacks had been the highest in a municipal election in the history of Dallas.

Studying the way precincts voted in the last election and analyzing polling data, Clack calculates the messages that would appeal to people who vote the way these people vote and answer as they do when called by pollsters. Her work can make the difference in a close election.

Clack arrived on February 28, 1990, less than two weeks before the Democratic primary election, at a time when Richards was in big trouble. The campaign was underfunded: many television markets had to be eliminated and very tough decisions made about when and where Richards' ads would go on the air. The consultants were whispering among themselves that their candidate was doing crazy things, and nobody argued with the fact that Ann Richards was very angry.

By the time Clack got to Texas, many people around Richards thought the candidate had lost confidence in everyone, but especially in herself. She was dropping in the polls: she was losing support among minorities and labor; older women were abandoning her. She was watching her cozy relationship with the press curdle. Nobody liked her television ads. The rumor was abroad that she had a bad temper and was chewing out everybody around, especially her children.

Kirk Adams understood that since his mother-in-law is a perfectionist and knew how to run a political campaign, "it was hard for her to let go. . . . She knows everything from the phone bank rap to index cards for supporters. She had done it all twenty-five years ago. She had strong opinions about the way things ought to be done, and sometimes she had to tell you about it!"

A skilled debater and a willful woman, she had begun playing one staff person off against another and outside "experts" against the staff. She would grill people relentlessly. Consultants were not always prepared to respond to her questions, and she was seldom satisfied with the answers they gave.

According to Anne Schwartz, the legal counsel at treasury, Richards characteristically trusted her staff and, in turn, expected them to give her the best information available. In normal times, she had developed an uncanny knack for asking the one question they had not anticipated. If she came across sloppy preparation, she could be scathing and would reduce a hapless person with a few acerbic words. Ordinarily, she reserved her ire for those who had earned it. The campaign was anything but "normal times," and many on the team felt like targets that an expert markswoman was reducing to shreds.

When she was presented with a series of options and a preference, Richards often called people outside the campaign framework and asked, "What would you do?" It was not uncommon for a staff member to get home and discover that Richards had called ten people after a meeting had broken up and wailed, "Listen to what they're trying to do to me now!" One weary consultant remarked: "Ann probably keeps the group of people around her making decisions at any given moment pretty small because that gives her the chance to go to all the people who weren't there and ask their opinion."

Glenn Smith, as campaign manager, would present Richards with alternatives, along with a recommendation, and she would usually leave the decision to him. But after he made it, he would find himself ambushed by two or three others whose opinions she had solicited. Smith's decisions were not necessarily overturned, but an extravagant amount of time and energy seemed to be lavished on the process.

Richards was not only a perfectionist—she was pushing herself to exhaustion doing something whose effectiveness neither she nor anyone else could measure precisely. During most of the primary campaign, the two people with whom she had worked most closely in the past—Mary Beth Rogers and Jane Hickie—were not involved. The men she hired had never worked with her before and had no idea what to expect. They were unprepared for her to ask, Why? and to ask it obsessively.

One key participant observed that three central characters in the drama were temperamentally alike: Ann, her daughter Cecile, and Lena Guerrero. They are all willful, articulate, tough, and excitable. Glenn Smith came to believe that a big part of his job was keeping everyone calm, which he would have found easier if fewer people had been convinced that the world was caving in. As he puts it: "They were always looking for the monster hiding behind the rock. When you're doing that all the time, you run into a lot of rocks."

But ambitious women had grown up in a world full of rocks with monsters behind them, and they had learned long since that to get where they wanted to go, they had to work incredibly hard and pay microscopic attention to detail. A man who had got his best stories at the watering hole shooting the breeze with the boys had learned and practiced his craft in a world radically different from theirs. His equanimity had to strike them at least now and again as obtuse, and when he insisted that all was well, they must have thought he had skipped lightly over some of the evidence.

One conflict played itself out over the much-maligned "grandmother" ad, which Squier had designed to show that Richards was not a shrill feminist or an "overly ambitious bitch," as one staff member put it, and to work as a counterweight to the drug charges. It was intended to be a tone-setter, a picture of a radiant Ann Richards surrounded by her children and grandchildren, which put the emphasis where patriotic Texans wanted to see it put—on the family.

The campaign was perched on a precarious ledge: the drug question was hovering, and the national press was coming in platoons to write overviews on Texas politics and the wisecracking woman who was running for governor. The level of stress was skyrocketing, and perhaps as a way of working it off, Richards began to take the ad to small fund-raisers and ridicule it. As a key staff member put it, she "criticized the hell out of it, told them what a piece of shit it

was. And her message became: 'Oh my God, Ann's gonna lose because her television's so bad.' She was blaming it on everybody else.
She was saying, *'Look what they're doing to me!'* "

Another instance came during the debate preparation, when some
disagreement arose and Glenn Smith presented his views in an offhand manner. Richards suddenly started yelling that she couldn't
take it any more: people who weren't compulsive drove her crazy
and he was driving her mad! So Smith stood up and threw his pen
against the wall, yelled, "How's that, Bitch?" and then sat down
calmly. Both were trying to be funny, but nobody laughed.

As Smith confessed later, "The hardest thing was watching it tear
Ann Richards' soul apart. And knowing that I had to let her unload
on me and not take it personally. Nobody who ever works with a
politician should take it personally! But the volume and amount of
[rage] were enormous, and it was harder than I'd imagined. I'm a
laid-back guy, pretty easygoing. I assumed at the outset that it
wouldn't be much for me to take with my feet up on the desk. But
it took a bigger toll on me than I normally admit."

"I've never seen a candidate be so hands-on," Clack says. "She'd
lost so much confidence she always wanted to know what was happening. I'd have sent her away in January. At least I'd have kept her
out of the decision-making process." Under such intense pressure,
the staff was not only trying to make sure the campaign functioned
properly on an organizational level—that the blockwalks happened,
that the fieldworkers actually worked, and that radio spots got out—
but trying to help each other out with the candidate. A good many
of them were "trying to cover their asses with Ann Richards."

Months later, each consultant was likely to name others who had
thrown up their hands in despair, or just plain given up, and no
account can be conclusive because everyone tells the story differently.
The only thing they agree on is that it was awful.

While those running the campaign kept trying to do their jobs,
everybody else in Austin seemed to be speculating about why Ann
Richards' campaign was so astonishingly inept. Bob Squier, who loves
Austin and lived there for several years, claims that 100 percent of
its citizens are media consultants. Some of them do other things as

well: they bag groceries, they teach at the university, they paint, they practice law, and so on. Richards' friends worried most of all.

As the Democratic primary contest degenerated, a schism developed within the Richards campaign that no one had anticipated—or for months even understood. In a *Texas Monthly* article that came out in the fall, Mimi Swartz described it as a schism between "the boys" and "the girls," but this made little sense to people who had watched Ann Richards play "good ole girl" politics—which is a way Texas women have of being one of the boys.

Like many feminists, Richards had deep and abiding friendships with men. Bill Hobby was a close friend and mentor, and so completely did he trust her that when he had problems in his personal life, she was one of the people he turned to. Bob Armstrong and Don Kennard "ran the river" with her. Bud Shrake, Jap Cartwright, Fletcher Boone, and Jerry Jeff Walker were among her drinking buddies—and stayed friends after she got sober. Although she was prone to saying things like "Women have to work twice as hard as men," she is as male-identified and as much a flirt as most attractive women of her generation.

Still, Mimi Swartz was on to something. There apparently was a schism, not literally between women and men, but between Richards' support groups, broadly defined, which were predominantly female, and the pros she brought in to run her campaign, most of whom were male. Each spoke from divergent male and female cultures that had evolved from the impact of industrialism on the American economy in the early nineteenth century. In her best-selling book *You Just Don't Understand* (1990), Deborah Tannen analyzes the different expectations men and women often bring to conversation in order to understand why they so often end up at loggerheads. In the 1990 primary campaign, many women who sustained Ann Richards found themselves repeatedly at loggerheads with some of the men.

Richards' friends held to their primary purpose, which was to minister to her well-being. The pros wanted to elect her governor. Though each was vital, the two goals were not always compatible.

On the one side were people who wanted to keep her happy, and since they knew her, they knew the positions with which she was comfortable. An astonishing number of them adored Ann Richards, and some idolized her. They wanted to protect her from a world that would give her pain. And under a barrage of abuse that no one should have to bear, much less a woman who was brought up to be a good girl and to please, their support was life-sustaining. At the same time, those who had been involved in Richards' two campaigns for treasurer were convinced they knew how to run her for governor.

To them, in turn, she brought a lifetime's habit of pleasing—an ineradicable desire to replicate that period about which she could write, "I wanted to be, and I was, everything to everybody." It was in some measure because of them that she was accused of running a cult campaign. Being surrounded by people who adore you can be both wonderful and misleading. One man put it bluntly: "I think Ann was startled to discover that the rest of the world wasn't going to fall down at her feet."

On the other side were people who asked harder questions and made tougher demands. They dismissed the friends' claims to expertise and did not care whether Richards was comfortable. As Glenn Smith says: "In a campaign, you have to be able to recognize, on an hourly basis, the worst in yourself and the worst in the opposition. Because the public's going to see and hear that, and you have to deal with it." They insisted that if she wanted to win, she had to make very unpleasant decisions.

This potential conflict, as a close observer saw it, created on the one hand "a weird psychological inertia" and on the other "an unusual tension within the campaign that wasn't always negative. Sometimes it could lead to openness. Other times it could lead to bizarre instances of dishonesty. I never saw such a pronounced case of 'want-to-be's.' [The friends] wanted the world to be different from what it is. And you can't make campaign decisions based on that."

When the two goals were in conflict, Richards' support groups inclined both to speak from their own idealism and to tell her what they thought she wanted to hear. The pros sometimes tried to impose on her the truth as they saw it.

The support groups did what the weaker people have always done: they sniped and undermined. And the pros did what people in control have historically done: they blinded themselves to the importance and subversive power of the other side. As one of them later admitted, "Ann's inner circle needed to be at the table. If they weren't, they were going to be outside the table."

Despite the problems within the campaign, the grass-roots organization Kirk Adams had been building for almost a year was becoming a fine-tuned machine. "We could call our volunteer base," Nancy Clack says, "and activate them—and then motivate them to do *anything!*" That meant she had excellent material to work with to accomplish her job, which was to make sure the phone banks were working and kept on working.

The job at hand was to stop the erosion of support in the minority communities and among older women that Harrison Hickman's research disclosed. Clack insisted on defining her role: "I'm not saying I know how to win the race. I'm saying I know who she has to go after and where she has to go and what she has to say." Richards' schedule was changed so that she could spend more time addressing the audiences Clack targeted.

Glenn Smith would ultimately be convinced that the things that seemed important at the moment—the friction between people, the disagreements, the confusion over who was authorized to make what decisions—made no difference whatever to the outcome of the election. All campaigns suffer more or less from such problems. Someone called "political organization" itself an oxymoron, and, as Jane Hickie says, campaigns are barely controlled insanity involving a bunch of crazy people on deadline. Seen in the larger perspective, the daily problems were trivial. What counted were Richards' daily labors in the vineyard, the Get-Out-the-Vote efforts, and television.

"The simplest things are always the most difficult to do," as Richards said later. "The hard part was doing what I knew was the right thing to do." She was clear in believing she had to live one day at a time, and she knew basically how to do that. "I planned ahead, but I did not think ahead," she explained. "You lay out a strategy, and you lay out goals, and you lay out ideas about how you're going to accomplish what you're going to accomplish. And then you can always refer back to that to refresh your memory. But you don't get up in the morning anticipating what's ahead of you. You live in the moment. Anticipation adds to the stress; it adds to the anxiety; and it is totally self-defeating.

"Often, if it was a very long day, I would break it up into components and live each of them at a time. I would say, 'All I've got to do now is do my best at this breakfast.' And then when that breakfast was over, I would say to myself, 'All I have to do is to do my very best at this brunch, or gathering, or rally.' And so I tried to live in the moment. That way, life is manageable.

"I would go to bed at night, and I would have a conversation with my Higher Power. And I tried to concentrate on things that had gone well that day. I would tick over a list of things that were good, rather than concentrating on all the things that might be going wrong. Because it was important for me to continue to feel secure about the decisions we made early on in the planning process."

She was keeping faith in herself—and keeping faith *with* herself. And she could do that because she knew that she was not the Ann Richards being reviled by the public. "My identity is not caught up in public perception," she said firmly. "It's very important for those of us who are in the public eye to develop something I call the inner light. Your identity has *got* to be inside you. It *cannot* be external.

"Of course my family plays an enormous part in that inside-of-me person. And I have to *touch* that person a lot. I have to get in touch with what's going on inside this person who is a candidate. It was such a joy to run into my daughters on the road, or see my granddaughters, because that's like touching base with who you really are."

In 1990, the pros insisted that a candidate who is attacked has little choice but to counterattack. Consultant George Shipley echoed Bill Zimmerman in saying that "negative commercials are ultimately forced on candidates by the logic of circumstances." After the second debate, Ann Richards accepted that logic, to the dismay of many friends and supporters.

On Saturday, March 3, the day after the second Democratic debate in Dallas, Richards' gloomy advisers gathered in Shipley's office to decide what to do. A banner headline in the *Dallas Morning News* read "Democrats quarrel on drug abuse, taxes." Richards had fallen to third in the polls, and several thought it was all over.

Bob Squier was there, and so was Jane Hickie, whom Shipley had

brought back into the campaign after a hiatus of nine months. Although the "grandmother ad" was obviously a response to drug and
lesbian charges from Richards' opponents, neither it nor any others
that Squier had done found many defenders. As Hickie says, "All
people knew about Ann Richards was that she didn't hate her children." Dave McNeely of the *Austin American-Statesman* had complained that "with potentially one of the best media candidates in
Texas political history, Squier has produced television ads that might
be capable of selling lavender doilies to grandmothers. Maybe."
Squier, he said, had turned a silk purse into a sow's ear.

Richards' response to the drug question during the debate had
only goaded Mattox and White into ganging up on her afterward to
say she had to stop hiding from her past. The rumors circulating
were so dire that Kaye Northcott wrote, "Her story is probably much
less damaging than the speculation." Hickie was convinced that Richards should attack Mattox and White: "They were just beating on
her. They'd spent $5 million saying she was a drug addict, and she
was not felt to be somebody who was coming back." To get people's
minds off the drug charges, Hickie argued that it was "better to let
them debate her dirty campaign." So they designed a new ad.

Richards had been trying for months to nail her opponents on
shoddy financial ethics. While Mattox and White were pandering to
the pro–death penalty sentiment in Texas by competing to see who
could convince the electorate that he would pull the switch at the
state penitentiary in Huntsville more frequently and with greater
enthusiasm, Richards had released her income taxes and called upon
her opponents to do the same. They had ignored her.

So overconfident had White become that he had sent emissaries
to George Shipley and Glenn Smith demanding Richards' surrender:
she should drop out of the race, endorse him, and then together they
would go after Mattox. But the Richards camp knew the *Dallas
Morning News* was coming out with a story about White's suspicious
connections to state bond transactions during the time he was governor, as well as about a million-dollar home mortgage he had gotten
with no cash down that they knew the voters would find hard to
understand. White's former law firm had been the underwriter's
counsel on $2.7 billion worth of bond deals while he was governor,

and reporters suspected that White had retained an interest in the law firm, which he rejoined on leaving public service.

On Monday, March 5, Richards called a press conference, and within forty-five minutes, two hundred reporters, cameramen, and fans had crowded into her headquarters. As Hickie describes it, Richards walked in and "let 'em have it! She took their hides off!" She said, "I said just what I intended to say about my alcoholism during the debate and afterward. I haven't had a mood-altering chemical for ten years. I didn't even take aspirin after the last debate. Ten years is a lifetime to me." Then she started asking hard questions about her opponents.

The next day, in a lead story, the *Dallas Morning News* reported that Richards had come out slugging—insisting that "voters should be more concerned with how Mr. White became wealthy while serving as governor and on Mr. Mattox's acceptance of large, questionable contributions." Columnist Molly Ivins threw in a touch of sanity: "Anyone in our generation who hadn't smoked dope was such a twerpy goody-two-shoes we wouldn't want them leading the country anyway."

The same day, the *News* ran its first account of Mark White's dubious ethics under the headline "White's ex-firm got bond work." The subhead read "Appointees steered jobs to former law associates."

The Richards thirty-second attack ad, which was finished that morning, included a shot of the front page of the *News* with its bold headlines slamming White. The spots were then shipped to fifty television stations all over the state.

The ads ran on Wednesday, hitting both Mattox and White, and implying they were pigs feeding at the public trough: the former for accepting a $200,000 gift from entrepreneur Danny Faulkner which got him indicted, and the latter for getting rich enough on a state salary of less than $100,000 to report an $800,000 income the year after he left public service—rich enough to move from the governor's mansion into a house in Houston worth $1.3 million and to buy a Mercedes-Benz and a BMW. Her opponents, Richards said, had "lined their pockets" while enjoying the public trust. She even claimed that White "took our tax dollars to line his own pockets."

The ad played to a general perception, which had never been

substantiated, that White lived beyond his means; in the parlance of the experts, the ad had resonance. It ran for only two or three days, and few voters can have seen it. But the public furor was far out of proportion to the number of its putative viewers because it unhinged Mark White. He was so outraged that he called a press conference to protest his innocence and denounce Richards. (At the same time, he was running radio ads in east Texas that were quite as vicious as Mattox's.)

He could not have played more completely into the hands of the Richards camp. As a key adviser said later, "It was like putting a lure in front of a bass." At the press conference, White held up the top page of his 1040 federal income tax form, which listed a $200,000 dividend from an unspecified source.

Robert Riggs, a capitol reporter for Dallas television station WFAA who had been a chief investigator for the Joint Committee on Defense Production in Congress, began grilling White: "Could I get a million-dollar house with a mortgage like that?" White was red-faced with anger when Riggs said, "Let's talk about your taxes!" White responded, *These are my taxes!* but since the former governor was only offering the first two pages of his tax return, Riggs replied, "I beg to differ: where's Schedule D? Where's Schedule B?"

Other reporters followed suit: "If you didn't take that $200,000 from your law firm, we need Schedule E to show it." "By the way, how did you finance your two $70,000 cars?" "You made $55,000 your last year as governor, practiced law for ten months, and then paid taxes on $800,000! How do you explain that?"

Riggs was unrelenting. The deed records showed that Rice University had loaned White the money to buy his house in Houston, but a Rice official had refused to discuss the loan. "There's no down payment here," Riggs declared, and in the heated exchanges that followed, White admitted that Rice had also loaned him the money for the improvements. Riggs said: "Wait a minute. The average person asking for a home-improvement loan can't get one if any of the mortgage money is borrowed. Why did they loan you so much money for home improvements?"

The Dallas television audience is the largest in the state, reaching approximately 34 percent of the Texas market. Riggs's program gets

to many more people still because, as a first-rate investigative reporter, he is put on satellite and then picked up by seventeen other
stations. The noon press conference made the five o'clock and then
the ten o'clock news. People watching throughout the state could see
Mark White, as George Shipley put it, "caught in his pride," and
many were convinced he was lying.

Subsequent articles in the *Dallas Morning News* revealed that
individuals or political action committees (PACs) connected with
sixteen of the twenty-two bond firms that did business with the state
when White was governor had contributed at least $209,000 to his
campaign. And Dallas reporters leaked the story that the $200,000
on the first page of his tax return was a dividend from his old law
firm in payment for his steering the bond deal business its way.

Billie Carr, national Democratic committeewoman from Houston, whose calling card reads "Bitch" and who makes the most of a
laconic drawl, said to White, "When you live by the mouth, you die
by the mouth!" To counter his indignation, she pointed out to him
that he had run an ad that asked how you could know when Jim
Mattox was lying and answered its own question by retorting, "When
he opens his mouth!" Every campaign Mark White had ever run,
according to Carr, was a dirty campaign. Now he was turning green
from his own poison.

At the same time, many supporters of Richards, much less Mattox
and White, were incensed because the Richards ad was deliberately
misleading. It violated the fundamental principle of American ju-
risprudence: that a person is innocent until proved guilty. Noting
that Mattox had been found innocent in his bribery trial in 1984,
Northcott called the Richards attack "wretched," and McNeely
wrote that "her use of that unfounded charge [against White] removed her aura as a high-minded candidate and put her in the desperate ranks of [candidates] who have developed reputations for
saying and doing whatever they think they must do to win."

Mattox had made a television buy for the last two weeks of the
campaign that a Republican consultant called gargantuan, and it
worked for him. White's campaign was disintegrating because he had
run out of money and his organization was virtually nonexistent.

The Richards ad, and his response to it, compounded his troubles and popped him out of the race.

White finished a poor third, with less than 20 percent of the vote. So galling was his public humiliation that he refused to endorse Richards, and, just before the November election, refused even to say he would vote for her. Such churlishness in a former Democratic governor was thought unseemly, and it appeared likely that Mark White was politically dead in Texas.

CHAPTER 4

> *You accuse Ann Richards. . . . Why don't*
> *you come forward with the evidence? Be-*
> *cause if you don't . . . isn't it somewhat like*
> *McCarthyism? You know: "I have this piece*
> *of paper?"*
> —LESLEY STAHL on "Face the Nation"

Mark White had been a Democrat more nearly of the John Connally stripe than his opponents: he was a moderate leaning toward conservative. Mattox and Richards had both been described as liberals, though she was less overtly ideological than he. Since the primary runoff would be between candidates who drew from the same base of support, it had the ingredients of a family feud. And it lived up to the expectations of those who dreaded it: when it was over, friends and even families had split, and there was a good chance the wounds would not heal. It had the inexorability and some essential elements of Greek tragedy.

Mary Beth Rogers was not yet officially involved, but she went to see Mattox's campaign manager and lamented "the tone and tenor" of the race on the grounds that whoever won would have "a helluva time winning in November." It used to be, says Rogers, that "when the primary was over, you had two to four years to heal. But now you just hand the poison to the Republicans." The Mattox camp was unmoved. "Everything was set in motion at that point," says Rogers. "There was probably no turning back."*

Labor was split. The unions that were predominantly male—the Steelworkers, the Teamsters, the building trades—supported Mattox. The unions that were predominantly female—the Service Employees International Union, the Communications Workers of America, the

---

*Months later, when Mattox was asked whether he had worried about the viability of any Democratic candidate who emerged from the fight he started, he replied that his polls told him he could beat Clayton Williams.

American Federation of State, County, and Municipal Employees (AFSCME)—supported Richards. The state AFL-CIO remained officially neutral.

Texas is a right-to-work state, and unions are not strong there. But they provide a disproportionate number of vital workers in Democratic campaigns, and both sides received substantial amounts of money from the national unions.

The feminist community was solidly behind Richards, although Mattox's record on women's issues was excellent, and he had been among the first to join the amicus curiae brief that the state attorneys general submitted in the 1989 landmark *Webster* case. Unlike Richards, he had also signed on to the National Abortion Rights Action League's National Advisory Committee, which was formed before the United States Supreme Court announced the decision in *Webster* that subsequently inspired women all over the country to organize to protect freedom of choice. Presumably because she was downplaying her feminism to attract a broader base of support, Richards had declined her invitation.

The most shocking defector from the feminist camp was Sissy Farenthold, who had run for governor in 1972 with the overwhelming support of Texas women and been the first chair of the National Women's Political Caucus. Her own gubernatorial campaign had been a reformist crusade, however—a bootstrap operation that was quite different from Richards' mainstream effort.

Farenthold had filed at the last minute because she was deferring to former Senator Ralph Yarborough: "If he ran for the Senate, I'd run for governor. If he ran for governor, I'd run for attorney general." Since Yarborough had not made up his mind until December 1971, Farenthold's was not "a planned campaign." She had written her own speeches and flown around the state in a dangerously rickety little plane to make twenty-six different appearances in two days to announce her candidacy. Liz Carpenter captured the flavor of the Farenthold operation when she called it a "Volkswagen campaign": whenever she traveled to speak for Sissy, "I was always met at the airport by a Volkswagen."*

---

*Carpenter worked for three of the four Texas women who have run for governor. In 1944, she had served as press secretary to Minnie Fisher Cunningham when Minnie Fish, as

On principle, Farenthold, who practices law in Houston, refuses to duck a direct question. Acutely uncomfortable with her dilemma, she got through two interviews on the governor's race without being queried about her preference, but when a third reporter asked her outright which candidate she was supporting, she answered, "Mattox." As attorney general, he had been responsive to her political commitments to Latin American peace efforts, and she found his programmatic liberalism more congenial than Richards'.

These arguments did not mollify feminists, who felt betrayed. Many of them—including the core of women who started the Texas Women's Political Caucus—had first thrown themselves into politics when they worked on Farenthold's gubernatorial campaign. Her insistence that she had warned Mattox that his attacks on Richards would only lose him votes seemed a flimsy response to his systematic campaign of character assassination. The generous world view that informs liberalism was so fundamentally at odds with Mattox's scurrilous attacks that many women remained incredulous that Sissy Farenthold could blink at a discrepancy so marked.

The Harris County Democrats, the most influential liberal organization in the state, had made their choice earlier in the primary, supporting Richards after screening all three candidates. Billie Carr, a Harris County stalwart, says of Mattox that his record deserved the liberal community's support, but his behavior cost him much of it. During the screening process, he was asked about gun control. When he said he didn't know much about that, he was asked specifically about Saturday Night Specials and AK47s—to which he replied that he wished the Chinese students had had some. His flippancy cost him the Harris County endorsement. Now it seemed to Carr that "Mattox went a little crazy.... He was saying, 'If you're not for me, I'm going to remember.' "

Richards had gotten just over 2 percent more of the primary vote than Mattox did: in a seven-candidate field, she had 39.3 percent to his 37 percent. Meanwhile, Midland rancher and oilman Clayton Williams had won the Republican primary in a field of four with 61

she was called, ran to give people an alternative to Coke Stevenson, "whom nobody expected," as Carpenter puts it, "to end up being Robert Caro's hero."

percent of the vote, and *Dallas Morning News* columnist William Murchison, delighted at the prospect of two liberal Democrats self-destructing, wrote that Williams "might as well start writing his inaugural address."

The day after the primary, the Democratic nominee for attorney general, Dan Morales, publicly pleaded with both gubernatorial candidates to run a clean, issue-oriented campaign because "a runoff marred by personal attacks and mudslinging could hurt all Democrats in the November general election." But Clayton Williams was the kind of candidate Mattox lusted to run against, and Morales was whistling in a Gulf hurricane.

Mattox immediately hinted that he knew things about Richards' work at the treasury that might damage her. According to the *Corpus Christi Caller-Times*, he refused to be specific and, when pressed by reporters, acknowledged that he had no proof she had done anything illegal.*

Still, Mattox said he might reveal unspecified acts unless Richards ran a clean runoff campaign. *Austin American-Statesman* columnist Billy Porterfield decided that "the state's highest public defender and prosecutor appears willing to foul at close range, and appeal to the lowest instincts if that's what it takes to win." Richards, whom Porterfield credited with Sissy Farenthold's class and Barbara Jordan's brains, countered that she expected Mattox to try to turn the race into "a mud wrestling match."

Glenn Smith and his counterpart in the Mattox campaign, Jim Cunningham, met for five days in a row with Texas Democratic party chairman Bob Slagle to try to work out a truce so that whoever lost would not be simply handing the other's nearly severed head to Williams in November. Although they reported progress, no more than a week later, the *Austin American-Statesman* ran an outsized headline on the front page: "Mattox claims he has evidence of Richards drug use." In the article he was quoted as saying: "She must answer what she used, how much, for how long, and who supplied them, or she has disqualified herself in the eyes of

---

*Questions would be raised about Richards' connections to Gary Bradley, an Austin developer; Thomas Gaubert, a former thrift executive who was tied in with Jim Wright; and Ruben Johnson, an Austin banker who went to prison. Nothing was proved except that she had trusted people who were not trustworthy, a common enough experience.

the law enforcement community in Texas, and I would think in the eyes of all citizens *if she won't answer those very basic questions.*" His rationale was that "she had a flawed judgment that would re-emerge."

Each campaign was now trying to secure the areas it had won and build its strength in borderline districts. The typical problem in a primary runoff is that few people turn out to vote, but on this score Richards seemed to have the advantage. Since she had won most handily in central Texas and the big cities, while Mattox had carried south Texas and most rural areas, her voters would probably be easier to mobilize.

Many rural voters go to the polls primarily to decide local races so that except in districts where there were runoffs, those people were more than likely to stay home. Yet a high proportion of Richards' support had come out specifically for her. The Republican crossover vote, for instance, which was dominated by pro-choice women, was obvious in places like the sedate Alamo Heights section of San Antonio and prestigious North Dallas, where old-time precinct watchers said after the primary that they had never seen so many young professional women as those still in line when the polls closed. Such women invariably have a high rate of turnout and could be expected to come back to vote in the runoff. San Antonio, furthermore, was one of the few areas with a large Hispanic population where Richards beat Mattox by two to one, and her strength there could be traced to former Mayor Henry Cisneros' support—which he could be counted on to redouble.

Mattox had already outspent Richards by two to one: Richards reported outlays of just under $2.3 million between July 1, 1989, and March 3, 1990, while Mattox had spent over $4.5 million. Richards had $175,000 on hand, plus another $185,000 in pledges. Although his coffers were nearly empty, Mattox had the advantage of his office and a highly developed arm-twisting style to coerce law firms and businesses that had already given to him into giving more. Both intended to put at least $1 million into the runoff, and within three weeks, they had reached their goals. (Over $100,000 of this chunk of Richards' money came from contributors to EMILY's

List, the national PAC that supports pro-choice Democratic women.)

Meanwhile, many of Mark White's supporters were so inflamed by Richards' "lined his pockets" commercial that they resolutely refused to back her, and Liz Carpenter, Sam Dawson of the Steelworkers, and Austin consultant George Christian were among the most prominent Richards admirers who looked on the White ad as the biggest mistake of her campaign. White had already run out of money before she ran the ad, and his support had been steadily leaching away. Her close friend and adviser Bob Armstrong conceded in retrospect that they had not needed to hit White so hard to knock him out of the race, but the polls had not yet registered his losses and they had acted on the basis of the polls.

The week before the runoff election, White called a news conference in Austin to say that he would never endorse, never support, and never vote for Ann Richards. He compared her campaign tactics to those of Nazi storm troopers. What she did, he said, "would make Himmler blush." (Jane Ely of the *Houston Chronicle* subsequently chided White for whining over his defeat and for not knowing the difference between Joseph Goebbels, the Nazi propagandist, and Heinrich Himmler, the Gestapo chief.)

Newspapers such as the *Beaumont Enterprise* continued to run columns saying Richards should answer "The Question"; until she did, "a nasty campaign will swirl around personal issues that do not relate to the state's real problems." With breathtaking understatement, David Broder of the *Washington Post* wrote, "Women are discovering—as if they didn't already know—that men will not yield the real power positions without a fight."

The press wrung its hands daily. Making an implicit contrast with an "issueless" gubernatorial campaign, a *Houston Post* article recalled the stands Sissy Farenthold had taken in 1972—many of them controversial. Despite being a Roman Catholic, for instance, she had supported the pro-choice position. She had argued, furthermore, that children in poor districts should have the same quality education as children in wealthy ones, advocated lowering first-offense possession of marijuana from a felony to a misdemeanor, backed a corporate profits tax and state utilities regulation, and endorsed sweeping reform in Austin, where special interests were running state government. The papers did not underscore the fact that Farenthold had lost.*

Kirk Adams and Cecile Richards were spending fifteen-hour days getting their field operation in the top eighty-nine counties into maximum working order. Since most old-school party operatives were lined up with Mattox, Kirk and Cecile had built a Get-Out-the-Vote organization that depended on people who had never done such work before or had done it at a lower level of responsibility.

Many had been eager for the chance to take on more—people Kirk and Cecile had met through their union organizing or supporters who had been with Richards for years, some of them since she ran for treasurer in 1982. Still another group had been attracted by her 1988 keynote speech, and some were tied to issues like choice that she represented. Adams had worried about how the drug controversy would affect their volunteer army and was thrilled to find that, if anything, it had hardened their resolve and improved their efficiency: "They were still coming, and they were coming back!"

Others were out in the field working with Adams. Embarrassed that Mattox had won so many votes on his home territory, for instance, County Clerk Billy Leo in Hidalgo County threw himself into the job of whipping his folks into better shape.

Two days before the runoff, newspapers across the country ran articles showing frames of television ads from one or both Democratic gubernatorial candidates in Texas. The headline in the *Washington Post* read "Texas Campaign Takes the Low Road." In the *New York Times*, it read "Texas Campaign Tests Limits of Politics." The *Post* showed two frames of Mattox's ad showing Ann Richards' face, over which were superimposed the statements: "Did she use marijuana, or something worse like cocaine" and "Not as a college kid, but as a forty-seven-year-old elected official sworn to uphold the law?"

Richards' ads showed first a caricature of Mattox throwing mud

*Money, however, was at least as important to Farenthold's defeat as ideology. In the primary, her opponents outspent her more than seven to one; in the general election, conservative Democrat Dolph Briscoe, one of the wealthiest men in Texas, outspent her almost six to one.

at a picture of Richards holding her granddaughter Lily, and then one of Mattox with the mud all over his own face. There was nothing for it but to try to laugh, and one Democrat was heard to mumble, "When it comes to issues, I'm afraid our party has gone to pot."

Meanwhile, Richards got extra political mileage out of Republican Clayton Williams' "joke" comparing bad weather to rape: "If it's inevitable, just relax and enjoy it!" She injected into her speeches the line: "It's time we had a governor who knows the difference between a joke and a violent crime." Mattox compared his own persecutions to Christ's. And the *New York Times* referred to the campaign as a harrowing drive without brakes to the limits of modern politics.

On the Sunday before the election, Jim Mattox appeared on television screens across the country in a CBS interview with Lesley Stahl on "Face the Nation." Stahl challenged him:

> You accuse Ann Richards. . . . Why don't you come forward with the evidence? Because if you don't come forward with it, isn't it somewhat like McCarthyism? You know: "I have this piece of paper?"

Mattox replied:

> Well, Lesley, [for] the same reason you would not give up a confidential individual that would come to you as a journalist. . . . The individuals came to me and said we feel strongly enough that Ann Richards should not be in the governor's office.

Stahl asked:

> But you are the only one on the record making the charge, right?

Mattox answered:

> Well, there are other people who have made it on the record. They've just simply not disclosed their names. . . . We're not talking about pot; we're talking about cocaine. . . . When she was a forty-six-year-old county official, sworn to uphold the laws of the state of Texas. . . . I believe she went for treatment in the St. Mary's Chemical Dependency Center for both cocaine and alcohol addiction.

Stahl:

> Are you saying that she was addicted to cocaine at the age of forty-six, and that that's one of the reasons she went to this clinic?

Mattox:

> I believe she had a multiple addiction, and that's the reason she went to the clinic, that's right.

After an equally dispiriting series of exchanges about Mattox's refusal to release his income tax returns, Stahl ended by saying that Richards had "declined an invitation to be on this broadcast, but called us to deny that she has ever been treated for cocaine addiction." The nation had been offered the spectacle of Texas' attorney general making unsubstantiated accusations in a performance that a top-flight journalist could compare to that of Senator Joe McCarthy. As Billie Carr said, Mattox had gone a little crazy.

"Face the Nation" had been taped on Saturday in Houston, and according to WFAA reporter Robert Riggs, Mattox pulled out all the stops from then on. He insisted publicly that mutual friends had told him that Richards had been addicted to cocaine. In response to Mattox's claim that a man in New Mexico had seen Richards use it, reporters said, "Produce him!" In the absence of proof, WFAA refused to do anything with the charge—and others like it—but some stations built stories around them and ran the stories.

Kaye Northcott wrote that "unsubstantiated rumors are the staples of the current campaign." Newspapers printed charges made by nameless sources to other newspapers, as well as charges by people whose credibility was dubious, and excused themselves by saying they had had no time to check them. As Riggs put it, the press went a little crazy along with Mattox.

One Richards consultant observed wearily that running for thirty days against Jim Mattox was like running for ninety days against anybody else. The sensational had driven out the serious, and Harrison Hickman lamented that Richards' media did not do her justice. "I think the real blame is on us," he says. "We did not communicate well that [her answer to the drug question] was part of a bigger belief.

People didn't understand why she wouldn't answer. We never got that across to voters."

Hickman was convinced that Mattox's best shot had been to stay with the lottery, which had won him support, but by diverting his attention to the drug issue, he had forfeited the voters' respect. "Everybody knew everything about the drug stuff that they needed to know," Hickman says. "[Mattox] only seemed unfair in the way he treated her. That's one time being a woman helped her: people were protective of her."

And indeed, as the weeks passed, the momentum seemed to be building for Ann Richards. With the Mattox attacks backfiring, huge crowds met her wherever she appeared like a wave cresting across the state. The last weekend before the election, Henry Cisneros traveled with her, and they were met by four thousand people in El Paso and fifteen hundred at churches in conservative Lubbock.

On election day, *Fort Worth Star-Telegram* reporter Joe Cutbirth traveled with Jim Mattox, and when the campaign stops were done and the last voter's hand shaken, he followed him to Campisi's restaurant in Dallas, where his mother had been a waitress and where he sat talking about the "Old Mattox."

Cutbirth saw then that Mattox knew it was all over. "Old Mattox" was the guy who for eight years had taken on the insurance companies, the guy who had been named one of the ten most feared attorneys general in the nation. He had fought the toughest liberal fights in the state legislature and the Congress. And now, as Jim Mattox would see it, Texas Democrats didn't care about competence or record: they just wanted to elect a woman. As many others would see it, Mattox had turned himself into a snake.

Nancy Clack did her background work by studying the demography and recent voting history of each of Texas' 254 counties, using the 1986 election as a benchmark for turnout because it was a nonpresidential year, as this one would be. She had weighed each county's bias in political trends and philosophies by looking, among other things, at the 1984 Democratic primary with Doggett, Hance, and Krueger. She had gone minutely over Hickman's polling data, checking especially for trends.

In the Democratic primary election a month earlier, 1.4 million people had voted. She expected fewer to come out for a runoff for a statewide office, although in counties with hotly contested runoffs for judge, sheriff, or some other local office, the turnout might be as high. She had factored those races into her calculations.

After doing all that, and after working the figures repeatedly, Clack had given Richards a list of the counties, her projected turnout, and an estimate of the way each county was likely to vote, based on its past history and the Hickman data. She projected that Richards would win the runoff with 54 percent of the vote. When Virginia Whitten unscientifically predicted 57 percent, everybody laughed.

On election day, Clack sat at headquarters calling around the state to find out how the phone banks were working and whether the volunteers were out in force. Matching the fieldworkers' reports of the numbers showing up at the polls against the numbers of 1986 voters, she then would calculate what those figures might mean for her candidate. If she estimated that Hidalgo County, for example, might go for Richards 60/40, and more people were coming to the polls there than in 1986, that was good for Richards. If fewer, the candidate would have to make it up in another county.

The figures, as Clack tallied them, were far better than she had dared to hope. The turnout was as she had predicted, but Richards was getting a higher percentage of the vote. In a small county, she might exceed by one hundred the projected number on Clack's sheet. Richards was even winning county after county in macho west Texas! And when she won Lubbock, in the conservative Panhandle, with 65 percent of the vote, Clack knew it would be what they call in the trade "an early evening": nobody would be up until dawn waiting for returns from Dimmit County, or Angelina, or Gillespie.

By 8:45, less than an hour after the polls closed in El Paso, Clack was convinced by her figures, and not long after, Richards called to ask, "What are we going to do?" Clack replied slowly: "I'm conservative and I don't like to call things this early. And we don't have Dallas." Finally, she relented: "But it's going to be an incredible win."

Before 10 P.M., Richards strode into the ballroom at the Hyatt Regency Hotel and stood ecstatically before the cameras to say: "We're at fifty-five percent and climbing!" In the final count, with a beaming Virginia Whitten looking on, she won with 57 percent of the vote, beating Jim Mattox by 14 percent.

Jack Martin saw now that Richards evoked an enthusiasm and excitement that might elect her regardless of campaign mechanics. She had won the runoff "by hook and by crook," as he put it: "It was the old-fashioned 'we're gonna make it' . . . 'we're gonna Band-Aid it together.' " She just might be able to do that again in the general election.

CHAPTER 5

Money is how you keep score.
—CLAYTON WILLIAMS

As the *Washington Post* put it the day after the runoff, Ann Richards moved "into the general election campaign bruised and broke, a certain underdog against the Republican nominee, West Texas cowboy millionaire Clayton Williams." She had come out of the 1988 Democratic convention with her positive rankings in the polls high among Democrats and her negatives high among Republicans. She came out of the primary runoff with her negative rankings among Democrats as high as her positives. David Broder wondered in the *Post* whether she had much credibility left. It would take all Richards' tact and skill, as well as a certain glinty-eyed shrewdness on the part of former Mattox and White supporters about their own self-interest, to get the Democrats in trim again for their next performance on the high wires.

And Richards' opponent was like no candidate the Grand Old Party in Texas had ever imagined, or for that matter, could have imagined. With 61 percent of the primary vote, Clayton Williams had overwhelmed three of their best-qualified candidates. He was a grinning, jug-eared, guitar-playing, high-energy guy in chaps who had come out of the Texas recession with $110 million of his own money, after paying his debts.

To the amazement of bystanders, he had even ridden a horse up the capitol steps to publicize his telecommunications company's fight against AT&T. George Christian, a prominent Austin consultant and Lyndon Johnson's press secretary, had warned him, "That horse is liable to fall flat out there on that pavement!" But Williams only grinned, and "he came galloping right up the front walk and roaring off that horse like a real cowboy." Christian was dumbfounded: "Nobody ever sees that in the flesh! They see it in the movies maybe, but they don't see a *person* riding a horse like that!"

With nothing short of genius, Williams exploited the cowboy myth—far and away the most powerful in Texas culture. Not only did he wear a ten-gallon hat and boots, but he said he didn't even own a pair of shoes. Admitting that he had "decked" an employee in an office dispute, he said he would do it again, and his audiences loved it. He confessed to ABC's Judd Rose that he would like to be John Wayne, of whom he had two statues and a portrait, and Rose concluded that since Williams had "brawled, boozed, and whored," he was "a throwback to the old West, not unlike the image his ads promote relentlessly." His corporate jet was even nicknamed *Lonesome Dove.**

Williams had the gall of a daylight bank robber, as well as the zest, and journalists who went to scoff were abashed to find that they really liked the guy. He spoke cowhand Spanish with gusto, teared up whenever he heard the Texas A&M fight song, and danced on tables when he was deep enough in the sauce. When he was young, he had announced that he would make a million dollars, kill a lion on an African safari, and marry a beautiful woman, and he had done all three, though not in that order. Jan Jarboe of the *Texas Monthly* said he reminded you of your favorite grandfather, and Judd Rose of ABC's "Prime Time," who spent a month, off and on, following him around Texas, said he was having the time of his life.

For Texans with long memories, he evoked W. Lee (Pappy) O'Daniel, a flour salesman who asked his radio audience on Palm Sunday in 1938 whether they thought he should run for governor and got in the race after more than fifty thousand messages came in cheering him on. (Only four told him not to.) To the accompaniment of his Lightcrust Doughboys strumming their guitars and singing in the background, he brought out mammoth crowds all over the state. With the Ten Commandments for a platform and the Golden Rule

---

*Anyone who doubts the power of the cowboy myth or the appeal of the Old West should learn from Larry McMurtry's example. As early as the mid-1960s McMurtry began to rail at friends and critics who wanted him to write a sequel to *Leaving Cheyenne*, an early novel set in the Panhandle that he claimed had been overpraised. The cowboy myth, he said, had been worked through sufficiently, and nothing more need be said about it. In 1985, however, McMurtry published the granddaddy Western of them all, *Lonesome Dove*, which won the Pulitzer Prize and made him a fortune. The myth appeals because the era it describes is so much simpler than modern times: men don't have to deal with women, cities, or machines, and you have to have a mighty hard heart not to have some sympathy.

as a motto, he overwhelmed a field of qualified candidates and won
the primary without a runoff. When he was reelected in 1940, he
was the first candidate to poll more than 1 million votes in a Texas
election. In 1941, in a special election, he defeated Lyndon Johnson
for the United States Senate by stealing ballot boxes at the last minute
in east Texas—thereby teaching his opponent a lesson he would never
forget. Although O'Daniel was a master of populist rhetoric, his votes
were on call, as one writer put it, for "some of the most uncivilized
wealth on the North American continent."

In his most popular television ad, Clayton Williams' background
chorus was not the Lightcrust Doughboys but a gaggle of film extras
playing convicts "bustin' rocks," the punishment he proposed for
people dealing drugs. Like Pappy O'Daniel, he made people think
he could go down to Austin and clean up the mess. Like Pappy, he
wanted Texans to believe that the less he knew about it beforehand,
the better he'd be at the job, and there was no question that Williams
would cast his votes the same way Pappy had.

During the Republican primary, Williams' opponents had ganged
up on him to try to expose his innocence of government, and he had
outfaced them by sitting on camera grinning. One of them said,
"Claytie, you can't ride into the twenty-first century on a horse,"
and he came back fast: "You can if you've got a good horse." He
later admitted he would never win a debate—that wasn't his strong
suit—and the armies of people who distrusted government found in
him a champion.

His platform left something to be desired. On the stump he said,
"We stand for God and our country, and our own basic values of a
day's work for a day's pay, for honesty and integrity and the Boy
Scouts!" But Williams did not need to be an expert because he knew
how to find and use experts. Bob Armstrong, the former land commissioner, remembers that when they auctioned off oil leases on state
land, "Claytie," who had never employed his own geologist, would
see EXXON and Shell bidding against each other, figure if the big
guys wanted that tract it must be good, and simply outbid them.

His fortune had come in on New Year's Eve 1975, when a deep
gas well, Gataga No. 2, on his wife's land in far west Texas erupted
in a blowout so spectacular that the county seat had to be evacuated.
Within days it was producing almost $50,000 a day, which Williams

used to borrow more so he could buy oil and gas leases on huge tracts and get himself half a million acres of Texas and Wyoming ranch land. Fifteen years later, he operated an alfalfa and oat farm, as well as twelve ranches, where he ran over eleven thousand head of cattle, including more than two thousand purebred Brangus. The National Cattlemen's Association ranked him the nation's seventh-largest commercial cow-calf producer. He had a mansion, a hotel, and a third interest in a hospital in Midland; a ranch house in Alpine with a boot-shaped swimming pool; a Sabreliner corporate jet, a helicopter, and a Beechcraft twin-engine turboprop airplane. Clayton Williams was not just rich: he was *Giant* rich. And now he had a hankering to be governor of Texas.

For Harrison Hickman, May and June were the most depressing months of the entire campaign. When he did polling and focus groups immediately after the primary, he found that Williams was trouncing Richards by as much as twenty-two points, and her negative ratings had soared above 50 percent. The drug issue itself had not hurt her so much as her refusal to "answer the question," which "took away one of the great advantages of a woman candidate—that people think you're going to be honest and forthright." And although she had not lost much support among Democrats—she had just given those who were not voting for her a justification—"unfortunately, this little group of people participating in the primary," Hickman says, "are being observed by the folks in the grandstands who are going to vote in November."

The changing demographics of Texas, furthermore, had transformed a state that had belonged to the Democratic party since the Civil War into one in which the Republicans were reaching parity. Three Democrats voted in the 1990 primary elections for every two Republicans, but many of the former had come out for local races, which the Democrats still dominated, and at the top of the ticket, they might well cast their votes for the other side. Texas had had a Republican senator, for instance, since John Tower was elected in 1961.

In 1981, Bill Hobby had been chair of the redistricting board, and he observed that as people moved into Texas over the period of time reflected in the last three censuses, "almost all the growth has

been in the suburbs and the metroplex. And they're Republicans."
The 1980 census had also shown that of the 254 counties in Texas,
probably 180 had lost population.

Preliminary figures for the 1990 census showed that the movement from the farms and towns to the cities had continued: urban
areas had grown substantially during the 1980s, while 108 rural
counties lost population. (Loving County, where Clayton Williams'
Gataga No. 2 had made his fortune, lost one-third of its residents
by dropping from 91 to 62.) According to Hobby, the inner city,
which traditionally votes Democratic in overwhelming percentages,
is declining in population: the increase is in the suburbs.

Dallas County had added almost 350,000 people, for a 21.6
percent increase. Fort Worth and its surrounding Tarrant County
had gained just under 310,000, or 35.9 percent. Travis County had
grown at the rate of 38.2 percent by adding 160,000, and its three
surrounding counties had growth rates that ranged from 63 to 94
percent.

The Texas Republican party is largely white, and as Chandler
Davidson's *Race and Class in Texas Politics* makes clear, its spectacular growth since the 1950s can be traced in good measure to
voters' perceptions that the Democratic party caters to minorities. In
1988, for instance, blacks made up 1 percent of the Republican
presidential primary electorate and only a shade over 0.5 percent of
the state Republican convention. Richards' long commitment to civil
rights was therefore at odds with that party's history in Texas. Now,
as she tested her appeal to Republican women and to upscale, well-
educated suburban voters, she would have to pitch her messages
carefully and be very selective about the audiences she courted.

The good news was that her national popularity would draw into
Texas a significant amount of money—not only for her own gubernatorial campaign, but for voter-registration and identification drives
sponsored by pro-choice and civil rights groups as well as labor. A
well-coordinated Democratic campaign could use that money to get
voters who were traditionally theirs to the polls in November, and
their numbers still exceeded those of Republicans in Texas.

This time Texas voters had a very real choice: a moderate-to-
liberal Democratic woman was pitted against a conservative Repub-

lican man. Both were not only flamboyant but given to self-parody. And while Richards evoked "the new Texas," albeit vaguely, Williams traded on nostalgia: "I want to restore that Texas my father handed to me years ago." Late in the campaign, when Richards tried to think of things they had in common, the best she could come up with was that they both cried at movies.

Nevertheless, it seemed likely that the election would turn on personalities rather than issues. Even before the Democratic primary runoff swept to its lopsided close, Clayton Williams became as garrulous as a gabby old circus barker, and what he said chilled many a Republican spirit.

He first made national headlines when he joked to reporters at his ranch about the drizzle that was spoiling his roundup: "Bad weather's like rape: if it's inevitable, just relax and enjoy it." He made headlines again when a reporter asked if he had ever fancied prostitutes and he admitted that as a teenager he had crossed the border to visit the Mexican brothels: "It was a lot different in those days. The houses were the only places you got serviced then." When he explained that he was using the term "service" agriculturally, Molly Ivins pointed out that it was cows that got serviced—not bulls—and the talk in Republican circles began to focus on handlers.*

Rumors of "honey hunts" at Williams' ranch electrified the media, and despite his denials, ABC reportedly spent $100,000 on a team with instructions to comb the area around his ranch in Fort Stockton for anyone who could confirm them. As the core story would have it, Williams had brought in a passel of prostitutes, told them to hide in the brush on his ranch, and then sent out his buddies on horseback with nothing but jockey shorts on their loins and lassoes in their hands to bring them in. One journalist quipped that it was probably the first time penicillin had shown up on a reporter's expense sheet. The ABC team found nothing conclusive.

All this was followed by a great deal of hand wringing, both in press and establishment circles. But the dirty little secret of Texas politics was that a lot of people found it very funny. (Williams' polling

---

*Five days after the rape crack, a woman in Austin was raped by a man who held a knife at her throat and, citing Williams, told her that since it was inevitable, she should relax and enjoy it. Just before the election, he was sentenced to fifty years in prison.

indicated that only 6 percent disapproved.) *Fort Worth Star-Telegram* reporter Joe Cutbirth refused to call Williams' comments gaffes because he was convinced that Williams knew exactly what he was saying and how best to appeal to his audience. They were comments that invited the familiar snickering apologia—boys will be boys!—with which generations had dismissed the high-handed vulgarity of certain men. When he was accused of "playing to the 'Bubba' vote," Williams chortled triumphantly "I *am* Bubba!"

With so daunting a challenge before her, Richards looked at the more than seven months that lay ahead until the general election and gave first priority to reorganizing her staff. She had found Glenn Smith's managerial skills less impressive than his political savvy and his way with the press. Smith, in any event, no longer wanted to manage the campaign because he considered the strategic planning on which Richards insisted impossible: "She was dying for plans and goals she could check on almost hourly, and they don't exist in a campaign—except in fund-raising."

She asked her former deputy at treasury, Mary Beth Rogers, to come in on an interim basis. The two had worked together for almost twenty years, and as Kirk Adams said, they could communicate almost without talking. Like most people who had watched Rogers at her work, George Shipley called her "a great manager," but even more important, there was no one whom Ann Richards trusted more or who understood her better.

Although Rogers had never managed a campaign, her late husband, along with Jack Martin, had run John Hill's losing race for governor in 1984. After spending every night at headquarters, she understood the pressures and knew it was necessary to be clear about "who your real friends are [and] who's flattering you." Her commitment to bringing ordinary people back into the political process, expressed in her book *Cold Anger,* meant that she knew how to reach constituencies that most men and women involved in electoral politics do not.

Jane Hickie then approached Jack Martin to join with her, Rogers, and Glenn Smith to decide what they needed to do and where they needed to go. He agreed, and for three weeks in June, the four of them met together. While Rogers reluctantly continued as acting manager, they tried to think of a man they could put in the managerial chair who would appear professional but take directions from them. Sometime in July, and almost by default, Rogers realized she was there for the duration and officially took on the job until November.

Bob Squier would describe this reorganization as brilliant: "Putting Glenn and Monte [Williams] in charge of communications, at which they're superb, was a great idea. Preserving George [Shipley] as the outside, local guy working with them, as well as with the press and the people coming through, was first-rate. . . . Mary Beth had the total confidence of the candidate. . . . Everyone was just the right amount afraid of Mary Beth. . . . The candidate, the campaign staff, the consultants—all of us needed her."

Although Hickie continued to refer to Martin as part of the troika running the campaign, after June his connection with it became more and more tenuous and he shied away from any official responsibility. Since Richards did not want the general election campaign to be as "consultant-driven" as the primary, she remained vulnerable to the charge that hers was a cult campaign, run by women for women.

The Richards team realized that in a race they would begin with an almost twenty-point disadvantage, their first priority had to be raising money; unless they were competitive on television for the last two months of the campaign, they had no hope whatever.

By now Richards had already brought in twice as much money as Lloyd Bentsen had raised at a comparable point in his 1970 campaign against Ralph Yarborough. But the costs of campaigning had skyrocketed, and she needed far more. By reactivating her direct mail operation, Richards could draw upon thirty thousand contributors by the end of September, and she also had to galvanize labor, the Democratic National Committee, and the big Democratic fund-raisers in Washington, New York, and Los Angeles.

George Bristol and Martha Smiley would make their fund-raising pitch even harder. Cecile Richards, who was by now pregnant with twins, moved from the field operation to fund-raising, a job at which she would prove almost as effective as her mother. Ann herself would spend at least one day a week in the office "dialing for dollars." And for six months, Carol Yontz, a lobbyist for the American Federation of State, County, and Municipal Employees, who had been one of the small group that ran Sarah Weddington's 1972 campaign, moved down from Washington to work on special events like a Willie Nelson fund-raiser. Money, then, came first.

Second, the Richards campaign needed to help secure the Democratic base vote, which meant working with Unity '90, the state party operation that would construct a massive Get-Out-the-Vote operation among traditional Democrats. They moved Lena Guerrero from political director of the Richards campaign to Unity '90 as co-chair, along with Bob Slagle, the state party chairman. And Rogers and Kirk Adams began coordinating their work with that group as well as with the managers of the other statewide campaigns to maximize the Democrats' efficiency.

Third, the Richards team needed to tell Clayton Williams' story, to get behind the figure so brilliantly crafted in the television ads— as Hickman put it, "to make people see Clayton Williams himself, rather than Clayton Williams starring as John Wayne"—and to trigger the innate public skepticism of Republican businessmen.

Fourth, they needed to tell Ann Richards' story. Since most of the electorate's information about her was negative, they needed to give voters a reason to support her. They needed to turn her experience in government into a plus with people angry at government, and they needed to show that she knew how to manage money.

Fifth, they had to extend the grass-roots organization Kirk Adams and Cecile Richards had built to reach all 254 counties in Texas. (In the primary they had not even worked some of the rural areas where Mattox had beaten them badly, especially in west Texas.)

Finally, they had to galvanize the women of Texas and make them see this as a crucial election for them, for Williams and Richards differed fundamentally on freedom of choice regarding abortion.

Since 1990 was the first general election after the Supreme Court's 1989 *Webster* decision, which allowed states to curtail abortion rights that *Roe* v. *Wade* had seemed to guarantee to all American women, the political professionals could only speculate on how important the choice vote might be. According to Richard Murray of the University of Houston, only 7 percent of the Texas electorate called choice the number one issue, and of the 57 percent who considered it important enough to influence their vote, most were conservative. Half of all Texans claim to be evangelical Christians, fundamentalists, or both—

and such people tend to be anti-choice. And since anti-choice forces had taken over the Republican party machinery in many Texas cities, Republican candidates had less than ideal flexibility.*

But the Richards people believed that the choice issue had political momentum, forcing Republican pro-choice women, of whom there are many in Texas, onto the horns of a dilemma. With varying degrees of dismay, they had tolerated George Bush's switch to an anti-abortion position. But after *Webster*, many Republican women, like their Democratic counterparts, had begun to make abortion a touchstone. Since Williams was anti-choice, as well as a man whose comments about women were at best embarrassing, Republican women would have to ask themselves which of the two gubernatorial candidates was the less offensive.

Since Clayton Williams had rolled over his opponents in the Republican primary, instead of dissipating his strength in a runoff, he had been able to do in April and May what the Richards campaign could not even begin until June and July. Mary Beth Rogers had expected to have the campaign in order by the first of May, but she quickly discovered that her goal was unrealistic. It took longer than she expected just to find out what had been going on, and for a while, she felt as though she was wading in molasses. People were exhausted. Many, including the candidate, were still in pain, and as Rogers put it, "a whole lot of reaching out had to be done."

Richards took it upon herself to do much of the reaching and spent most of May on the telephone to Mattox and White supporters, soothing hurt feelings and rallying support for the cause of the Democratic party. In those conversations, and at the state convention in mid-June, she would say they had just had a little family feud. The Hatfields had been shooting at each other, and now that a truce had been called, they needed to rally their forces and start shooting at the McCoys.

She called state senator Carlos Truan in Corpus Christi, for instance, and he agreed to co-chair her campaign in Nueces County

---

*As the election drew nearer, Williams blurred his stand by focusing on parental consent and deploring abortion for the purpose of selecting an offspring's sex, thereby reflecting a common GOP strategy after *Webster*.

while she in turn agreed to go to Corpus for a mid-October party for him. She talked to state senator Gonzalo Barrientos in Austin, who had remained officially neutral, and told him how much she needed his help in the Hispanic community. She heaped praise on County Clerk Billy Leo in Hidalgo County for helping her whip Mattox in what was assumed to be the heart of Mattox territory. In a state so big, Richards could not reach everyone, and some were unrelenting in opposition. But she did try.

For a long time the headquarters operation itself remained a mess. Margaret Justus, whose background was in television news, had started as a volunteer in the field operation nine months earlier, before she was moved finally into the press office and a paid position on the staff. Justus still had to work with inadequate material. Darla Morgan, who spent late spring in the press office, found the campaign in desperate need of administrative help. There was no computer manual, no file of Richards' positions on issues, no media kits, and no bumper stickers. The only surrogate speakers were members of her family, and there was no surrogate speech.

The campaign's ability to respond quickly to breaking news was undermined by inefficiency. When the Norwegian tanker *Mega Borg* exploded and burned fifty-seven miles southeast of Galveston and spilled 3.9 million gallons of light crude oil into the Gulf of Mexico, Justus sent word upstairs to Rogers, who could not get hold of Richards for two days. By the time she reached her, Clayton Williams had already been to the coast and held a press conference. As Kaye Northcott observed, Richards was a strong environmentalist, and "Ann had missed the perfect opportunity."

Beyond Austin, where Richards was so popular she could ride like Lady Godiva down Congress Avenue and get elected, people still did not know what she stood for. All around the state, even people who were well disposed said she had not given them a reason to vote for her. Her "New Texas" was amorphous. Clayton Williams seemed clearheaded, honest, and forceful, and after the drug fiasco, she did not. Some recalled the 1980 Roger Mudd interview with Teddy Kennedy, when Kennedy fumbled badly after Mudd asked why he wanted to be president. He seemed to feel like the heir apparent: he did not need a reason. So far as the vast Texas electorate could see, Richards, too, did not feel called upon to be explicit.

In mid-July, Richards named Bill Hobby, Barbara Jordan, and Henry Cisneros honorary co-chairs of her campaign, making both a symbolic gesture to the Democratic electorate and a shrewd calculation that when the time was right, people of such stature would be persuasive on her behalf. But during the summer, if she was moving at all in the polls, she seemed to be moving in treacle. In early August, *Austin American-Statesman* columnist Dave McNeely wrote of the race as "a war of soft images": "The Ann Richards Texans thought they knew is in danger of disappearing. . . . She is dancing to the tune fiddled by Williams' handlers. . . . Those who had come to think of Richards as witty and urbane, able to handle any situation, too often have encountered a churlish whiner offended at tough questions."

She was running hard up against the Clayton Williams phenomenon, which was largely a function of the enormous amounts of money he had spent on television promoting himself. His campaign for governor had arguably started some five years earlier when he began appearing in person in the ads for ClayDesta, his telecommunications company. He was ebullient and vivid—as a Panhandle friend put it, "stronger than horseradish"—and the TV personality was authentic Williams: he really could "drink beer and dance on the table and sing Mexican songs all night, every night." By 1989, he already had 12 percent name identification among Texans, which is unheard-of for anyone short of a football hero, a movie star, or a successful politician. Then he hired savvy, efficient managers to run his campaign, and together they had created a wellspring of good feeling for him.

All the public knew of Clayton Williams, of course, came from four or five minutes of television he himself had chosen. The major question was whether, under the intense pressures of the campaign, the image would hold. As McNeely wrote, "If Texas voters ever get the idea that instead of a hero from a John Wayne movie Williams might actually be a flatulent cowpuncher from *Blazing Saddles*—a silly goofball with more smile than smarts—a compassionate, competent, capable woman might become governor." But Williams continued to hold a better than fifteen-point lead in the polls, and in midsummer McNeely's hypothesis seemed a long shot.

The positions Williams took were popular with a conservative electorate. He had preempted not only the cowboy myth but the crime and drug issue, which was foremost in people's minds. His proposal to set addicts and criminals to "bustin' rocks" brought people out of their chairs at every appearance. That he was offering a simplistic solution to a complex problem and that Texas' prisons were already so overcrowded they were under federal court order to reduce their populations did nothing to dampen voters' enthusiasm. Nor did Molly Ivins' observation that when Williams' own son had a drug problem, he put him into a $10,000 drug rehabilitation program that did not include "bustin' rocks."

Despite the dire problems confronting poor people in Texas, Williams took the position that the Department of Human Services could meet an expected shortfall by eliminating waste and bureaucratic excess. Five of the agency's six board members were Republicans, however, and its chairman was the Republican candidate for lieutenant governor, Rob Mosbacher, Jr. Ron Lindsey, Governor Clements' former budget chief, had headed the agency for almost a year, and Williams' position seemed to indicate, at best, an ignorance of the problems Texans faced in the 1990s. At worst it showed indifference to the fate of millions.

This indifference was not likely to be politically damaging to Clayton Williams. Poor people do not vote in proportion to their numbers, and their problems are not foremost in the minds of those who do vote. The sentiment is strong in Texas that people are poor because they are too lazy or stupid to work, and at least in the last half-century, no statewide candidate has ever won by running on a full employment platform.

If Williams had winning positions on drugs, crime, and poverty, Richards might nevertheless be able to exploit the public skepticism about big money and its influence in politics. During the 1990 electoral campaign, its disproportionate power over legislation was registering in the public mind to a degree more pronounced than at any time since 1971, when the Sharpstown stock fraud and banking scandal sparked Sissy Farenthold's historic candidacy, brought down an incumbent governor, and destroyed the lieutenant governor's promising political career.

Lobbyists had spent $2 million entertaining members of the Texas legislature during the most recent biennial session and far more in contributions to legislators' election-year campaigns. As Dave McNeely put it, "Politics is, after all, economics. A great deal of what goes on in any legislative body is deciding ways to slice the financial pie." And Richards did not miss a chance to point out that while she was saving the people of Texas $2 billion as treasurer, Williams and his friends were amassing mammoth personal fortunes.

But those who kept hoping that Ann Richards would deliver a full-scale populist appeal—and there were many—were doomed to frustration. Commissioner of Agriculture Jim Hightower, the nationally celebrated Texas populist, for example, was convinced that all Democrats should run for office by running against "The Interests." Hightower argued that east Texas was drifting toward the Republicans because the Democrats had failed to stay with the "true" Democratic message, which was class-based. "That still is in their hearts. That's what they want to hear." In places like Nacogdoches, when he talked about the rich getting richer, the middle class being ripped off, and the poor getting poorer, Hightower expected his audience to "come back home" and vote Democratic.

Harrison Hickman took a very different position, based on a theory about the way stereotypes work in a general election. He argued that a candidate has to play *against* form. People inferred that Ann Richards was a liberal—she was a Democratic woman and she lived in Austin—and to win, she needed to broaden her natural base. If what the voters knew about her already had been sufficient, she would not have been 15 percent behind.

The strategists who were stitching Richards' numbers together so that on election day they would equal 50 percent plus 0.1 percent believed that people in the suburbs liked Ann Richards because they figured that anybody with so much Ultrasuede must be a Republican at heart. Such people might respond to a politician who could persuade them she could keep the middle class from getting ripped off, but for the most part they still believed in the classic American fantasy that anyone can get rich if they work hard enough and get lucky. The Hightower message is not likely to win votes in suburban Dallas or El Paso or San Antonio.

So Richards designed a message for people in the suburbs based on a core belief that Democrats and Republicans wanted the same thing from government. "People want to know that government is going to do right by them," Richards said, "and that they are going to get their money's worth." She emphasized the importance of managing the public trust—a message that plugged in to her work as treasurer. "I wanted people to understand," she insisted, "that that's the way I feel about it too."

Beyond that, Ann Richards would not run against "The Interests" because, apart from rhetorical flourishes, she did not think in class-based terms. As she proved in small gatherings all through the general election campaign, she could galvanize an audience with her rousing promise: "In January, we are going to lock arms and walk up Congress Avenue and take the Capitol back for the People of Texas!"

But Richards did not imagine herself in opposition—as "Ann against the other side." "She's not a populist," Kaye Northcott said. Like her late friend Helen Farabee, she "doesn't really think in terms of challenging big business. She thinks about how she can help various interests come to agreement."

When Hickman's polling indicated that an attack on the high costs of health insurance was a winner, Richards made the attack. But she expected many of the other "interests" to support her, and many did. She did not think she could run on Hightower's issues and win. Neither, it would turn out, could Hightower.

Two candidates paired so brilliantly raised the question of the whole purpose of government. By pitting a multi-millionaire entrepreneur who despised government and talked about cutting fraud and waste against a civil servant dedicated to providing services for people who needed them, the 1990 gubernatorial campaign in Texas presented the alternatives as clearly as the American political system was likely ever to present them.

The tax issue blurred the lines between them.

Williams swore to veto any new taxes, and although the state faced a shortfall that responsible people estimated at between $2.5 and $3 billion, polls indicated that voters loved his stand. Richards refused to say she would veto a tax package, but she did persist in claiming that the deficit could be managed without new taxes.

For the voting public, Richards' position on taxes was less reassuring than Williams'. To editorial boards and newspaper columnists, it looked like political cowardice. For Bill Hobby, who had gone all over Texas arguing for an income tax, Richards' insistence that she could cope as governor without new taxes "foreclosed Ann's talking about the things she knows best and feels most strongly about—and that's the quality of health service and education."

But voters remained hostile to taxes even though, as Richard Murray's polls showed, 73 percent of all Texans refused to believe candidates who said they would not raise them. "Every other governor has lied to them about it," Murray said. "Why should they believe [these candidates]?" George Christian thought the voters were simply looking for a commitment from a politician that he or she would fight to the last against raising taxes. They got that commitment from Williams.

The Richards campaign was still struggling to come up with a message that would tell voters "what Ann would do for Texas." They had not yet found an equivalent of Williams' "bustin' rocks."

Jack Martin and Glenn Smith had taken Hickman's position that Richards needed to establish this message, whatever it might be, by running positive ads, and both had argued that she should do that in early summer to mitigate the damage she had suffered in the primary. "No matter how much money you have," Martin insisted, "spend it in June because that will help you raise more and stay in the race later."

The consultant who had taken the opposite position in the primary and had won the internal debate was, of course, Bob Squier, whose name was identified with negative advertising. And for two months after the primary, it looked as though Richards might jettison Squier, thereby strengthening the hands of those who wanted to "accentuate the positive." Shortly after her victory, and with Squier standing by her side, Richards had publicly embarrassed him when someone asked what she would change if she were doing it over, and she said she would probably change the television ads. Rumor had it that she had reamed him out in private for the backlash her negative ads had sparked and then had fired him. For nine weeks his firm had no connection with the Richards campaign.

Shopping around for another media consultant in late spring, Richards hired Rindy and McKinnon of Austin to work with Hickman on focus groups to discover how much damage the primary battle had done her. With devastating results in hand, they had called a meeting in their offices, and McKinnon had told her bluntly, "Right now, you couldn't be elected dogcatcher, and here's why." After McKinnon delivered the message, Richards killed the messenger.

Rejecting several other options, Mary Beth Rogers and Jane Hickie then called Squier and flew to Washington for "a little makeup session." According to campaign insiders, he had said, in effect, "I've worked for seventeen heads of state, I'm a regular on the 'Today Show,' I run U.S. Senate campaigns, and I've never been treated this way." But Squier had always assumed the call would come, and when it did, he said, "Let's start over. You decide who's running your campaign; you people come to Washington; and let us do a presentation for you. Then you decide whether you want to hire us."

Over the big conference table in his northeast Washington office, Squier insisted, "I still believe this woman is going to win the election." He did not know what a secret ballot taken in the room might say to that question, but he honestly believed what he said—and Richards' emissaries were "pretty desperate." His win/lose record remained the best, and he was a known quantity. They were going to have to "tell the Clayton Williams story"—to bring out the reality behind the brilliant television advertising—and they knew he would be good at that. And despite their turbulent relationship, he and Richards basically liked each other.

Rogers and Hickie asked him back. It was the only time in twenty-two years that his firm had been hired twice by the same campaign, and because of the abuse to which they had been subjected, it was not easy to reconcile his partners to trying again. Still, they went back tanned, fit, and rested.*

Squier rejected Martin's proposal to run positive ads early in the summer, giving the same advice he had in the primary: save your money and wait. His idea was for Richards to "hang in there" until

---

*Four years before, Harriett Woods, the Democratic candidate for the United States Senate from Missouri, had fired Squier after he ran an ad that backfired so badly it was credited with losing ground she never recovered, and Squier had subsequently gone around Washington denigrating her campaign. According to campaign insiders, Richards rehired him to keep him from doing the same to her and to prevent anyone from saying, if she lost, that she just wasn't up to sticking it out with the tough guys.

four weeks before the election, when voters would start paying attention and Clayton Williams might be forced to engage with her in what Glenn Smith would call *mano a mano,* or hand-to-hand combat.

This meant they needed to get Richards into October with her candidacy still viable, with money in hand to get her on the air and with the public's attention focused clearly on Williams. "Once she was there," Squier says, "we all believed she could do it. [Williams'] campaign also knew that if we could get her there, she could do it. The only person who didn't believe it was Clayton Williams. He didn't get it until it was over."

This strategy did not allow much room for introducing Ann Richards to people who did not know her. When staff members tried to explain why people did not understand what she stood for—when they tried to account for the fact that a gifted, capable, astute woman was not known to be such outside Austin—they invariably said the problem was a function of money. But the $4 million plus that Richards spent on television in the primary and general election could have bought a lot of image. In deference to Bob Squier's advice, the available money was spent for the most part on negative ads. Fortunately for Richards, the ones telling "the Clayton Williams story" would have the flair of genius.

The campaign had another way to use television to present a cool, savvy Ann Richards to the public, and so Squier's budget did not account for all Richards' media expenses. As early as midsummer, Cathy Bonner had begun to organize satellite feeds, which are televised news releases. For instance, when Richards went to Liberty County to call attention to a disputed toxic waste dump, the campaign took its own camera crew and filmed her signing a local petition to protest the use of the site. An edited version was then offered via satellite to television stations across the state.

A satellite feed costs between $2,500 and $3,500, but if enough stations use it, it can be worth $40,000 in television time. Bonner would get stations to pick up the feeds all during the general election campaign, beginning with one a week and ending with as many as three a week. On a slow news day, thirty stations might use one.

If the campaign wanted to talk about something important to a specific part of the state such as east Texas, ten or more television stations would be called and told that Richards would be in an Austin studio at a given time. Any anchorperson who was interested could then arrange to interview her for five minutes by satellite as an exclusive local story, which could be videotaped and run on the late afternoon or evening news programs.

Meanwhile, the Republicans were running against her by using techniques Richard Wirthlin had pioneered in California in the 1970s—techniques that evoked the 1960s Democratic campaign line against Richard Nixon: "Would you buy a used car from this man?" Wirthlin had discovered that if he could convincingly portray an opponent as "socially undesirable"—as someone you wouldn't invite home—she would have trouble connecting with voters. If the Republicans could make Richards seem out of the mainstream—corrupt, deviant, or simply "not like us"—she was likely to lose.

The Republican arsenal of weapons against Richards included drugs, alcohol, divorce, liberalism, Travis County, softness on the death penalty, and the damning images of Dukakis, Mondale, and Carter. In that context, the potent strain of misogyny in Texas, combined with Richards' gay support, could be crippling.

On July 17, Williams began a tour through rural east Texas, accusing Richards of supporting gun control, backing repeal of the state's anti-sodomy law, and being at once fainthearted on crime and questionable on patriotism. On the twenty-seventh, the Republican party began running ads on country-and-Western radio stations across the state trying to taint Richards by association: she was backed, they claimed dourly, by Hollywood liberals in general and actress Jane Fonda in particular, along with inmates on death row and the gay and lesbian caucus. The Williams strategists got hold of Richards' schedule and made sure that reporters who met her at each stop were fed information that prompted them to ask about gun control, Fonda, the flag, and gays.

Gay-bashing was to become a familiar technique in the 1990 election. Polls showed that 10 percent of the population was gay, while another 20 percent was either sympathetic or indifferent. For cynics, that made it a 70/30 percent issue, and 70 percent of the voting population is a tantalizing lure for anyone hell-bent on winning.

Fred Meyer, state Republican chairman, was unabashed about

his party's use of the gay issue against Democrats: "There's really basically about four areas in which Democrats and Republicans disagree, and one of them is in what's called traditional family values, traditional social values." The state Republican platform opposed child custody for a gay parent, and according to the *Texas Observer*, Wes Gilbreath, the Republican nominee for land commissioner, told an audience, "The first one of those guys I see hitting on my grandchildren, I may consider getting rid of them right there."

Primarily through radio ads, the Republicans attacked Richards for favoring repeal of the state's old sodomy statute, which she claimed was unenforceable. And during Richards' appearance at a lesbian meeting at the University of Texas, a woman who, according to later reports, had worked for Williams held up a sign reading "Ann Richards: Honorary Lesbian," an image the media spread all over Texas.

Even had she wanted to, however, Richards could not have managed without the substantial contribution gays made to her campaign. The most conspicuous gay involved in the Austin operation was Glen Maxey, executive director and chief lobbyist for the Lesbian/Gay Rights Lobby of Texas. He had organized Travis County in the primary and, by all accounts, had done it brilliantly. As field director Kirk Adams put it: "If we could have duplicated him, we'd have won by much more than we did." In the primary, he had worked with no money whatever, and for the general election, Adams had allotted him no more than $15,000 for expenses. In September, he would take a leave of absence from his job and throw himself obsessively into the campaign. Anyone who came to the headquarters at 3 A.M. was likely to find Glen Maxey already there.

Maxey had made the most of fruitful territory by identifying early on who was going to help. He then made sure the Richards volunteers contacted potential voters at least four times, whether by telephone, leaflet, or a knock at the door. On election day at about 5 A.M., he put up lemonade-like stands in parking lots where volunteers could pick up lists of Democratic voters they needed to get to the polls. According to Adams, Maxey not only "found every Democrat in Travis County" but kept as many as seven different interest groups happy and working together.

All through the summer of 1990, then, Clayton Williams and the

Republican party used radio ads and speeches around the state to insinuate that Richards was neither tough, nor patriotic, nor straight. Late in July, Richards personally asked Williams to withdraw a particularly vicious spot, but it continued to run for at least five weeks longer. Williams later told reporters it was a good ad and he had no control over the state GOP. In mid-September, arguing that the National Organization for Women was on record opposing discrimination on the grounds of sexual orientation, Williams even castigated Richards for accepting money from NOW.

The point was clearly to keep her off balance by forcing her to respond to charges like these—diverting her attention and the public's from major problems facing Texas, as well as from questions about Williams' own fitness to be governor. It was a strategy that would backfire in ways no one could have anticipated, but this became apparent only much later.

The newspapers gave the Richards campaign some help in telling the Clayton Williams story. In early August, both the *Dallas Morning News* and the *Houston Chronicle* carried banner headlines and long articles analyzing Williams as a businessman. The former read "Williams' image, business history differ," and the reporter summarized: "The portrait of Mr. Williams that emerges from public records is that of a super salesman who disdains organizational structure, doesn't get along with partners and who sometimes exaggerates his achievements." He noted that Williams had even told Vance Packard, author of *Ultra Rich: How Much Is Too Much?*, that "money is how you keep score."

The articles revealed that probably only two of the twenty-six companies Williams had founded had made money, and half had been sold or dissolved. In 1987, for instance, he had sold Clajon Gas in a leveraged buyout financed by junk bonds. In 1989, when he sold ClayDesta, the telecommunications company that had run the ads featuring Williams in chaps, he had lost $15 million. The company had been sued by a former employee who said Williams had stolen his idea, but like almost three hundred other suits in which Williams was involved, it had been settled out of court and the records were sealed at his attorneys' request.

These revelations did not seem to affect Williams' standing. As she had with her opponents in the primary, Richards challenged him all summer to release his income tax returns and to debate her. Refusing to do the former, Williams claimed that "it would take a Mack truck to haul it," and as he ducked the latter, she goaded him to fight like a man. But the chasm between them in the polls stayed as wide as ever, and Williams continued to hold the power to set the agenda.

Meanwhile, the Texas Democratic party was struggling to mobilize the potential Democratic vote in November. The Democratic National Committee, under its new chairman, Ron Brown, and political director, Paul Tully, was working to revitalize the party so that it could once again win presidential elections, and a disciplined and accountable chain of command was high on its agenda. Toward that end, it had stipulated that money raised nationally would go only to state Democratic parties that produced a written plan for a coordinated campaign endorsed by all statewide candidates. Unity '90, the Texas Democratic party effort, which was expected to turn out the base Democratic vote for statewide candidates, began to come alive around the first of August. The Dukakis/Bentsen effort in 1988 had spent $3.5 million to get out the Democratic vote in Texas, but Unity '90 set a more modest fund-raising goal of $1.6 million.

If reapportionment made 1990 more than merely a dry run for the presidential year of 1992, it also gave the DNC a chance to see what it took to forge the disparate elements of the traditional Democratic coalition into a functioning campaign organization. It turned out to take a great deal. The candidates had trouble agreeing which voters should be targeted and how much each campaign would contribute to the kitty.

Although Richards released Lena Guerrero to run Unity '90, her team was reluctant to commit other resources. "The DNC wanted a plan that was reflective of the real budget," Guerrero remembers, "and that was too hard to do. What you want is to get national money early, and then run the [money the candidates contribute to the joint effort] late. What happened to us was that nobody was willing to give money early, including Richards, because she was committed to getting on TV from September on into November."

Garry Mauro and Jim Hightower wanted to spend between

$400,000 and $600,000 of Unity '90 money targeting registered Democrats who fell into two categories: Hispanics for whom the primary is the principal election because it determines the local candidates who affect their lives, and people who vote Democratic in presidential elections but who ignore state races.

The Democratic National Committee was game to back the Mauro/Hightower strategy, and labor said it would contribute substantial amounts if the Texas Democrats were united behind it. But they were not. Richards refused to go along with it, and some of the other candidates said that even though it virtually guaranteed 5 percent of the November electorate, at an estimated $3 to $4 a vote, it was too expensive. Guerrero was also opposed. "Had I spent $400,000 on 100,000 voters," she insists, "I would have really jeopardized the operation for Ann, and I personally took that onto myself to deny—whatever the fallout." One group of strategists suspected another of being putty in the hands of consultants with a specialty to ride, and the deal fell apart.*

One reason her campaign seemed to dally with the DNC was that for Ann Richards, many traditional Democratic voters were problematic. "Those are swing voters for us," Jane Hickie explained. "They need to be treated as a group we have to persuade. Older men, women over forty-five, rural men—we've got to go after them! We need to say Ann Richards is a wonderful person and talk to them again and again." Many of those people were going to vote for Phil Gramm, and if they voted Republican in one race, there was no guarantee they wouldn't in another.

"If you look at the hard-core Democratic constituency," Hickie said, "you're looking at four counties in the Valley that are really solid, and 90 percent of that vote is Hispanic. Next, you're looking at black and Hispanic voters. [Then you have] east Texas, [where] folks are going to vote for Bob Bullock. But for Ann and for Dan Morales—they have to be worked and persuaded that it's OK to

---

*Eventually—but very late—all the statewide candidates signed on to a written plan for Unity '90 that met the DNC conditions, and national money began winging its way into Texas. Guerrero believes that "the DNC was going to give money, and they were going to give it late . . . because they've got limited dollars and they are going to play where they can play." The lateness of the hour meant that the big checks would come less than a week before the election, and the total Unity '90 raised was $850,000, less than one-fourth of the amount that Dukakis/Bentsen had spent in 1988.

vote for a woman and a Hispanic. They aren't just lever-pullers any more: they're much more inventive.

"We try to piece together our numbers like a quilt so they'll add up to that 50 plus 0.1 percent. We think the Democratic party has abandoned the suburbs, and we've spent a lot of time and energy and effort trying to organize the suburbs. We think Ann is the kind of candidate who can bring those folks back."

To appeal both to suburban voters and to minorities is no mean challenge. As Hickie recognized, the urban Democratic strongholds are typically the inner city—not the suburbs—and most politicians assume that winning one automatically means forgoing the other.

Richards was trying to bring together a voting constituency that was virtually unique. She needed not only the traditional Democrats but people like Amarillo columnist Kathie Greer, who considered Texas a conservative state where "the old-fashioned principles of hard work, independence, and responsibility are deeply ingrained." Richards needed to convince many voters, as she did Greer, that "when it comes to the rock-solid foundation of sound management, good government, fair representation, and political ethics, she may be more conservative [than Clayton Williams]."

Though Richards remained mired some ten to fifteen points behind Clayton Williams, depending on the poll, Mary Beth Rogers refused to panic. After whittling down the "dream budget" of about $9 million she had originally imagined, she put the minimum necessary to raise at $4 million. At summer's end, that goal at least looked attainable—and everything else hinged on it.

The ad campaign was about to begin, and the fortune that had put Clayton Williams so far in the lead in the race for governor had also made him vulnerable. The super-rich were a fair target—as Richards would put it, not sailboat-rich, but yacht-rich—and a tangible one for a well-crafted campaign. Hickman had polled extensively on Williams' business dealings to discover what was potent in voters' minds so that the Richards ads could focus on two or three points.

In mid-August, Richards began a series of ads, "Meet Clayton Williams," designed to reveal him as a shoddy businessman deeply in debt, with millions invested in junk bonds—a man whose court records were sealed and who refused to disclose his income taxes. With Williams' business history working on voters' stereotypes of Republican businessmen, Hickman was concerned lest he too play against form by sounding like a Democrat on education or health or some other social issue. Instead, he came out for a voucher system in education, which simply rallied the teachers for Richards. (As Hickman says, "That's the way issues frequently matter: with a select audience who really understands [them]. To the rest of the people, it just sounds like a bunch of politicians talking.")

Characterizing Williams as "a wheeler-dealer who has been sued more than three hundred times and accused of everything from fraud and price-fixing to not paying his employees," the Richards ad campaign was a concerted attack on his claim to a wide variety of skills he could transfer from the business arena into government to the advantage of the people of Texas. It ended effectively with the portentous words "Stay tuned!"

If that first ad was punchy, it was also problematic. Squier, by his own account, inadvertently cut a headline from the *Houston Post* in two, slicing off a comma and the last two words, "Richards Discloses." The ad then read "Lawsuits Allege Williams a Dead Beat," implying that the charge was objective truth, rather than a partisan interpretation. Squier blamed the mistake on a technical step in the videotape process called "paintboxing."

At about the same time, the *Boston Globe* contended that Squier's firm had violated federal copyright law by using a *Globe* headline in an ad for John Silber's gubernatorial campaign that David Broder of the *Washington Post* called "one of the sleaziest ads of the year." (Squier blamed this one on a dispute between *Globe* columnists.)

But if Richards worried about Squier's ethics, she nonetheless depended on him more than ever. As George Christian put it in September, "For Ann, there is no other strategy than to attack. She's behind and she's got to bring him down."

In response to Richards' attacks, Williams proposed to provide the "missing chapters" of Richards' autobiography, *Straight from the Heart,* and by the end of August had aired four new ads. But they turned out to be shoddy, which was startling since his ads had won him the Republican nomination in the first place. According to Sam Attlesey of the *Dallas Morning News,* "One contained an outright mistake regarding the state budget. Another contained apparently false claims about Ms. Richards." Attlesey found that the third said nothing and the fourth was confusing.

In late August, a Texas Poll gave Williams a 10 percent lead—roughly the lead the same poll had given him in the spring. Richards pointed out that the $2 million he had so far spent against her had not moved his figures a fraction. But the gender gap seemed to be working in Williams' favor: 57 percent of Texas men would vote for him, while only 44 percent of women would vote for Richards—just 4 percent more than for her opponent.

With charges and countercharges rocketing through the press as the summer ended, Democratic National Committeewoman Billie Carr thought the time had come for some clarity. "Negative campaigns are just something people do," Carr said matter-of-factly. "But I think we ought to define what 'negative' is. When you say that someone was sued by their employees . . . isn't that something we voters need and want to know? I draw the line at personal things. But when [Clayton Williams] says he's a good businessman, and there's evidence to the contrary, I think you need to talk about that." Exasperated with the media, she noticed that whenever they discussed the governor's race, they invariably put "the mud-slinging" first: "They do as much to perpetuate the idea that we're having a horrible campaign as the candidates do."

Journalists refused to accept the blame. Dave McNeely excoriated standard political practice: "Consultant-driven distortion and lying . . . eventually leaves people thinking they've been bamboozled, that all politicians are liars and cheats, that everything is a scam. And that makes it difficult for whoever wins to have the trust necessary to govern." Haynes Johnson had already pointed out in the *Washington Post* that the Texas primary campaign had been the sort that bred public cynicism about politics: only three out of ten eligible voters had participated.

As Labor Day approached, and with it the traditional beginning of the campaign season, the chance that those figures might improve seemed negligible.

CHAPTER 6

The very idea of shootin' little animals makes Ann Richards laugh.

Naw, she's thinkin' about shootin' reporters.
(exchange between reporters)

Seotember 1, 1990, was Ann Richards' fifty-seventh birthday, and she spent it in a way that would have dumbfounded most women of her generation. She had flown almost four hundred miles the night before from the south Texas Gulf Coast to Kaufman County just east of Dallas so that she could get up before dawn to hunt for doves.

Someone innocent of Texas politics might think it odd for a gubernatorial candidate to take a morning off for sport so near the election. But the National Rifle Association had attacked Richards for favoring gun control—a position it could make politically fatal in Texas, even to a candidate for justice of the peace. Ann Richards had come into east Texas to give them the lie.

The newspapers had told her it was a waste of time because her Republican opponent, Clayton Williams, already had "the Bubba vote." Richards might win a trophy for shooting and bag a brace of doves, one paper opined, but the guys with the pickup trucks and six-packs would still belong to Claytie.

Perhaps she was just stubborn. She had grown up in the outdoors, and her father had first taken her hunting when she was ten. She canoes; she hikes; she shoots the rapids; she's known as a terrific campfire cook; she sleeps happily on the ground. And she has been an environmentalist as long as the term has had any meaning. Clearly, if the National Rifle Association could shove Ann Richards into political oblivion, no woman was safe.*

---

*Oddly enough, the most recent Texas Poll had shown that more Texans favored Richards' position on guns than Williams': 69 percent wanted to ban the purchase of assault rifles; 89 percent wanted at least a seven-day waiting period before someone could buy an assault rifle; and 62 percent wanted the same for a handgun.

Adding to the day's incongruities, the host for the shoot, state senator Ted Lyon, an affable man in his forties, was a leader of the anti-choice forces in the state legislature and had sponsored a bill prohibiting abortion during the third trimester of pregnancy. On the issue of dove-shooting, however, Richards and Lyon could agree.

The route to the hunting site led off the interstate onto an obscure country road that turned after a quarter of a mile into a rutted dirt trail. One convoy after another of cars and trucks tossed over the last several hundred yards until they pulled up near two striped tents flapping in a soft dawn breeze.

Twenty feet away from long wooden tables awaiting the celebratory feast sat a six-foot-long, black metal butane tank made into an oven. Its long side rested on a trailer hitch, and the barbecue chef lifted a door to show off a mixture of oak and mesquite logs on which sixty pounds of brisket had been cooking for the past fourteen hours. A man with a beaked cap and a happy morning grin stirred a caldron of beans with a five-foot-long spatula, and once in a while someone tossed more wood onto a fire being readied for doves.

Knots of men in blue jeans and khakis stood chatting with the ease and patience of those long accustomed to slow country rhythms. By seven in the morning about forty people were milling around, of the seventy expected from the ten counties of Lyon's district. Some had already gone into the field, and now and again the still of a heavy east Texas morning was broken by sharp bursts of shotgun fire.

The host groused: "The only place in Kaufman County where it rained last night was here." The wind, Lyon said, had blown at seventy miles an hour. The tents had gone down. His truck had foundered in the mud, four-wheel drive and all, and they'd been up past midnight getting the place back together again.

"Gonna be a blessing, Senator," said a hunched old man with grizzled stubble on his chin. "Keep the dust down, and maybe the fire ants."

The *Dallas Morning News* was there, as well as the *Houston Post*, the *Austin American-Statesman*, the Associated Press, and two Dallas television stations that between them reached virtually all east Texas. To a restless reporter, Lyon spoke reassuringly: "Birds'll be flyin' till 10 A.M."

A man with an accent that made it doubtful he had ever left Kaufman County, even to go to Dallas, was asked the name of a lovely gray-green wildflower and he said abashedly, "We call 'em niggerheads."

Just then a truck came lurching to a stop carrying two fine pointers with their paws dangling over the tailgate, ears pricked forward, and tails moving fast. Their eagerness spread impatience through the camp, until finally, at 7:30, the waiting clusters spied a Land Rover rocking up the road that seemed the likely carriage of Lyon's special guest.

In east Texas, "you" is pronounced in a way that defies spelling. One man suggested "yeuuu"; another, "yeouww." However it is properly rendered, there were a lot of "you's" in the next few minutes, and the accents fell in a lot of different places.

"Senator, how're yeuuw?"

"Miss Ann, proud to have yeouww here."

"What yeuuw say, Yates?"

"I got this special blind for yeouww."

A reporter called, "Start killin' somethin', Ann!," and nodding toward Chula Reynolds, an old friend who was taking the guns from the back of the Land Rover, Richards joked, "I brought my ringer with me. I'll put whatever she hits into my bag." When Reynolds handed her a light, twenty-gauge shotgun, she said, "Gonna use my daddy's gun to shoot. Won't wear me out." To a reporter who was leaving after the first few minutes, she grinned, saying, "It's a shame you're not gonna git to go with me."

On the way to the blind, the small party around Richards and Lyon skirted a water tank and clumps of mesquite bushes with wicked two-inch thorns and then made their way up a little rise, while the reporters who followed began harassing Bill Cryer, Richards' press secretary.

"Hey Bill, what's the official purpose of this trip?"

"Hittin' doves, puttin' food on the table."

"Pity there aren't any high wires you can shoot 'em off of."

"Got a cage somewhere? Let loose a buncha doves just at the right time?"

"Come on, Cryer: the Republicans wouldn't go out without knowing where the doves are comin' from."

A full quarter of an hour was given over to a brace of photographers shooting "Miss Ann" at the blind in khaki hunting gear, and to the surprise of the press party, she handled her gun like someone who knew exactly what she was doing. No more than a handful of the faithful would actually see Ann Richards today, but her political purposes were served by media images that would flash all over Texas on the evening news and appear on the front pages of the next day's papers. In a race in which the polls showed only 12 or 13 percent undecided, and Richards 10 to 12 percent down, she needed every vote she could get.

When Richards said she was afraid of shooting someone, the reporters moved off the rise as somebody grumbled: "She prob'ly wouldn't say that if Clayton Williams was around." Hearing a distinctive guffaw from above, another wisecracked, "The very idea of shootin' little animals makes Ann Richards laugh," to which a third responded: "Naw, she's thinkin' about shootin' reporters." And when Sam Attlesey of the *Dallas Morning News* shouted to her, she quipped, "I been readin' your trash, Attlesey, and this is my chance."

As they waited for birds that did not come, the reporters swapped information: the latest Texas Poll showed that 45 percent of Texans thought Clayton Williams would be perceived in the rest of the country as a better representative of their state, compared to Richards' 30 percent. Two Williams supporters, when asked what they considered their candidate's greatest liability, had said he was an idiot.

By 8:15 not a single dove had flown near the Richards blind, and the reporters started harassing her host again: "Ted, you're not gonna git a good appointment if you don't git some birds over her." "Your chances of bein' secretary of state're goin' down the tubes."

At 8:22 her party took its first shots and missed. A dragonfly lighted on a camera case, and that was all the action for the next half hour.

Finally Lyon shot a dove, which his eight-year-old son retrieved to catcalls of "Child abuse!" from below. When Richards held it up for a picture and then put it in her pocket, one reporter quipped: "Ted's contribution to Ann's campaign." Another ducked behind Cryer when the Richards party turned the guns in their direction, but Cryer said laconically, "I wouldn't count on that; she's been tellin' me how many minutes of Dallas airtime my salary's worth."

The blind itself was an eight-foot piece of netting stamped with a camouflage design and stretched over three five-foot rusty metal posts. Since it seemed after forty-five minutes that the doves had not been fooled, Richards moved downhill under the shade of a mesquite tree, while Lyon grumbled that the big rain the night before had dispersed the doves' watering holes, and besides, the reporters were scaring the birds away.

He used his unwonted leisure to explain why Richards' being there mattered: "The east Texas blue-collar types—the good ol' boys who aren't sure they can vote for a woman—they'll see Ann here and think again. Dukakis wouldn't touch the issue of gun control. We begged him. If only he'd just addressed it." Texas had always had gun control: "You can't carry a pistol in your pocket. We're talkin' about the right to hunt." And he mused: "Ann's daddy took her huntin' when she was ten. My son Peyton's gonna remember today all his life." The old images, he said, still play well: "When I first ran in this district, I rode a horse from Bonham to Tyler. Took me eight days. By the time I got there, the blisters had healed and I had four TV stations coverin' me."

At 9:20, Frank Branson, Richards' overnight host, shot a dove that fell into the water tank and began drifting slowly toward the bank. At 9:45, Ted Lyon shot another. When Peyton tried to give Richards his father's bird, she said, "I already got one, honey." At about 10:15, with the temperature nearing 95 degrees, they decided to call it quits.

As Richards walked back into camp, hunters began coming over to shake her hand. "Glad to be back," she said. "Made an Industrial Day luncheon speech in Terrell maybe five years ago. First time they ever let a woman speak." Then she sat down at the table the press had preempted, pulled two doves out of her jacket pocket, and as reporters began firing questions, she began to pluck the birds.

The most important point she made all day—and she made it over and over—was that Clayton Williams had spent $2 million on television over the summer trying to knock her out of the race. According to the polls, his percentage of the voters had not increased a fraction, and if he had not been able to beat her by now, he was not going to beat her at all.

Many informal decisions, she went on to say, were made on

hunting trips like this, and years earlier, Billy Clayton, the Speaker of the House, had begun asking her to go along. "Wish I'd got to show off a little more for y'all," she grinned. When asked what she liked best about hunting, she answered, "Bein' outdoors."

She went on plucking and talking, and by the time she got around to Clayton Williams' money ("I'll never outspend him. But money can't buy grass-roots support and passion"), the naked carcasses were lying on the table in front of her. When a reporter visibly shuddered at the dangling heads and scrawny wings, she explained: "My daddy taught me: if you're not willin' to clean it, you shouldn't kill it. And if you clean it, you gotta eat it. And if you eat it, you gotta cook it first."

When she and David Richards had started courting, he was the better shot, she said, but she could pull the heads off the birds and clean them. "I think that's what charmed him. He called yesterday and said, 'Ann, you're not gonna take those guns we had down in the basement, are you? They're not real safe.' " One reporter heard wistfulness in her voice and turned away.

She got back to business. Williams had come out for a voucher system in education, and she called his ideas ridiculous: "It's time for him to give us specifics. I want to know how he thinks his voucher system is going to work. What exactly does it mean to Highland Park High School? What does it mean to Hockaday? What does it mean to the students?"

Both she and Bob Bullock, the Democratic candidate for lieutenant governor, were convinced there had been a census undercount, especially in south Texas: "The administration doesn't want any more Democrats in Texas. . . . If they counted right, all south Texas would belong to the Democrats." It would belong to the Democrats, that is, unless a district were bizarrely gerrymandered: "Like 'Tiger' Teague's, you remember: if you drove the length of it with your car doors open, you coulda hit every voter."

She had given the reporters their time, and now she needed to work the crowd. "I saw y'all gettin' my birds," she would say to a new batch of hunters. "Glad to be back. . . . Gave a speech here on Industrial Day. . . . First time they let a woman speak." She firmly shook hand after hand. She looked people dead in the eye. And if any had been doubters before, they were Richards people now.

138 CELIA MORRIS

Before lunch, she addressed the crowd. "It's traditional that women do one thing and men do another, and we all miss out on a lot. We don't get to know each other very well. Informal settings like this help us get over that. . . . It's time we had a governor who gets up in the morning and puts in a full day's work like the rest of us. . . . If you liked Bill Clements, you're gonna love Clayton Williams."

Then it was time for serious barbecue, the way it is done in Texas. And despite a temperature that broke 100 degrees, there under the striped tents, with two giant fans clunking and roaring away, and people sitting and laughing at their leisure, it was as good as it ever gets.

Richards spent the afternoon officially opening county Democratic campaign headquarters, the first one in Rockwall, which the chairman claimed was the smallest county in the state, then in Greenville in Hunt County, and finally back in Terrell. She went through the day hugging and shaking hands with her own: "Appreciate y'all comin'. Been standing' out in 105 degree heat. Shot one dove, took credit for two. I'm lookin' for Virginia Clower." "Here I am, Ann." "Hey, Virginia, I been askin' about you. . . . Hey there, Carleen. Wally, my gosh, thanks for comin'. Can I just move around a while?"

She shook hands with an eight-year-old: "Hello, Stephanie, my name's Ann. I'm glad to meet you." To a man who told her he was running unopposed for justice of the peace, she quipped: "That's the best way. I've done it both ways, and that one's the best. Real glad to come see y'all. Good to be here. I love you." And so on.

Lyon introduced her each time by saying, "I been shootin' dove with this wonderful lady all mornin', and she can not only outtalk Clayton Williams, and outthink him, she can outshoot him too." After the guffaws, he went on: "I cannot afford to spend another four years with a governor who is aggressively dumb. Ann Richards has made $2 billion for the state of Texas in her seven years as treasurer, more than all the other treasurers in the history of Texas put together."

And when Richards took over, she said, "We had so many reporters with us, that's why we didn't see many birds. . . . It's like havin' a buncha scarecrows with you . . . all those white shirts." (As the day got longer, the number of reporters at the hunting site grew: "Hardest thing I ever did was try to shoot doves with thirty reporters around.")

Then she moved on to the issues: "Education is our number one priority. . . . Unless we do the job in education, you can forget about economic development. . . . Eighty percent of the people in the Texas Department of Corrections didn't finish high school. . . . Eighty percent committed crimes under the influence of alcohol or drugs. . . . Can you believe we're behind Mississippi in education?

"We can't afford to keep electing these know-nothings to run the state. . . . Medicare/Medicaid reimbursements ought to be as generous for country hospitals as for the ones in cities like Dallas. . . . Women don't like criminals any more than men do. . . . Women are the most victimized group in the country. . . . I believe people don't mind payin' their taxes if they get their money's worth." After ten minutes she wound up: "Come January, we're all gonna march up Congress Avenue, and we're gonna take that Capitol back for the People of Texas."

At 5 P.M. the reporters' pool had dwindled to nothing, but Richards was heading back with Lyon to see if the doves were flying better at dusk. By this time, she had already been at it for twelve hours, and she might have another five to go.

CHAPTER 7

*Ann took the campaign to [Claytie]! . . . She
broke through all the money, the ads, the
hiding, the vacations. . . . And there they
were—finally in the ring. He had on his ten-
gallon hat and his boots, and nothing else.
And she said, "OK, Claytie, let's do it!" And
he was petrified!*

—BOB SQUIER

On or about Labor Day, Ann Richards decided that she had a
real chance to beat Clayton Williams and become governor of Texas.
Virtually the only people who agreed were those closest to her, and
whenever they confessed their faith to the visiting press, they were
likely to be met with the patronizing glance reserved for those whose
hearts have taken over for brains that have turned to mush.

Any inquiring reporter who poked around outside Austin in the
month of September would have been forced to conclude that the
Richards campaign effort was feeble. The minority communities of
Houston and San Antonio, for instance, are key to any Democratic
victory in Texas, and the voices of those communities were beginning
to sing a dirge over Ann Richards' candidacy.

To be sure, prominent black politicians like Houston's state senator Rodney Ellis and representative Al Edwards said they were upbeat and support was building. (Ellis pointed out that "black folks
are used to character assassination" and can see through it.) But
people closer to the ground sang the song differently.

Janie Reyes, a leader in Houston's Hispanic community, had
backed Richards in the primary, though her husband, Frumencio,
had supported Mattox. For the first time in thirty years, they had
taken opposite sides politically, and now she wondered if she had
made a mistake. Although she was on a Richards advisory board,
she had heard from the campaign only twice—and then about trivia.

Even within her own extended family, she found herself on the defensive: Clayton Williams actually spoke Spanish; he was having a great time working the Hispanic communities; and he was giving people jobs in south Texas.

Billie Carr thought the Richards style played superbly in the black community: "Those black women think, 'What a ballsy woman!' " Nonetheless, Sheila Jackson Lee, a Houston city councilwoman, lamented that the Richards campaign had mobilized neither the black sororities nor any other powerful women's networks within her community. Like Janie Reyes, she was on a Richards advisory board, but no one had contacted her.

Alma Butler, a longtime Houston activist and a woman not easily put off, had been discouraged by the Richards campaign during the primary: "You'd get [to the headquarters] and run in out of the rain—you'd have gone to a lot of trouble to make it—and they wouldn't have anything for you to do!" Her friends had had the same experience, and now, within the black community, she could find no enthusiasm for Richards.

Franklin Jones, a professor of political science at Texas Southern University, confessed that "a number of black women took a feminist line in supporting [Richards] that was much stronger than a lot of people anticipated," but six weeks before the November election, it seemed to him that her campaign not only lacked clear direction but was very nearly dormant. Blacks were not going to vote for Clayton Williams, but unless Richards gave them a better reason than she had done to date, they might not vote at all.

Since members of the press for the most part found Richards appealing, they were dumbfounded. Jane Ely of the *Houston Chronicle* was surprised that "Ann's has been one of the absolutely worst campaigns I've ever seen." Tim Fleck of the *Houston Press*, who clipped the papers daily, said the campaign had not come alive in Houston: not a single story it generated locally had made the front pages.

And while Clayton Williams was jumping into his plane every morning and having the time of his life campaigning, Richards gave the opposite impression: she had long since stopped having fun. In late September, Ely reported that the *Chronicle* editorial board had

found her testy. To Fleck, she seemed defensive and strained: "A lot
of us have had the sense of a deflating balloon, of the energy going
out of that campaign."

At a Houston fund-raiser that George Bristol expected to pull in
$350,000—a figure he had lowered from $500,000 because of Richards' standing in the polls—the take at the door was $4,000. The
campaign had received $45,000 in anticipation, and more might come
in later. But the fund-raiser had clearly been a fiasco.

In San Antonio, a wide-ranging chorus of voices told the same
jumbled story. Writer and historian Juan Sepulveda pointed out that
relying on Henry Cisneros, as Richards was doing, meant campaigning at the Guadalupe Art Center, on the fringes of the barrio, with
the upscale set. "Amigos for Clayton Williams," by contrast, appealed to working people. With mariachis and beer and tamales,
Williams was drawing crowds to places like Rosedale Park in the
heart of the barrio. His rallies were reminiscent of the padron system
of the 1940s and 1950s, which Robert Caro had immortalized in his
work on Lyndon Johnson, but however regrettable that system might
be, people were enjoying Williams' parties, and so was he.

Sissy Bravo, who sells textbooks throughout Hispanic south
Texas, saw scores of Clayton Williams bumper stickers on pickup
trucks in boondocks that traditionally went Democratic. An Anglo
married to a Hispanic, Bravo heard Hispanic men dismissing Richards as too tough and outspoken: qualities they admired in Williams,
they hated in her.

Indeed, it was a truism in the 1990 campaign that Hispanic men,
especially those middle-aged and older, had trouble accepting Richards. Their culture had taught them that women were properly re-
spectful and serene—they did not mock vice-presidents on national
television, drink whiskey, take drugs, or encourage other women to
defy their husbands, their bishops, and the pope himself to assert
authority over their own bodies. In addition, the Republican radio
ads were playing on the homophobia that is strong among Hispanics.
Although Bob Brischetto, research director of the Southwest Voter
Registration and Education Project, thought most Hispanics would
vote Democratic because they understood their economic self-
interest, he admitted that the Republicans were speaking more forcefully about the drugs that were terrorizing Hispanic communities.

San Antonian Linda Chavez Thompson of the American Federation of State, County, and Municipal Employees was optimistic
about Richards' support from labor and saw people volunteering
who had never been involved before. The local branch of the Texas
Women's Political Caucus was Richards territory, and its members
were canny, determined, and upbeat. Still, they were mainly Anglos
in a city in which the majority is Hispanic, and they were scrambling
to raise $500 just to keep the headquarters open. Longtime organizer
Kathleen Voigt had even been told by one of Richards' running mates
that her campaign was hopeless.

The street patter—the voices in the coffee shops and bars and
bodegas—was about Claytie, when it was about politics at all. And
when seasoned observers talked, the rhythm seemed the same: at first
wistful and then solemn. Hollis Grizzard, for instance, an investigative reporter for KSAT, the ABC affiliate in San Antonio, who had
seen politics from the inside as Lloyd Doggett's press secretary in
1984, knew that campaigns are barely controlled disorder. So when
Richards blew her chance for about $4,000 worth of free television
by failing to arrive at his station in time, he didn't assume that she
was self-destructing. Still, he said, Williams managed to get to San
Antonio more often than she did, and as Grizzard put it: "He exudes
this magnetic warmth: he chatters in your face, your pores come
open, and you think, 'What a lively, energetic guy!' "

In mid-September the Williams handlers seemed to be doing
things right, keeping people at bay who would embarrass their candidate—or provoke him into embarrassing himself. And since Williams so superbly exploited people's sense of disfranchisement and
their rage at government, Grizzard was ready to call the race.

Nor had Richards used her distinguished honorary co-chairs. In
early fall, Cisneros was spending a great deal of time out of state,
and Hobby observed that he had no formal duties. Barbara Jordan,
however, had always been available. When Richards spent a few days
relaxing at the beach after the primary, Jordan had taken her place
at a workshop, which prompted Billie Carr to comment, "If Barbara
Jordan's willing to fill in for you, you oughta be absent a lot." But
on October 9, Jordan told a reporter that she had "not yet been
asked to do anything for the next six weeks."

Perhaps the nadir of public disenchantment was reached in late

September, when Richard Murray came out with a poll showing
Richards fifteen points behind Clayton Williams and the October
issue of the *Texas Monthly* hit the newsstands. The cover was a
clever mock-up photo of Richards and Williams grinning as they
danced together, and the headline read "Dirty Dancing." In the special section devoted to the governor's race, a legend knocked "an
unenlightening and uninspiring campaign." Mimi Swartz's article on
Richards was subtitled "How perfection led to failure." And with a
disdain so cavalier an Astor might have envied it, editor in chief
Gregory Curtis dismissed both candidates as "minor phenomena."

Richards' old river-running pal Molly Ivins subsequently pointed
out that only half of one paragraph in Swartz's article touched on
Richards' fifteen-year record in office. But Ivins went on to say that
her campaign "has no focus, no issues, and is too fractionated to
respond quickly to targets of opportunity." Nor did she stop there.
"She doesn't seem to stand for anything," Ivins concluded. "Education, the environment, women and children's issues are all naturals
for her, but she hasn't made any of them her centerpiece."

About this time, Jack Martin was summoned to Richards' headquarters. "It was one of these deals where they needed to talk seriously to Ann," he remembered, "and they wouldn't start the meeting
until I got there." When Martin arrived fifteen minutes late, he discovered that Richards was sitting alone in a room "and nobody dared
go in there and talk to her until I was there."

The immediate problem was that the campaign was short $1
million, but the discussion turned inevitably to the question, "Where
are we?" While Richards began knocking the media and Squier, and
generally passing the buck, Jane Hickie sat "literally on the edge of
her chair looking at me and nodding, trying to get me to say something positive." But Martin talked straight. He said the numbers
looked bad, and "some internal things appear to be hemorrhaging."
The race was now a long shot, and winning would depend on what
Richards put on television.

"I felt sick about it," Martin said softly, "because I saw again
firsthand why I really want to see her as governor: it's her personal
magnetism and her intellectual honesty and her ability to cut through
a bunch of unnecessary bullshit. Here was somebody I care about a
whole lot—a wonderful person I think would be a wonderful gov-

ernor—and I'm having to sit there and say, 'You are going to have a hard time winning this race!' "

A month before the election, the Democratic National Committee appeared to be sending its money to Dianne Feinstein in California. The national press and, according to Martin, 80 percent of the Texas political community had written Ann Richards off.

For all that, what Glenn Smith said about the primary proved true in the general election as well: Richards turned out to be a stunningly resilient candidate and a great counterpuncher, and both she and her campaign held together while her opponent's collapsed. In the first war of attrition, White and then Mattox self-destructed. In the second, Clayton Williams shot off the lower half of his body.

As Jack Martin began to sense, under the dispiriting surface, all Ann Richards' carefully made political investments were coming to maturity—just in time—and enthusiasm was building. Though Martin could still say, "If she pulls this off, it won't be because of any conventional campaign technique," Richards could feel it happening. While her daughters, Cecile and Ellen, shook hands, gave speeches, raised money, and rode in parades—Kirk Adams calculates that through the sisters, the campaign reached a hundred more counties— Ann Richards' humor was coming back. In preparation for a debate that never took place, Bob Armstrong threw her an obvious question: "Why do you think you can beat Clayton Williams?" and she quipped: "First of all, because I'm bigger than he is."

At last she focused on a positive message she stayed with until the end. After touching on scores of issues over the course of the campaign, she picked up on the polling that told her people cared about insurance reform. It was not as strong an issue as the lottery had been for Mattox, but, as Harrison Hickman says, it gave her a chance to "connect all the dots—bad things about Williams, bad impressions of Republicans on business, good impressions of Ann." Squier cut a spot with Richards and her father, whose health insurance had been canceled when he was over seventy, and at last she showed people something she was for—something, as Armstrong put it, "that she will do for me."

Now, as she would claim the day after the election, she really did "let go and let God." Rogers had her organizational chart, and trusting her implicitly, Richards did what Rogers told her to do. Kirk Adams put it succinctly: "She let us do our job, and she did hers."

Day after day, Rogers had been discovering the truth of Ernie Cortes' belief that electoral politics is totally divorced from the politics of empowerment, from democracy with a little "d." It is an isolated activity with little relevance to anything else—and a hard business. Every day she had to gear up as though for war. But the last month was wholly engaging: the long-term planning was behind her, and now, every time she did something, she could see its effects.

What Edmund Wilson called "the shock of recognition" came sometime around the first of October. The campaign had decided to borrow the money they needed to stay on television from September 15 until November 6 and had gotten enough in addition to spend more than $200,000 on a million pieces of direct mail.

Rogers was sitting at her desk looking at the mailings, which were targeted to swing voters in about twenty-three counties, to senior citizens in east Texas, and to sixty thousand women on the choice issue. She knew the media was solid. The money was coming in more easily. And suddenly she knew: this was going to work! Her level of tension, she remembers, was so high that she had to get up and leave her office. She walked around downtown Austin for about forty-five minutes before she could go back inside. "I didn't know we were going to win," she says, but "I knew it was *possible* to win!" After that, the daily fight was easier.

Every day Rogers met with the staff. As Kirk Adams puts it, "She's an excellent manager, but that's a dry word. She's a leader, and she had a bunch of followers who were committed." She used the word "discipline" often; she was straightforward, open, and determined that nothing would push them off her plan.

Remembering the rigors of campaigning, Liz Carpenter remarked, "You get so tired, and so surrounded, that you don't ever have a moment. But Ann's got peace within herself and it shows." In those last two months before the election, when Richards was convinced she had a chance to win, she was extraordinarily focused. She knew the groundwork had been carefully laid and she had done everything she could to win the gubernatorial race. Now the election would be largely determined by things she could not control so that all she could do was live one day fully at a time.

The organization few had believed in proved to be there after all—the organization Richards would claim was "unequaled in the political history of Texas," with county coordinators in all 254 counties and phone banks in more than 190. Four weeks before the election, Barbara Jordan finally heard from the campaign, and so did Henry Cisneros and Bill Hobby.

And women began to "come home." In the focus groups Hickman did on October 3 in Dallas, although Richards was still double digits behind, he could hear the change in the tenor of people's voices. One seventy-year-old woman who had read the *Texas Monthly* profile the campaign had found so damaging had discovered in it a woman she could admire. "She's had her ups and downs," she exclaimed, "but she's human. She's OK!"

The pro-choice movement turned out to be the political equivalent of several hundred Cruise missiles. Representing Voters for Choice, Cybill Shepherd had made many trips through Texas and California, raising well over $100,000 for Richards, and in September, when the movie made from Larry McMurtry's *Texasville* premiered in Dallas, with Shepherd in a starring role, Richards was her special guest. Voters for Choice then helped raise money for a mailing targeted at pro-choice women across the state and cut a thirty-second television ad with Annie Potts, star of the series "Designing Women," which would air repeatedly in the Dallas–Fort Worth area the last eight days before the election. Until the 1989 *Webster* decision, residents of the Dallas suburbs had been decidedly pro-choice but unlikely to let that issue determine their vote. In the past six months, however, polls had shown that many women had begun to fear that their right to choose might be taken away. Before making her pitch for Richards, Potts said, *"Roe* v. *Wade* started here in Texas. It may end here!"

Phyllis Dunham, director of the Texas Abortion Rights Action League (TARAL), had pledged in May to raise $250,000, which TARAL would use to identify 250,000 pro-choice voters and get them to the polls on election day to vote for Ann Richards. They would concentrate on Independent, Republican, and, finally, young women. According to Dunham, the going was not easy because the received wisdom has it that you cannot do grass-roots organizing among middle-class people in Texas: you buy elections; you don't organize to win them. And you do it with paid media; you don't ever count on free media.

Since the *Webster* decision, however, which showed people who had been pro-choice all along that they were going to have to work hard on the statewide level to preserve choice, TARAL's membership had multiplied five times. The phone-bank money had come in slowly and late, but all $250,000 did come, and it came in time.

TARAL had to buy the voter lists and pay for the telephones, but except for the master phone-bank coordinator, the work was done by volunteers. Since, as consultant Celinda Lake puts it, "Texas is a very uneven state in terms of abortion—unlike California, which is dramatically pro-choice"—TARAL commissioned a poll in mid-September that was designed to help determine audiences to target. It showed that for the first time, women were convinced that Republicans might actually change the laws to limit choice, and therefore TARAL focused on Austin, Houston, and the Dallas suburbs. (The Greenburg/Lake poll put Richards only 6 percent behind and rising, and it was the first dramatic good news Richards had had since she beat Jim Mattox in the primary runoff.)

TARAL's work was unprecedented for a woman's interest group in Texas. The Austin phone bank, which also telephoned statewide, had begun calling in June and called through the election. The phone banks in Dallas, Houston, San Antonio, and Lubbock started late in the summer or early in the fall. During the last ninety days of the campaign, they logged fifteen thousand volunteer hours.

The power to which most male consultants had been blind emerged at last. As a clear-eyed Liz Carpenter said the day after the election: "Women didn't do it all, but there *is* a sisterhood—there's a feeling that she is one of us, and we are part of her. We'd have crawled to the polls on ground glass if it had been necessary."

Carpenter was speaking modestly. A longtime friend of Richards and co-conspirator in many a shenanigan and act of political skulduggery, she had decided early in the fall to act on her conviction that something important had gone out of politics. As a reporter in Washington and then as Lady Bird Johnson's press secretary, Carpenter had seen politics from more different angles than most people in the country, and she hated the turn the 1990 campaign took early on. "Politics should not be mean and ugly," she says decisively. "We're doing the most important thing a democracy does. It ought to have a sense of joy and spirit. It should not be something you want to shrink from, but instead something you want to embrace."

She remembered how much fun they'd had on the whistle-stop campaigns she made in 1960 and 1964 as part of the Johnsons' entourage. They would climb on the train in Washington, D.C., and head for Louisiana, stopping at every likely place along the way and more than a few unlikely ones as well. (One snapshot that entered political folklore was of Lyndon Johnson waving from the caboose as the train pulled away from the crowd and shouting, "What has Richard Nixon ever done for Culpeper, Virginia?")

Liz Carpenter knows how to make better lemonade out of lemons than practically anyone in Texas. She wrote a book about growing old happily, for instance, and her prescriptions include spitting in public, wearing purple, and baying at the moon. (She started a baying-at-the-moon society that meets irregularly at her home overlooking Austin from the hills across the lake.) Carpenter looked around the Richards headquarters and realized that since everybody running it was under thirty-five, they knew nothing of politics in its glory days. To teach the young and take some of the bitterness out of the campaign, she decided to do a caravan.

She called Judith Moyers in New York and B. A. Bentsen in Washington, along with a dozen women in Austin who had worked with Ann Richards for years, and they put together a "dog-and-pony show" to roll through central and east Texas appealing not to the "couch-potato" voters a television media campaign is designed to reach but to voters "who want some of the old-fashioned 'rough-and-tumble.' " A devoted supporter loaned them a giant Winnebago, and they plotted a route hitting eighteen cities in a week, starting off with Carpenter's hometown of Salado, some fifty miles from Austin.

They were all experienced women: Judith Moyers, for instance, runs her husband Bill Moyers' production company, and B. A. Bentsen has been working alongside her husband, Lloyd, for four decades. The rest included lawyers, photographers, philanthropists, and the founding spirits of Esther's Follies, a long-running musical company in Austin. They were also women who had grown up in Texas and were fiercely loyal both to their state and to Ann Richards. The candidate would be with them only one day, and they had no idea how many people they could turn out "in this year of our Lord 1990" without the drawing power of the star. But their venturesome spirit showed when Carpenter arranged to stop at College Station— home of Texas A&M University, the Williams alma mater known familiarly to University of Texas graduates as the "cow college"— remarking, "We're taking the bull by the horns."

The last week of September Carpenter's "truth squad" ended up being the hit road show of the season: it was corny, hokey, hard-hitting, and barrels of laughs. They would come into a town with the public address system on top of the van blasting out with carnival patter, "Come one, come all! The Ann Richards bandwagon has arrived!" As many as two hundred people turned out at their trial run in Salado, where Esther's Follies star Shannon Sedwick loosened up the crowd by singing favorite old songs with new lyrics that musical director Lyova Rosanoff had written for the occasion. To the tune of "Accentuate the Positive," for instance, Sedwick sang:

> You gotta accent the educational,
> Augment the way vocational
> Our task is inspirational:
>   Schools are the future of the state!

At Salado an enthusiast even gave Carpenter an "Aggies for Ann" T-shirt.

On the second day, they were joined in New Braunfels by Ann, her mother, Ona Willis, her daughter Cecile, and granddaughter Lily. The PA system rallied the folks to Bob and Kathleen Krueger's home on the banks of the Comal River, which natives boast is the shortest river in the United States, beginning and ending, as it does, in New Braunfels.

It was a clear, sunny day with puffy white cumulus clouds banked on the horizon and a soft breeze wafting off the water. Punch and cookies were laid out under seventy-five-foot-tall papershell pecans bearing a crop of two-inch nuts so heavy the tree limbs were breaking. Cypresses and cottonwoods lined the banks of the river, which is a backwater of the Guadalupe, and while Lyova Rosanoff played "The

Yellow Rose of Texas" on a collapsible Yamaha piano, a crowd of about one hundred watched a flotilla of canoes, rafts, and kayaks welcome Ann Richards to the Hill Country.

Standing tall, blonde, and striking on a grassy natural stage built up with native fieldstone from the terraced lawn, Shannon Sedwick took the mike with a new version of an old song, "Get off your can, and vote for Ann! Deep in the Heart of Texas!" while Carpenter stood beside her, grinning like a manic female Santa Claus. Then Sedwick began singing, "There's a little bit of Texas in everyone, but a whole lot of Texas in Ann!" as the Richards family climbed onto the stage, waving to the cheering audience: "Texas wants a winner who can get things done. Go! Go! for Richards, she's the one, one, one!" Liz's show was on.

"This is the way Texas politics really oughta be," she began, "under a canopy of pecan trees with babies on the quilt. Singing 'Shall We Gather at the River' and 'Amazing Grace' and all those good songs. . . . We are mommas, and grandmommas, and grand-poppas, and daddies. . . . And we want you to join a whole network of supporters all across Texas to work for Ann's election. You'll be walking with the tallest people in this state: Lady Bird Johnson, Bill Hobby, Henry Cisneros, Barbara Jordan. Now, you can't get better company than that in Texas." Recalling the days when a candidate ran for office on a three-plank platform—"paying your honest debts, saving your seed potatoes, and baptism by total immersion"—she laughed and said: "Well, Ann's for all those things, but a lot of other things too, and we want to give her a preview of the dog-and-pony show we're taking across Texas for her."

Judith Moyers' two-minute spiel was a classic piece of political persuasion. She gave her qualifications (her roots went back to the Stephen F. Austin colony and the Fredonia Rebellion), sounded the alarm (there was an emergency in Texas), startled the audience by citing the evidence ("The murder rate is higher in my hometown of Dallas than it is in the place where I live: New York. . . . A national study recently rated the Texas air quality among the worst in the nation"), and proposed the solution ("There are two candidates, but one has no experience in government, a questionable reputation in business, and in my opinion he is unfit to be governor").

After more testimonials and a musical interlude, Carpenter in-

troduced Martha Smiley, the state chair of the Richards finance committee, who prefaced her pitch with the comment that campaigns in
Texas are obscenely expensive and then reached in her pocket to
hold up what was in it: "I've got a check for $100, a $10 bill, a $20
bill, and I need you to reach deep into your pockets." Her son and
a New Braunfels girl went out to pass the hat, and when she got
back on the bus, Smiley had another $2,000.

When her turn came, Richards began by saying: "I have followed
some tough acts in my time. Probably the most difficult was Nelson
Mandela in Florida. . . . And now I have to come here and follow
this kind of act *in my own home state*. It isn't fair! I don't want to
ever follow Liz Carpenter. Not only is Liz going to be better than
you are, and more energetic than you are, when you get off she's
gonna tell you what you left out!"

Next Richards introduced her mother, who would be eighty years
old the next week—"I want you all to look at my momma and know
how much grit and how many years I've got left!"—the "most incredibly talented grandchild anybody ever had, Lily," and her very
pregnant daughter Cecile, and then she said, "I could not have made
this race, and I would not have been successful in the primary, without
these three women: my daughter, my granddaughter, and my
mother."

Then she gave a stump speech as good as stump speeches get, in
Texas or anywhere, touching on the environment, crime, addiction,
education, and abortion. Mocking her opponent's show-stopping
line, she began by saying, "It is time we started training brains instead
of spending money busting rocks." Introducing the insurance theme
that her campaign focused on in the last six weeks, she lamented:
"When my father was in his seventies, his health insurance was canceled. And he has no recourse, no place to go, because health insurance in this state is not regulated." She hit on the underdeveloped
state of the Texas economy: "We take every Texas hide and ship
them to Italy and to Spain, and you end up wearing Gucci boots and
carrying Spanish briefcases and handsome Italian handbags. It's time
we brought the processing and the jobs and the money that goes with
it home to Texas!"

Finally, she explained parental consent by noticing that the standard legislation would give a judge the right to decide whether a

young woman was mature enough to terminate a pregnancy: "If the judge decides that this young person is not mature enough, then this young woman must bear the child. Can you imagine anything more ludicrous? To say that a person is too young to make that decision but old enough to be a mother?"

Ending with the refrain "It's all up to you now," she called on Eleanor Roosevelt as her model, mentioning the time she looked out a train window to see clothes hanging on a line and wrote in her diary that she saw Thrift hanging there. "Most people in politics would have looked out that window and seen merely clothes hanging on that line. Would not have seen the *people* those clothes represent! But that is what we are about: we are about trying to secure government for that family represented by those clothes." Amid the applause, Carpenter called out, "Whistle-stoppers, we are on our way to San Marcos!"

Three-quarters of an hour later, more than three hundred people thronged to former Ambassador Bill Crook's white-pillared home in San Marcos. If the home in whose shadow they stood was imposing, the crowd on the side lawn next to a gazebo and grape arbor was the typical Democratic motley, including a girl with a ring through one nostril and a quiet child with Down syndrome. Jacque Goettsche, who had already given Richards over $50,000, presided over a table with campaign literature. One man wore an "Another Man for Ann" T-shirt, and as Shannon Sedwick caroled, "Let's help Ann ace / The governor's race," a child with thin, bright red hair who was just learning to walk fell on her back in the deep grass and lay there like a beetle waving her arms and legs.

Richards gave her speech a populist edge this time: "The rich and the poor don't pay income taxes. And I mean rich-rich. Not sailboat-rich: yacht-rich!" She had more fun tweaking her opponent by connecting him with the sitting governor: "The best part of the Clements administration is that he's been gone most of the time." After she wound up, the local CBS News affiliate honed in, and its televised interview was broadcast all over central Texas on the evening news. Martha Smiley left San Marcos with $3,000 in checks and enough cash to bring the day's total close to $5,000. The crowd had thinned by the time Carpenter's bus pulled out, but in front of the tall white mansion, Ann Richards still stood talking, listening, and smiling.

In seven days Liz Carpenter's caravan made twenty stops, and there were seldom fewer than a hundred people in the audience. She gave each speaker two minutes to make her pitch, and they focused on what Carpenter called the three E's: education, the environment, and the economy. "We ate our way through east Texas," she drawled. "You run out of adrenaline, and people gave us cookies and cakes to eat along the way." At every stop, they went to the local radio and television stations, and for twenty-four hours, the papers covered what they said and pictures flashed across neighboring television screens. As Carpenter puts it, "That's hard time to buy!"

Not only did they spread the word in all the local media, they energized local people who had been working for Ann Richards for months and even years. Buddy Temple, who had once run for governor himself, gleefully called Jack Martin from Lufkin to say, "They had a huge turnout and great press last night." At a time when virtually all the experts were conceding the race to Clayton Williams, Liz Carpenter and her friends were helping to turn east Texas around for Ann Richards. "It was jubilation to eat cornpone," Carpenter said, grinning. "It was the kind of thing that convinced you that's the way politics ought to be."

And finally Richards began connecting with the minority communities around the state. She went into the barrios; she spoke in one black church after another; she ran ads with Barbara Jordan and Henry Cisneros bearing witness. Each time what she said was a little different, but the core of her message was always the same: that she and they together were taking power at last from people who had held it too long and too jealously—and had made a mess of things.

In the third week of September Richards went to Texas Southern in Houston, a historic black university that Bill Hobby had said should be closed because of persistent problems in accreditation and financial management. She sat in the president's office and asked him, the chairman of his board, and a handful of trustees what they considered important in a damaging auditor's report, what was being done to correct it, and how long they expected the corrections to take. And she listened carefully while they responded.

Then she sat back in a deep sofa, stared up at the ceiling with her hands clasped behind her head, and began to tell them how she and her staff had turned an antiquated Treasury Department into an operation so streamlined that by the end of her tenure it would have made $2 billion for Texas. When they got there, she said, they found money lying around in boxes. She told them she wasn't interested in confrontational politics. More could be accomplished by erasing lines in the dirt than by drawing them: "This is the most integrated school we have in the state, and there's no institution that's higher on my list than Texas Southern University. I'm going to be a very good governor, and I look forward to the opportunity to help you. We can't afford to fight the same battles over and over again."

Next, she told a small group of students how she had changed the hiring policies at the Treasury Department so that 55 percent of its employees were female, 14 percent were Afro-American, and 27 percent were Hispanic: "When I went in, they told me I could not fulfill my commitment, which was that my office, both in the management and in the hiring and in purchasing, was going to reflect the population of this state. They said you couldn't find anybody who understood financial management who was black or brown. . . .

"And I had a tough time, I really did, because the guy who was running the personnel office was convinced he couldn't find them either. And when you begin with that perception, that's exactly what you're going to get. . . .

"So I just moved him out and hired a Hispanic female. And I didn't have to *explain* it to Aurora Sanchez so that she got it *intellectually*, because she already had a gut instinct. . . . Now the person who invests more money and runs the biggest portfolio of money in the state of Texas is a black female named Winsome Jean in the treasury: she manages $2 to $3 billion daily.

"I had directors who came to me and said, 'I know I'm supposed to be hiring minority employees, but I can't find any.' I said, 'Fine. We'll just leave this position open.' And it's amazing how quickly, when you need workers, that you can find somebody. . . .

"I made the head of purchasing a black male, and I didn't have to *explain* it to him. So 58 percent of everything we purchase over which I have authority is made by minority or women-owned firms. There is no agency in the state of Texas that can equal that. . . .

"I know how to do it. I've done it. That's where we're going to make a difference, and I don't care if it is too much trouble!"

Jane Hickie said of Richards that she is not an idealist—that she is a very practical woman. Her practicality, however, is informed by an abiding conviction that the people who have been left out of the process need to be let in. If that is not idealism, it is as close as you are likely to come in the workaday world of Texas politics.

Meanwhile, the acrimony between the Richards and Williams camps cracked like a ball in master's Ping-Pong: they quarreled over everything from savings and loan associations (S&Ls) to decorum. The newspapers kept busy adjudicating claims: she fudged here, he exaggerated there, and now and again one or the other flatly lied.

Richards' series of ads, "Meet Clayton Williams," got well under way with its catchy tag line, "Stay tuned!" and Sam Attlesey of the *Dallas Morning News*, quoting one of her spokespeople who called the second "a positive spot—Type O positive," quipped, "As in blood." While his handlers' eyes glazed over again, Williams put his boots back into his mouth by promising to "head and hoof her and drag her through the dirt."

Hoping to use the same strategy Mark White had used in 1982, when he defeated Bill Clements by running against inflated utility rates, Richards hammered away at insurance reform from mid-September on, giving Democrats who had begged for a spark of populism a candidate running at last against the big-money guys, albeit only one group of them. With barely disguised glee, she waved a letter from Matt Berry to the twelve thousand Independent Insurance Agents of Texas and then read in her Waco drawl, "If you want to protect your livelihood, you can't *afford* to vote for Ann Richards."

Not only the president and first lady, but the Gipper himself came to Texas for Williams. Richards put her money on a different audience, with Willie Nelson and Carol Channing. But she did not turn down political help when it came from the Democrats' first team. In mid-September Senator Sam Nunn came to a Dallas fund-raiser that brought in $400,000; House Majority Whip Richard Gephardt worked east Texas with her in early November; and after Congress shut down *sine die,* she got Lloyd Bentsen home to Texas and at rallies by her side.

*   *   *

The only subject on which the candidates actually connected with each other until well into October was on the question of whether they would have a debate. Williams had confessed during the Republican primary that his virtues did not show to advantage in debate, and he had survived the ordeal in the spring by flashing his opossum's grin while his three opponents tried to shake him from his tree. Still, even an opossum can play dead only so long, and now, when his opponent was a sharp-tongued woman with almost twenty years in government service, it made better sense to climb down and run.

Since running away from a woman would not endear him to a Texas audience, however, Williams found himself in a world-class dilemma. Casting about for a rationale that might rescue him with his political hide intact, his aides did the best they could: they agreed that he would debate Richards if she, in turn, would promise to run only positive ads until the general election. To the inattentive public ear, this stand would seem to lodge him with the angels.

It was Richards' serve. Since Williams' negative ads had had at least three-months' lead time over hers, and since part of her strategy involved "telling his story"—exposing his business dealings as suspect—he was asking her, in effect, to drench her clothes with gasoline and light the match. She said, "No!" He said, "Only if. . . ." Back and forth they went with little more than an occasional variation in phrasing until well into October, when they tired of the game.

Hickman's focus groups were beginning to show that although Richards was still double digits behind, Democrats were ready to come home, in part because of the national debate over the budget. People had come to feel that the rich were not paying their share, and for Democrats that was a good message. Even older women were ready at last to rally to Richards. And it looked as though Clayton Williams had outstayed his welcome. Hickman noted that "he had gone from being kinda interesting to being a goofball."

The gambling instinct that had served Williams well when he saw EXXON and Shell competing for the same oil lease and simply outbid them turned out not to be solid enough grounding to win high office, even in Texas. Hollis Grizzard had given Williams credit for capturing the public's rage against government, but despite their sense of disfranchisement, people turned out to believe in government after all.

The Richards camp kept telling the Clayton Williams story, citing, among other things, sworn depositions that a bank Williams controlled required people who wanted car loans to buy credit insurance through the bank—a practice that violated both federal and state law. They also charged Williams with suspicious business ties to a Houston banker, Lloyd Williams (no relation), whom the FBI was investigating for allegedly laundering drug money.

On the tenth anniversary of her sobriety, Richards had the panache to throw a party at Scholz's Beer Garden, where she announced that the TARAL poll now found her only 6 percent behind. When Williams heard this claim, he wisecracked, "I hope she didn't go back to drinking again!"—a comment so tasteless it awakened the unpleasant memory of his earlier offhand remarks about women.

When the endorsements began to come in, two were triumphs for Richards. The Sierra Club called Williams an "environmental disaster for Texas." The 8,500-member Combined Law Enforcement Associations of Texas were wordier: they ridiculed Williams' idea that "bustin' rocks" was a way to deal with crime, called his speech to their association "insulting" to men who patrolled the streets, and told him to "come out and start acting like a man and debate Ann Richards publicly."

On Thursday, October 11, Williams committed his most serious blunder to date. At a rare joint appearance before the Greater Dallas Crime Commission, and before an audience of more than one thousand, Williams whispered to a companion, "Watch this!" and went up to Richards and said, "I'm here to call you a liar today." Richards was startled but said, "I'm sorry, Clayton," and offered her hand while he went on: "That's what you are. You've lied about me; you've lied about Mark White and you've lied about Jim Mattox. I'm going to finish this deal today, and you can count on it." Richards stood there with her hand outstretched, and Williams turned his back and walked away. At the end of his luncheon speech, he looked right at Richards and alluded to Senator Joe McCarthy's unsavory tactics when he paraphrased Joseph Welch's comment in the Army-McCarthy hearings: "Ma'am, have you at long last lost all your decency?"

An open microphone had captured Williams' "Watch this!" and television cameras caught his refusal to shake her hand. When he subsequently told the press, "She came across the line when she attacked my business," he showed that the Richards attack ads based on George Shipley's research were reaching their mark.

Richards had told a columnist, "You don't get headlines with issues," and nothing so vindicated her judgment as the uproar that followed. An account of Williams' slight not only appeared in virtually every paper in Texas, it made the national news. The *San Antonio Express* titled a typical story "Williams loses cool in run-in with rival," and until election day, television networks showed him over and over refusing to shake her hand. The pollster Richard Murray in Houston said that for a man with a significant lead, Williams had done "the dumbest thing" he had ever seen in politics, and Richards, of course, made the most of it: "Texas men are not like that. Texas men are very supportive. They're very encouraging. They're gentlemen. They're not always looking backward, talking about the good old days."

"I think we can take full credit," Richards said later, "for the errors that occurred in the Williams camp. We knew, *we knew* that he was going to blow!"

As Bob Squier put it: "Ann Richards understood the transaction they were involved in and he didn't. His handlers did, but Claytie expected to be able to do his thing the way he'd always done it. Ann took the campaign to him! She made *him* the issue. She broke through all the money, the ads, the hiding, the vacations. . . . And there they were—finally in the ring. He had on his ten-gallon hat and his boots, and nothing else. And she said, 'OK, Claytie, let's do it!' And he was petrified! You could smell it at the end of that race: in the end, she unmanned him!"

From that day on, the Williams handlers seemed obsessed with keeping their candidate away from the press. They refused to allow reporters on his plane, and television cameras caught Williams being shoved into a car, the door slammed shut, and microphones pressed futilely against the rolled-up window. When a reporter quipped that Clayton Williams was the only man in Texas who could stir up controversy by talking about the weather, it appeared that the John

Wayne image had indeed been replaced by that of a buffoon. A new Richards television ad enlisted Williams against himself, beginning with his "most publicized verbal miscues" and ending with the question *"Governor* Williams?"

With the fortune at his disposal, however, Williams was no joke, and by mid-October, he had broken the record for the most money ever spent on a statewide campaign in Texas. His $16.6 million was dramatically higher even than Bill Clements' $12 million in 1986. Since midsummer, he had been outspending Richards two to one.

Still, in Hickman's polls, Richards was moving up slowly and Williams was going down. Although Richards' negative ratings did not vary much, they did go below 50 percent. In the third week of October, a Gallup poll showed that Richards had narrowed Williams' lead to five points, and a summary statement accompanying the poll credited Williams' loss of support to women offended by the handshake episode. In three weeks, Williams had lost 5 percent of his advantage, and if his slide continued at that rate, Richards not only could but would beat him.

By October 25, an Eppstein poll showed the race a dead heat, with 24 percent undecided. For Richards this was heady stuff, since Bryan Eppstein, a Republican consultant in Fort Worth, had given Williams a 13 percent advantage two months earlier.

Suddenly, the chief of criminal investigation in the Bexar County Sheriff's Department announced another drug charge against Richards. He claimed that a man he had sent to New Mexico on other business had happened across a former press aide to Jim Mattox who said he'd seen Richards take cocaine outside a Dallas bar thirteen years earlier after a fund-raiser for his boss.

This was the man Mattox had alluded to at the end of the primary runoff, and Robert Riggs of WFAA was convinced that Mattox was still so bitter in defeat that he would rather see the Democratic party go down than watch Ann Richards become governor. But Richards not only denied the charge: she refuted it by producing two witnesses who swore she was somewhere else that night with them.

Once more voters perceived that a man was picking on a woman, and as Jack Martin had predicted six weeks earlier, when Williams' support began to vanish, it dropped first in south Texas. Stumping for Richards in the Valley, Henry Cisneros called on men to defend a lady's honor: "In the Hispanic community, men must respect ladies. . . . It's a strong ethnic cultural tradition, and to turn one's back on [a woman] says a very ungentlemanly thing." Unity '90 mailed a message from Cisneros to all Hispanics urging them to vote the straight ticket, and the former San Antonio mayor cut a thirty-second TV spot for Richards in Spanish.

Until the last few weeks of the campaign, Bob Bullock, the Democratic candidate for lieutenant governor, seemed to be avoiding the top of the ticket, and his slogan, "An Independent Voice for Texas," implicitly dissociated him even from the Democratic party. But now he took on Richards as a cause: at a big *pachanga* in the Valley, he got on the platform and said: "You men, now you listen to me! In Texas a man shakes a woman's hand! I'm here to tell you Clayton Williams is no man!" His performance made the front pages and news programs all over south Texas.

Big-city newspapers began coming out with endorsements: for Richards, the *Houston Chronicle*, which was something of a surprise; the *Austin American-Statesman*, which was not; the *Dallas Times Herald*, the *Fort Worth Star-Telegram*, and the *Corpus Christi Caller-Times*. Into the Williams camp fell the *Dallas Morning News* and the *Houston Post*—the latter endorsement no doubt galling to Richards' campaign co-chair and the paper's former owner, Bill Hobby.

Then at the end of October, as Williams' campaign costs mounted to $20 million, he made yet another mistake. His excuse for avoiding a debate with Richards had been sufficiently plausible to the average voter that he had escaped humiliation. But for the sake of appearing both competent and confident, he had agreed to paired, albeit separate, interviews by television station KERA in Dallas.

Accustomed to being the man who controls the questions and indifferent to detail, he was vulnerable when the panel of reporters asked him about Proposition 1 on the November ballot.

"Now, Prop 1 is which, excuse me?" Williams asked.

He was told there was only one.

"Oh, on the education commissioner?"

No. It changed the timing on gubernatorial appointments. Was he aware of the problem?

No.

Well, it had been "a major problem in the legislature last year."

Then it should certainly be remedied, but he hadn't taken a position.

Hadn't he already cast his absentee ballot?

As a matter of fact, he had. Well, he thought he had voted for it. Yes, his wife, Modesta, had told him how to vote. In self-defense, he said he wasn't a politician but he could read: "If you'd put that in front of me, it would take me about thirty seconds to give you my opinion. I had the highest grade point in the school of agriculture at A&M my last semester."

The press was dumbfounded because the proposition Williams had failed to notice had to do with the powers of the office for which he was running. Once more, a Williams blunder made headlines all over the state. This excerpt from the interview was added to the televised catalog of such blunders, and even Governor Bill Clements began to poke fun at his would-be successor.

By now, Williams had run so many television spots the average Texan had seen him eighty times. According to media expert Kathleen Hall Jamieson, that is more than four times the saturation rate, and it had unintended consequences. Roy Spence, the Austin consultant who had designed Walter Mondale's media, put it clearly: "Williams was essentially elected governor two months ago in the minds of the public, so for all practical purposes he is the incumbent. With the anti-incumbency mood sweeping the country because of the budget problems and everything else, Williams has a real problem." The backlash against George Bush was catching him in its eddies.

The last Gallup poll before the election showed the race even but indicated, at the same time, that 51 percent of the voters would mark "none of the above" if they were given that option. Sam Attlesey reported seeing a bumper sticker that read "Does Texas Really Need a Governor Anyway?" Referring to "the unprecedented volatility of today's voters," Jane Ely confessed that "the Texas gubernatorial race has come unglued." And conservative national columnists Rowland Evans and Robert Novak noticed that because of self-inflicted wounds, the Republican candidate for governor of Texas might well snatch defeat from the jaws of victory.

By now it was clear that Richards and Williams were fighting for every vote. And when the electorate began to compare the two, as Hickman tells it, although Richards had very little margin to play with, her negatives began to go down. In the end, voters began to jump from "negative" to "positive," skipping "undecided" altogether.

In only two weeks, Clayton Williams had lost 10 percent of his support and was under sustained pressure. In early September, Dave McNeely had warned that when the option of hiding behind well-crafted television ads had vanished, the pressures at the end of a campaign could be murderous. Even seasoned politicians like Mark White and Jim Mattox had cracked under the strain, and a novice, however shrewd and gifted, was far more vulnerable. Williams' poll numbers seemed in free fall and the burden of his accumulating blunders heavier by the day. The question now was whether his handlers could keep him from making a slip that would be irreversible.

Ten days before the election, Sam Dawson of the United Steelworkers arrived in Austin and was amazed to discover that except for one problem, Unity '90 was functional and Richards could win. The problem was familiar: Unity '90 was almost broke. Dawson got on the telephone and stayed there with his message: "You've *got* to understand: if we can get our folks out, she's gonna win!" Within a week he brought in between $80,000 and $90,000, and the Democratic Get-Out-the-Vote effort was assured.

With the election a week away, the two candidates together reported spending $32.5 million, making this already the most expensive gubernatorial race in United States history. In the month preceding, they had spent nearly $10,000 an hour. Of the grand total, Richards had raised $12.6 million, an unprecedented amount for a statewide Democratic race in Texas. Williams, who had poured just under $3 million into television in September alone, went back on a public pledge by throwing another $1.4 million of his own money into his campaign.*

At last the Democratic National Committee money came in, trailing what had already come from labor. "Late money" usually means

---

*Between July and September, Richards could boast of almost fifteen thousand contributors: 86 percent of them gave less than $100, 58 percent were women, and 18 percent lived outside Texas.

the last week or ten days. This time it was sent the weekend before the election, with three payments in five-figure numbers, and the party had to charter a plane to fly "street money" around the state for the people who were paid to do the Get-Out-the-Vote effort.*

The gubernatorial battle had awakened deep anxieties seldom touched by conventional politics, sparking what even the densest onlooker had to recognize as a battle between the sexes. Reports began coming in from exclusive neighborhoods like Highland Park in Dallas that Republican women were switching to Richards. One told a reporter, "I'm a conservative Republican, I probably vote Republican 99.9 percent of the time, but no way could I vote for Clayton Williams." Another saw him as "a man who has hoof and mouth disease . . . he's going to make a national laughingstock of us."

In small east Texas towns, in parts of west Texas, and in rural areas all through the state, however, Richards was just as hard for men to take. The *Dallas Times Herald* reported that for many in Red River County, for instance, Richards was a tough sell: in a Democratic stronghold that had even gone for Lloyd Doggett in 1984 and Michael Dukakis in 1988, more than one man said flatly that he would not vote for a woman. An embarrassed Democrat said Richards would be lucky to carry his county by 55 percent, which he considered disgraceful.**

Minorities were moving from the apathy Bob Brischetto of Southwest Voter had observed only a few weeks earlier into something resembling active involvement. When Henry Cisneros and Barbara Jordan talk, a lot of people listen—Hispanic, black, and Anglo.

In the week before the election, Jordan called a press conference at which she declared in her most august tones that any minority person who voted for Williams was out of his or her mind. Afterward, as Nancy Clack tells the story, Chula Reynolds was taking Jordan back to the Lyndon Baines Johnson School of Public Affairs where

*Nancy Clack believes that if the money had come a week earlier, the election would not have been so close. Turnout reached 1986 levels, but the Richards campaign needed to reach 1988 levels to meet its goals. It did reach that level in certain south Texas counties, but overall, those counties had a 10 to 12 percent lower turnout than in 1988. In one county, the Hispanic organizer for Richards would say, "Clayton Williams got forty-four votes. I know forty Anglos. I gotta find out who those four Mexicans were!"

**She got even less than he had hoped, carrying it by 54.4 percent.

she teaches, when suddenly Jordan lifted her arms and called out in her resonant, deliberate voice that sounds like God, "We are taking the Capitol back for the People of Texas!" Reynolds stopped the car, or the car stopped itself, she is not entirely certain which. She looked over, and when she saw Jordan's radiant face, she asked if she was all right. When assured that she was fine, Reynolds started the car again and delivered her distinguished guest in due order.

On Friday, November 2, Clayton Williams did it again. He volunteered to a reporter that he had paid no income taxes in 1986 because, he said, it was a bad year.

Once more Richards' long-term strategy had paid off. She had been hammering at Williams since June to release his tax returns, and the press, goaded by the Richards campaign, had kept after him as well. In her stump speeches since Labor Day, Richards had asked her audiences: "What does a man who can write a personal check for $6 million know about you and me?" Finally, at a stop in College Station, Williams exploded in irritation, saying of course he had paid millions of dollars in taxes, but not in 1986.

The timing was crucial. The revelation came after a month-long congressional deadlock over the budget, when President George Bush's popularity had plummeted because the public perceived him as favoring the rich at the expense of the middle class and the working poor. In budget negotiations, Bush had held out for reducing the capital gains tax from 28 to 15 percent and had opposed any change in the infamous federal income tax "bubble"—a provision that allows those with incomes over $200,000 to pay a marginal rate of only 28 percent, while those just under it pay 33 percent.

Earlier in the year, Kevin Phillips, in *The Politics of Rich and Poor*, had revealed that in 1986, the wealthiest 1 percent of Americans took 14.7 percent of the national income—up 6.6 percent in only five years—while between 1980 and 1989, the net worth of the Forbes 400 richest Americans had nearly tripled. From Ann Richards' point of view, a Gallup poll released in September was good news: it showed that 51 percent of the voters linked the GOP to "rich, powerful moneyed interests"—up from only 18 percent in 1987.

On Friday evening, November 2, when Margaret Justus heard Channel 8 in Dallas say that Clayton Williams had told reporters in

College Station that he had paid no income taxes in 1986, she ran into the next office to tell Bill Cryer. He immediately picked up the telephone, called the Associated Press, repeated the story, and wondered pointedly how many other years Williams had not paid taxes.

Together they raced upstairs to Mary Beth Rogers' office, where she was waiting for Richards to call from a labor hall in Houston. The three of them called her instead, and Rogers told her she should play the story for all it was worth. It was the fifth or sixth stop of the day, however, and Richards was tired. When she seemed to be holding back, Rogers put Cryer on the speaker phone. He insisted: "This is the story tonight. You *have* to make an issue of it!" Richards said "OK," hung up, and turned the Williams blunder into another attack on him as well as a soliloquy on the injustices of the system.

In the midst of that soliloquy, Joe Cutbirth of the *Fort Worth Star-Telegram*, who had spent the day traveling with Richards, had what he calls an epiphany. Until that moment, he had thought she would lose and had grown so tired of hearing the same speech that day that all he wanted to do then was finish talking to Sissy Farenthold, with whom he was chatting at the back of the hall. But in the midst of Richards' speech, he heard her say, "We understand Clayton Williams didn't pay any income tax in 1986." He stood there thunderstruck that she had waited until 8 P.M., when all the reporters' stories were in, to make this announcement: "The old cliché 'Stop the presses!' was legitimate in this case."

"The minute she was through with her speech," according to Cutbirth, "we mobbed her," and as the reporters fired away with their questions, he could see Williams' "$10 million juggernaut crumble." Richards had the presence of mind to say: "This is why I don't support an income tax: wealthy people can hire accountants and not pay it. It's working-class people who end up paying it." And Cutbirth "knew it was over. Williams had lost every issue. His campaign had no theme."

Once more the lead story in papers across the state carried banner headlines embarrassing to Clayton Williams. A subhead in the *Houston Chronicle* read, "Richards says opponent out of touch," and the *Dallas Morning News* quoted her more fully: "Our opposition *does not represent nor can he understand* what it is like to be among the working people of this state, who pay their income tax, meet their payrolls, take care of their families, and scrimp and save to send their kids to college."

In the three days before the election, President George Bush campaigned with Williams, but if his popularity remained stronger in Texas than in many parts of the country, the budget debacle in Washington had nevertheless left him singularly unconvincing when he argued that Republicans could best be trusted with the voters' financial well-being.

That Sunday, accompanied by Barbara Jordan and Virginia Governor Douglas Wilder to one black church after another in Dallas and Houston, Richards would say, "1986 was a bad year for truckers, but they paid their taxes! 1986 was a bad year for teachers, but they paid their taxes! 1986 was a bad year for people who work in government, but we paid our taxes!" The man who had run against government now came to be seen as a clever but common cheat.

Barbara Jordan does not like to be seen in her wheelchair, and her strenuous and public effort on behalf of Ann Richards was immensely moving to the black community and to others as well. That evening in the tiniest hamlets of Texas—in places like Dime Box, Bug Tussle, Snook, and Carthage—television watchers saw dramatic shots of an ebullient group: Ann Richards, Barbara Jordan, and Doug Wilder with a changing group of local politicians but always with a lively bunch surrounding them. Election day now held the prospect of being downright joyful for Democrats.

Sam Dawson claims that Williams lost between 5 and 6 percent of the vote over that last weekend. "People tell me if he hadn't made that statement, she probably wouldn't have won east Texas." And to Dawson's mind, Richards became herself again: "The way she handled the tax statement after he made it was terrific!"

Her chances of winning improved ever so slightly at lunchtime on Monday, when Congressman Martin Frost was approached at a Citizens' Council lunch in Dallas by a disgruntled member who gave him a piece of advice. If he checked with the secretary of state, he would discover that in 1986, that bad year for Clayton Williams, he had given $10,000 to Bill Clements' campaign for governor.

Frost excused himself, went outside, and called his office, telling them to pass the message immediately to the Richards people. This is not the kind of research that takes all day, especially when the incentives for haste are attractive, and the information was available in time for the late afternoon and early evening newscasts. It was repeated on the late night news and appeared the next morning in the *Dallas Morning News*.

CHAPTER 8

> *What is it Bob Dylan says? "The first year*
> *we knocked on the door. The second year*
> *we banged on the door. And this year, we're*
> *gonna kick that sucker in!"*
> —ANN RICHARDS, November 5, 1990

On Monday, November 5, at 9:30 P.M., a crowd of almost two hundred was gathered at Austin Aero, which John Connally and Ben Barnes built for the private plane trade before the Texas economy went into free fall and they into receivership. It is bright red baked enamel, with rounded corners like a ship's turrets, and its lights were beaming out on an otherwise dark corner of Austin like a ship's onto a midnight sea. Wearing white masks with Ann Richards' grinning face, the people in the crowd were standing with the network cameras just behind a heavy iron fence. They were waiting for the sleek white jet that would bring their candidate home on the very last night of a two-and-a-half-year ordeal. The crowd was keyed up even higher than on most such nights, when the smell of victory is tangy, because this one was historic.

The din of jet engines swooping above and revving up on the tarmac obscured Barbara Jordan's brief remarks, but suddenly through the noise her last sentence leaped out: "After tomorrow, the state of Texas will never be the same!" A roar of sheer exultation followed, and when you ask yourself why politicians do it, a crowd like this gives one of the answers.

"We want Ann! . . . We want Ann! . . ."

Nancy Clack greeted a visiting reporter with a rhetorical question: "Who'd have thought we'd be putting our hopes on this race rather than on Dianne Feinstein's?" The most recent polling had been done on Halloween, just five days earlier, and Clack's figures were showing a 50.04 percent Richards win. "My heart says 54 percent," she added, "but the numbers say 50.04 percent."

Sam Dawson, who had been guarded and apprehensive a month before, called it a win but warned: "If she doesn't pull it out, it'll be ten years at least before a woman can run here again for a major office. We're still gettin' calls sayin' 'I just can't vote for a woman.' I think we're gonna do it, but the map's gonna be the craziest thing you've ever seen."

At the top of the crowd, closest to the gate, Dan Morales, the candidate for attorney general, passed the mike to someone who shouted, "Check your watches: in twenty hours and thirty minutes, Ann Richards and the Democratic party are taking back the state of Texas!"

Congressman Jake Pickle now had the microphone, but no one was paying attention. A wild spirit had seized the crowd, and a random cheer broke out now and again until the Richards plane landed and the cheers swelled to a crescendo. The white plane rolled to a stop, the door opened, and the spotlights gleamed on the halo of white hair.

"We want Ann! . . . We want Ann! . . ." It was more than ten minutes before the noise from the planes and the crowd settled enough to let her speak.

"All those attacks," she began hoarsely, "they weren't personal. We're talking about improving Texans' lives, and that's a threat to a lot of people. We're talking about regulating the insurance industry of this state. We're talking about seizing the educational system and allowing the teachers and the educators to take part in establishing what needs to be done. We're talking about equalizing opportunity. We're talking about the environment, about no longer allowing it to be poisoned by people from outside, we're talking about protecting the clean air and clean water and clean land that Texas should be. . . .

"Anything worth having," she said emphatically, "anything worth having, is worth fighting for. After two and a half years, and I don't know how many millions of miles, talking to people about what has to be done and what government ought to be about—*none* of the personal fatigue, *none* of the hard work—can really equate to the fact that people have given their lives for the freedom of this country: for civil rights, for equal rights, for the rights for us to have a free voice and to have privacy in our private lives.

"I am nothing more than an extension of the people. And . . .

I'm glad that at no time were they able to bring us *even* to our knees. I'm glad that at every instance, we stood up and we fought back. . . .

"This election means more, my friends, than all the issues we've talked about. This campaign has serious significance for the generations to come. There are gonna be a lot of little boys who are gonna be opening their history books, and they're going to see Dan Morales' picture. Their teacher isn't gonna have to explain it to them. They're gonna say, 'If he can do that, I can do that.' There are a lotta little black kids who are gonna open those books and see Morris Overstreet's picture. And they're gonna say, 'If Morris Overstreet can do that, I can do that.' What better example can you give a kid than the fact that if they stay with it, if they work hard, they can do it too. And a lotta little girls are gonna open those books, and they're gonna see Ann Richards."

"We want Ann! We want Ann!"

"And you know what they're gonna say, don't you? They're gonna say, 'If she can do that, I can do that.'"

"So this election is about opening doors. What is it Bob Dylan says? 'The first year we knocked on the door. The second year we banged on the door. And this year, we're gonna kick that sucker in!'"

Then it was sheer pandemonium for a while, but after she thanked the people with her—Lena Guerrero, Oscar Mauzy, Bob Krueger— she gave an admonition:

"I want to tell you a story about St. Francis. All of you know St. Francis: he was the one who came into the garden and all the birds loved him. St. Francis was standing in the garden when a preacher walked by, and seeing him in the garden there with all the gorgeous flowers and trees and birds singing, the preacher said, 'St. Francis, what a magnificent garden!'

"St. Francis said, 'It is my garden of prayer.'

"And the preacher said, 'Well, St. Francis, you must have prayed many, many times to have this garden flourish like this.'

"And St. Francis said, 'I did, I prayed a great deal. But every time I prayed, I picked up the hoe.'

"I want your prayers, but tomorrow I want you hoeing at the same time."

*   *   *

The next day Virginia Whitten picked up her old friend and three-year-old Lily Adams for their usual walk around the lake. The day was beautiful, and that made Ann Richards happy because it meant a good turnout for Democrats. Her voice was nearly gone, but after a few warming-up exercises, her old alacrity came back. On November 6, she took off on the trail pushing Lily in her stroller and left Whitten and half the accompanying press corps behind.

Meanwhile, the Richards people and Unity '90 were getting their people to the polls. Glen Maxey had set up his lemonade stands to give out the information his volunteers needed to turn out the votes in almost every precinct in Travis County. Billy Leo had some help from labor organizers and *politiqueras* working Hidalgo County and other voter-rich counties of south Texas. They dropped the last of seventy-five thousand leaflets they had begun handing out over the weekend. Sound trucks spent the day rallying people to go to the polls. Teams of walkers knocked on doors, and every telephone line in the Valley was humming.

In Fort Worth, Gary Lipe and his volunteers were combing the swing precincts for Richards voters and goading them into the voting booths. In Houston, Ken Bentsen, the senator's cousin, was pulling together the various Democratic field operations under the rubric "the coordinated campaign"—the Richards people, Unity '90, and Billie Carr's precinct operation, which she had put together for Bob Bullock. Kirk Adams was overseeing his field operation in the swing precincts of the big cities and the brush and winter garden counties of south Texas. Unity '90 was working to get out the traditional Democratic vote in the heavily Hispanic and black areas and most of east Texas.

Republican women were calling each other for courage and going to the polls, sometimes together, to do something they never thought they would. A week before the election, the Texas Poll had found that 23 percent of Republican women remained undecided, while 11 percent said they would vote for Richards. According to exit polls, 10 percent switched on election day.

Reports came flying in that people were taking the money Clayton Williams was plowing into south Texas for election day workers but voting instead for Richards. By noon, the CBS exit polls were showing her ahead 52 to 48 percent, and as one gleeful staff person put it, "Our vote doesn't even come out 'til after 3 P.M." They also indicated that nearly half the people voting for Richards had made up their minds in the final month—a quarter of those in the last week!

That afternoon Ann Richards played bridge with Dan and a handful of friends and then went to her meeting of Alcoholics Anonymous. Finally, it was time to go to Jack Martin's office, which was election central. Mary Beth Rogers and Jane Hickie went with her.

The numbers were being called in to Nancy Clack in Richards headquarters from the people in the field. The county clerk would call, or someone standing next to him who took the numbers down and passed them along. This meant they were getting results almost as fast as the secretary of state, and every few minutes, Jane Hickie would phone Clack from Martin's office to ask, "Where are we now?" At half past eight, the three of them gave up on an obviously circuitous way of getting returns, abandoning Martin's office for Richards headquarters.

They ran upstairs to surround Clack, and Richards stood looking over her shoulder as she filled in the empty column next to the list of counties and projected numbers on the sheets laid before her on the table. Clack would write in a new set of figures, and the comparison with the projections might show that she was two votes off on overall turnout and one on how many people would vote for her candidate. Richards would then slap her on the shoulder, and she would grin. For the small counties, her figures were rarely more than thirty or forty votes off, and Richards would smile and keep standing patiently. An hour passed and then an hour and a half. Every once in a while Clack would let out a few whoops, and Richards would grill her: "What do you mean by that?" And she would explain.

About 9:30 P.M., the Hyatt Regency Hotel called to say the crowd was unruly and likely to riot unless the Democratic candidate for governor got there soon.

Richards looked at Clack.

Clack was comfortable with her numbers: she had not been wrong all night, and she was feeling cocky. But she knew that when Richards got to the Hyatt, the networks would cut to her and she would be on national television. As Clack put it later, "Now I know what a stroke feels like."

Richards said: "I'm not going over there unless you tell me to. I'm not going until you tell me I'm going to win. Yes or no? I need to know: am I going to win?" Everyone was looking at Nancy Clack. And she said, "You're going to win!"

Then she added, "To me it feels like a 54 percent night." Richards said, "No," and Clack said, "I'll stick with my numbers: 50.03 percent. You've won." Richards grabbed her around the shoulders and skipped out of headquarters. Someone next to Clack said, "You sure as hell better be right."

Richards' old friend Bud Shrake was waiting outside with the car, and her mother and father piled in along with her, the children and grandchildren tumbling into the cars behind, along with Hickie and Rogers, in what became a makeshift caravan. Their party was strangely quiet—smiling but perhaps a little stunned. People waved and yelled as they passed down Rio Grande and then, after a couple of turns, across the bridge over Town Lake and left for the few blocks east to the Hyatt.

Inside the hotel, the security men had started moving in on the peripheries of the Richards crowd, and word began to snake through the ballroom that she had won. As Jane Hickie puts it, the guys with the suits and the wires coming out of their ears spelled victory. The Texas Department of Public Safety was positioning itself to mount guard over the new governor.

With Richards in the lead, her party came in the back way at the Hyatt, pumping hands, howdying, and thanking their way past the gaggle of well-wishers with the grace that had gotten them triumphantly through almost two years. They made their way into the kitchen and, from there, to the back entrance of the ballroom. When they finally opened the big door onto the tumult, the wild noise pouring out was so piercing that Lily, in Kirk's arms, clamped her hands over her ears—and kept them there.

Just as Richards started up the ramp to the platform, the telephone Hickie was carrying began to ring. It was Buddy Barfield saying that Clayton Williams wanted to speak to Richards. Then he added, "I see on television that she's just come out, so he'll wait until she's finished." Hickie said uncertainly, "Well, I can go get her," but by then Richards was standing before a crowd still edging toward riot.

It was almost fifteen minutes before they were quiet enough for her to speak, and they went off again when she held up a T-shirt that read "A Woman's Place Is in the Dome!"

After giving her acceptance speech, Richards made her way back into the holding room, where Hickie handed her the telephone and Barfield on the other end passed his over to his boss. Accepting Williams' concession and congratulations, Richards told him how gracious he had been—a line she underscored and embellished the next morning at her press conference in the senate chamber.

Then, with a phalanx of patrolmen, Richards, her parents, Hickie, and Bud Shrake made their way in and out of several parties the big donors were throwing up and down the Hyatt until Shrake could take the governor-elect home at last. After they left, Hickie came across Mary Beth Rogers wandering the halls in a daze, and it dawned on them as they looked at each other that for the first time in years, they had nothing to do. At about the same time, just outside the ballroom, Phyllis Dunham of TARAL was surrounded by phone-bank volunteers shouting, "It works! It works!"

Clack's figures were off by 0.05 percent. Richards won by 49.98 percent. (Omitting the Libertarian candidate, or "none of the above," she won 52 to 48 percent.) Out of 3.8 million votes, Nancy Clack had miscalculated by 2,000.

At lunch the next day at the Zona Rosa, Richards brought that discrepancy to Clack's attention. She said, "I'm real disappointed in you." As Clack says, "When she's happy, those blue eyes are as happy as can be, and when she's angry, they're steel. She looked at me with steel blue eyes. And she said, 'You were off by two thousand votes.' " Clack said, "There are four precincts still out: I'll find 'em."

Richards won every big city and, with the help of a 21 percent Republican crossover, 61 percent of the women's vote. Williams narrowly won the absentees with 49.4 percent compared to her 47.9 percent. Among Anglos, according to Richard Murray, the gender gap was probably the largest ever seen in a major race in Texas: "This race really drove white men and women in opposite directions."

Whether one accepts Billie Carr's estimate that a precinct organization can account for up to 7 percent of the vote, or Jane Hickie's that it can produce at most 5 percent, Unity '90 and the operation Kirk Adams put together turned out to be more than enough. Clayton Williams lost by less than 100,000 votes out of almost 4 million cast, or 2.49 percent of the total.

According to the exit polls, Hugh Parmer, the Democratic candidate for United States senator, who had the unenviable task of running against Phil Gramm, got 35 percent of the total male vote and 39 percent of the total female vote. As Lena Guerrero put it, Parmer's vote was "what Unity '90 got out: he didn't get any swing votes." Richards got at least 9 percent more of the total male vote and over 20 percent more of the total female vote, and a substantial part of that margin can be attributed to Kirk Adams' work in swing districts. Without either Unity '90 or her own field operation, Ann Richards clearly would not have won.

Even before the inauguration, Barbara Jordan proved to be right: Texas would never be the same again. The governor and lieutenant governor were both recovering alcoholics whose publicly acknowledged confrontation with their demon had only made them stronger. A Hispanic, Dan Morales, was attorney general, and a black, Morris Overstreet, was sitting on the Texas Court of Criminal Appeals.

Richards' first appointment—to the three-member Railroad Commission, which for decades had set the world price of oil—would have been unthinkable at any earlier time in Texas history: she chose a thirty-two-year-old Hispanic woman, Lena Guerrero.* Taking a first step toward fulfilling her promise to toughen ethical requirements for Texas legislators, Richards appointed Barbara Jordan to be her special counsel on ethics and John Hannah, a former federal and county prosecutor with a record for battling corruption, to be her secretary of state. As though the courts themselves were responding to the new atmosphere, only eighteen days before the inauguration, Gib Lewis, who had recently announced that he would run for an unprecedented fifth term as Speaker of the House of Representatives, was indicted for violating state ethics laws. And as her chief of staff,

*In a special election, Richards' prize volunteer, Glen Maxey, won the seat in the state legislature that Guerrero vacated.

Richards appointed Mary Beth Rogers, a woman who believed, along with Ernesto Cortes, in empowering the insulted and the injured.

On January 15, 1991, the suspicion was abroad that the most powerful female in Texas for the next four years would be a little girl named Lily Adams, whose Nanny was about to start running the show. The Lone Star State was bracing itself to swear in a governor with a cat named Tina Turner and a penchant for watching the university's crack basketball team, the Lady Longhorns. And at 10 A.M., a crowd some twenty thousand strong with a white-haired woman in the lead really did link arms and walk up Congress Avenue to take back the Capitol for the People of Texas.

CHAPTER 9

Set it up!

—DIANNE FEINSTEIN

Dianne Feinstein was an abused child: she had an alcoholic mother with a brain disorder that went undiagnosed until Dianne and her two younger sisters were grown and the damage she could inflict was long since done. And until 1984, when she told a San Francisco reporter about watering her mother's booze and hovering protectively over her sisters, only the people closest to Feinstein knew her tumultuous story. Others saw simply the woman she became, in some measure because of it: a wealthy Jewish matron who turned in crisis to a black minister, the Reverend Cecil Williams, and to Glide Memorial Church, where the addicts and outcasts of San Francisco's Tenderloin district find what hope they can in a world that despises them. A woman who defied her own insecurities by putting them to tests the toughest would fail. A Stanford University Quad Queen who made common cause with Sweet Alice Harris, a black woman who put small change together to run shelters for homeless men and women and a school in Watts for children "at risk."

Not even the most astute observer could tell from watching Feinstein that life for her has been anything but a blessing. With a face that could sell Valentine chocolates, she cuts a grand figure at six feet tall in the high heels she wears and the bright colors she fancies. When Great Britain's Queen Elizabeth II visited San Francisco, its denizens tittered that their mayor was the more regal. She has a resonant, cultivated voice and a mode of speaking that radiates confidence. Taking a voter's hand in both of hers, she looks directly into his or her eyes as though to plumb the soul's mysteries. She is so earnest she is positively Victorian.

In fact, she recalls those deep-chested, high-collared women with ropes of pearls on bodices of bombazine over whalebone stays. Her gifts seem executive rather than maternal, and her repeated insistence that she would be tough on crime struck many an onlooker as superfluous. She is said to have a bawdy laugh, but it rarely surfaces in public and is quickly suppressed.

Feinstein had been seriously considered for the 1984 Democratic vice-presidential nomination and had more name identification than any other potential gubernatorial candidate in her party in 1990. Nevertheless, when she decided to run, she had neither a full-fledged staff nor a network of support outside San Francisco. This meant pitting herself, in the Democratic primary, against Attorney General John Van de Kamp, whose base was Los Angeles, a city with roughly half the votes in California and one where Van de Kamp was not only known but honored. So in April of 1989, she hired Darry Sragow, who had managed Alan Cranston's triumphant Senate campaign in 1986 and Lieutenant Governor Leo McCarthy's losing campaign in 1988, and told him to teach her about Los Angeles.

Sragow set up a meeting with Kenny Hahn, an aging white man who is a Los Angeles County supervisor with a largely black constituency and whose son is the LA city attorney. As Sragow puts it, the pictures hanging on the wall of a house in Watts would most likely be of Jesus, Martin Luther King, John F. Kennedy, and Kenny Hahn: he was a beloved institution. A series of strokes had left him in a wheelchair, and when they met in the spring of 1989, Feinstein came into the room forcefully, sat down next to him, and started asking questions.

"Dianne has been responsible for starting a school for kids at risk in Hunter's Point," Sragow says, "not in the glare of the spotlight, not for publicity. So she's describing this to Kenny Hahn. And he says, 'I've got somebody you have to meet: she's Sweet Alice Harris.' She runs something called Parents of Watts, and she gets sent kids by the LA School District that are 'at risk,' which is a term of art that means they've been arrested, they're in gangs, they're at the end of their rope.

"Dianne turns to me and says, 'Set it up!'

"I've lived in LA six years, I'd run two statewide campaigns. I had never been in Watts."

So Sragow went down to meet Sweet Alice Harris in the shadow of the Watts tower, which is an amazing work of folk art, and arranged to bring Feinstein. Then the three of them sat for hours talking shop.

"By this time," Sragow says, "I'm in love with Dianne Feinstein. Any candidate I'd ever heard of went to Watts, or any place like Watts—if they went at all—late in the campaign with the cameras trailing them."

In the time since then, Feinstein's relationship with Sweet Alice Harris has become, as Sragow says, "a real relationship. It's not some ritual: the white candidate pays homage to the black voter. Dianne identifies with the underprivileged in her gut."

Very much the same thing happened at a meeting Sragow organized with a group of school principals, when a woman got up and asked, "Why don't you spend some time in the LA schools?" Feinstein said to Sragow, "Set it up!"

"These visits are unannounced," Sragow explains. "Dianne's not waiting for the cameras. She talks to the teachers, she talks to the administrators. She absorbs. That's how she learns what life in LA is about." She was accustomed to learning in ways others might label unconventional.

On November 27, 1978, eleven years before Darry Sragow took Dianne Feinstein deep into the Los Angeles ghettos, San Francisco was still in shock from news of the Jonestown massacre nine days earlier. Most of the nine hundred members of the Reverend Jim Jones's People's Temple who had committed collective suicide in Guyana had come from the Bay Area, and people who had been friends and neighbors were still coming to terms with the enormity of the disaster. Feinstein was president of the city's Board of Supervisors, and on that bleak day, she was working in her office in City Hall when she looked up to see former Supervisor Dan White running down the hallway with a pistol in his hand. A few seconds later, she heard gunshots and raced into Supervisor Harvey Milk's office a few doors away. She ran over to the body on the floor, bent down to find a pulse, and put her thumb through a gunshot wound in his wrist. Within minutes she discovered that the freewheeling, popular mayor, George Moscone, was dead as well.

People who were at City Hall that day still look grim when they tell what happened. Coro* director Martha Bredon says: "The whole range of emotions that were swirling around the second floor was unbelievable. It was the most confusing, threatening, sad, terrifying, angry time. And Dianne was . . . absolutely exemplary in saying, 'This is the way this has to be handled.' "

As president of the Board of Supervisors, Feinstein was Moscone's successor. Twelve years later, the television ad that turned her political fortunes around struck a resonant chord: "Forged by tragedy!" The picture that faded into stark black and white showed her on the steps of City Hall that November day announcing gravely that Moscone and Milk had been shot and killed.

The sheer horror of that time cannot be exaggerated, and Feinstein rose to the occasion with awesome dignity. The *San Francisco Chronicle* wrote that she had "provided a voice for the city's sorrow and its aspirations. She was poised. She was eloquent. She was restrained. And she was reassuring and strong."

What most people did not know was that the murders came at a hard time for Feinstein herself. Only hours before, she had told reporters that after running for mayor and losing badly both times, she had decided to get out. Her husband of sixteen years, Bertram Feinstein, had died in April after a long battle with cancer, and she had emotionally withdrawn from those around her. So bereft that she could barely manage to get through each day at City Hall, she would go home in the evenings and shut herself in her room until it was time to get up and go again. Finally, her eighteen-year-old daughter, Katherine, had come in to plead: "Momma, you can't do this any more. You've got to live your life and get on with things." Feinstein had heard the wisdom in her daughter's advice and was trying to take it, but "getting on with things" did not have to mean staying in electoral politics.

In just a few terrible moments, the assassination changed all that, and Feinstein took what Martha Bredon calls a "developmental leap." "You could see it in her poise," Bredon says. "She became suddenly in charge, and that validated her sense of mission, [her] sense of destiny. When this horrible thing happened, she was *chosen* to serve the public purpose."

*See footnote Chapter 1, page 19.

To Bredon's mind, Feinstein gives noblesse oblige a good name because she incorporates in an approach to office that some denigrate as elitist the promise "The buck stops here!" And although many politicians are beguiled by the blatant power of office, as Bredon understands, "It's a terrible life unless you're fueled by a sense of mission—the kind of thing we apply ordinarily, if only in fantasy, to the Founding Fathers, to the thinkers. Feinstein definitely thinks."

As Sidney Blumenthal wrote in the *New Republic*, "If Dianne Feinstein appears controlled, polished, even stiff, it may be because she was raised between the poles of decorum and derangement." She was a child who endured her mother's beatings and threats, who watched her father violently shake her mother when she was co-matose and made her vomit the sleeping pills she took to kill herself, and, later, a girl who spent the night before her college board exams sleeping in the car because her mother had locked her out. The woman that child becomes has two options: she can emerge timorous and shriveled, or she can grow resilient far beyond the common measure. Feinstein did the latter.

The other pole in Feinstein's life was her father, Leon Goldman, a prominent surgeon and professor who embodied the upper-middle-class Jewish culture of commitment. On the memorial tablets in Mt. Zion synagogue, Goldman's name is prominent among those who have given, and so is Morris Bernstein's, his old friend and her honorary uncle. Since San Francisco is a compact city, the wealthy Jewish community was never isolated in gilded ghettos but instead has been fully integrated from the days of the gold rush. Families like the Levi-Strausses and the Fleishhackers set the pace, and men who achieved a measure of success were expected to honor the social ethic that required them to give back to the community.

Michael Schneider, a longtime labor activist from the International Brotherhood of Electrical Workers, remembers that Dr. Goldman liked to present his United Way contribution in public but at the same time was adept in behind-the-scenes negotiating. He arranged access to people, he was a facilitator, and on the campus where he taught, he was essentially a rabbi—advising, listening, consoling. Although apparently unable to shield his daughters from his

Sarah Weddington, surrounded by the women who ran her 1972 campaign for the Texas House of Representatives. Ann Richards (far left) was beginning to make the transition in her political career from volunteer to professional status. Carol Yontz, who would raise substantial amounts of money for Richards' 1990 gubernatorial campaign, is to the right in the bibbed dress. (Alan Pogue)

Frances ("Sissy") Farenthold, Ann Richards, and the late political satirist John Henry Faulk at a 1970s gathering of Texas liberals. Farenthold's 1972 campaign for governor brought Texas women by the thousands into active electoral politics for the first time and inspired many to found the Texas Women's Political Caucus. (*Texas Observer*)

Treasurer Ann Richards sharing a light moment with Lieutenant Governor Bill Hobby in the Texas senate chamber, while Stephen F. Austin looks on. Hobby, along with Barbara Jordan and Henry Cisneros, was honorary co-chair of Richards' 1990 gubernatorial campaign. (Senate Media Services)

Richards relishing the spotlight after her keynote address to the 1988 Democratic National Convention. Her quip that George Bush had been "born with a silver foot in his mouth" alienated many Texas Republicans. (AP/Wide World Photos)

Jane Hickie and Kirk Adams analyzing the political map of Texas. Richards' administrative assistant when she was Travis County commissioner, Hickie ran Richards' first statewide race for treasurer. Adams is married to Richards' oldest child, Cecile, and ran Richards' field operation in 1990. (Ave Bonar)

Three of Ann Richards' children—(left to right) Ellen, Cecile, and Dan—played crucial roles in her gubernatorial campaign. (Ave Bonar)

Former Governor Mark White, Treasurer Ann Richards, and Attorney General Jim Mattox, the three contenders for the Democratic nomination for governor in 1990, observing formal courtesies before their first televised debate in Houston. (*Houston Chronicle*)

Richards and Mattox, in an unguarded moment during a January 1990 labor convention in Austin, reveal the personal antagonism that splintered the Texas Democratic Party. (Ave Bonar)

Lena Guerrero, political director of the Richards campaign in the Democratic primary, with media guru Bob Squier, telling the incredulous candidate immediately after the Houston debate that she had made a damaging verbal slip. (Ave Bonar)

Richards' advisers Bob Squier (left) and pollster Harrison Hickman—considered by many to be the best Democratic political experts money could buy—in Dallas for the second debate during the primaries in March of 1990. Richards' opponents, Mattox and White, were expected to insist that she "answer the question": had she ever taken drugs? (Ave Bonar)

Campaign manager Glenn Smith, in characteristically "laid-back" style, during preparations for the Dallas debate. (Ave Bonar)

Harrison Hickman (left), along with consultants George Shipley (center) and Mark McKinnon, clowning away their tension in Dallas. After the debate, key Richards advisers—and some say the candidate herself—thought the bitter drug issue had cost her the election. (Ave Bonar)

Jane Hickie (foreground) and George Shipley (standing to the right) with press secretary Monte Williams (seated) and deputy treasurer Paul Williams, just before Richards' Austin press conference on drugs. After Richards lambasted her opponents for shoddy financial ethics, her political fortunes, many believe, began to turn around. (Ave Bonar)

For nine months Dan Richards campaigned around Texas with his mother, traveling extensively in private planes. In order to relieve the stress and tedium, Dan often resorted to reading thrillers. (Ave Bonar)

Clayton Williams galloping up the capitol walk in Austin in May 1987 to publicize his telecommunications company's fight against AT&T. In the primary, Williams defeated three highly qualified rivals to become the Republican candidate for governor in 1990. (*Austin American-Statesman*)

Richards with state senator Ted Lyon at a dove shoot in Kaufman County on September 1, 1990, her fifty-seventh birthday. (Ave Bonar)

THE
GODMOTHER

Richards in a tender moment with campaign co-chair Barbara Jordan, formerly a Democratic member of congress from Houston. (Shelley Boyd, Texastock)

Democratic National Committeewoman Billie Carr was a key member of the Harris County Democrats, an influential liberal organization that supported Richards in the primary. (courtesy Celia Morris)

Liz Carpenter, longtime newspaperwoman and Lady Bird Johnson's press secretary, organized a caravan of prominent women to travel for eight days through east Texas promoting Ann Richards' candidacy. Here Carpenter broadcasts a call for folks to come to a rally in New Braunfels. (Ave Bonar)

Richards teasing former San Antonio mayor and campaign co-chair Henry Cisneros before he introduced her at a rally in south Texas. (Ave Bonar)

Clayton Williams refusing to shake Richards'
hand—a moment of incivility that damaged
the Republicans. (Ave Bonar)

Barbara Jordan (left) and Chula Reynolds
(second from left), a King Ranch heiress and
longtime friend of Ann Richards, enjoying the
prospect of victory with Wendy Sherman (center) and Ellen Malcolm (right) of EMILY's
List. EMILY is a Democratic women's political action committee that gave Richards more
than $400,000, becoming her single largest
donor. (Ave Bonar)

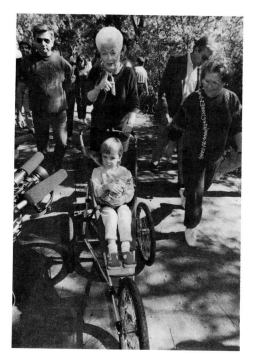

Richards pushing granddaughter Lily Adams
on a bike trail election morning, with old
friend Virginia Whitten (right) and press secretary Bill Cryer (left). (*Houston Chronicle*)

Jane Hickie (left) and campaign manager
Mary Beth Rogers (center) with Richards at
her home on the afternoon of the election.
(Ave Bonar)

Unity '90 co-chair Lena Guerrero (left) and consultant Nancy Clack happily adding up votes on election night, November 6, 1990. (Ave Bonar)

Governor-elect Ann Richards at her victory party at the Hyatt Regency Hotel in Austin, with her parents behind her, along with daughters Ellen and Cecile Richards, and Kirk Adams holding Lily. (*Houston Chronicle*)

Richards and Mary Beth Rogers on the day after the election, holding a newspaper with the banner headline "She Whups Him!" They are surrounded by headquarters staff and key volunteers: Glen Maxey is in front of Richards, with Ellen Richards at his elbow; Margaret Justus from the press office is seated at bottom left. (Alan Pogue)

wife's abuse, he nonetheless healed other people and made things work. His eldest daughter's style derives in some measure from his.

When Dianne was young, her uncle Morris Goldman came to live with her family and held nightly political arguments with her father, a Republican who preached self-reliance and looked dimly on unions. Morrie, by contrast, was a street-smart urban populist in the garment business who took her to meetings of the Board of Supervisors and walked her all over the city, pointing out the seedy delights of places like the Tenderloin. From these radically different brothers, Dianne learned to weigh all sides of an argument and to imagine life in terms far more complex than the typical girl her age.

Even more than most daughters of her generation, Dianne Goldman would have dreaded the possibility that she might grow up to be like her mother. Since most women of Betty Goldman's class were not well-read, well-informed, or passionately committed to anything—they were ladies, a condition in life that some of their daughters found at best a bore—there was little Dianne could take from her mother that could teach her how to live in ways she could both honor and enjoy.

That left her father and uncle, who became at once the inspiring and sustaining forces in her childhood. It is therefore hardly surprising that Feinstein has surrounded herself with men. Apart from the nuns in the Convent of the Sacred Heart, where she went to high school, her mentors and most close advisers have been male.

In recent years, however, she has begun to reach out to women. Cynics see this as a purely practical gesture because in the 1990 gubernatorial race she needed their votes to win. More than 52 percent of the California electorate is female, and to run as a woman who by virtue of that elemental fact represented a change from the "gray suits" of the past, she needed to identify more explicitly with women—or at least to persuade other women to identify with her.

Jan Williams, who works at Glide Memorial Church with her husband, the Reverend Cecil Williams, does not believe a political analysis is germane. She noticed well before Feinstein decided to run for governor that she was beginning to form trusting relations with women and gradually enlarging her circle of intimates and advisers to include them. After Feinstein "broke silence" about her mother's illness and abusiveness, Jan, who is Japanese American and was also abused as a child, began to recognize at once Feinstein's pain and her compassion for others who have been oppressed.

Vicky Rideout, who joined Feinstein after serving as deputy campaign manager for her primary opponent, John Van de Kamp, was surprised at how quickly she developed a close relationship with her new boss. "It's different working for a woman," Rideout discovered. A domestic policy adviser for Michael Dukakis, she had traveled with him for two years, compared to the four months she spent with Feinstein, but "it was literally years before we felt close."

Feinstein, however, had quickly begun to reach out and gone "out of her way to say nice things. She's given me a couple of books, and we talk a lot about books we're reading and about relationships. She's talked about her different marriages. She's a nice person! She'll call up and say, 'You know what's really great about you?' Some of the men I've worked with didn't even say the two words 'Thank you!'—even if you'd busted your butt for them."

Although both men and women close to Feinstein speak of her complexity, reporter Susan Yoachum, who has covered her for twelve years, adds that she is "very human. She'll call you up and say, 'Hi, this is Dianne,' and then complain hotly about something you've just written. She's also capable of laughing within the same conversation. It's not all business with her."

With a survivor's gut instinct that she can handle anything, Feinstein leaps repeatedly into situations others think her ill-suited and ill-prepared to handle. And then she puts herself through the grueling process of clearing the hurdles.

As Sragow says, "The advantage of doing it the way she does it is that when she gets it, she's lived it, and she can relate it then to the voters." Susan Yoachum agrees: "She doesn't have ideology: what she has is her own personal experience." When Feinstein *doesn't* get it, or her personal experience is insufficient for the challenge she faces, she is hard on herself and other people.

Feinstein's equivalent of Ann Richards' confrontation with her alcoholic demons is the series of calamities she has survived, which have made her deeply fatalistic. Yoachum discovered that she would talk "very matter-of-factly about death" and saw that such a woman "can also have burning ambition to reach great heights."

Although Feinstein lacks Richards' long identification with the women's movement and a network of women who have worked with her over the course of decades, many women nevertheless identified with her: they found her strength through all manner of disasters— insanity, murder, death, divorce, defeat—a powerful testament to female fortitude. In lieu of psychotherapy or a twelve-step program like the one that brings Richards serenity and gives her a means of coping under stress, Feinstein is of "the school that toughs it out."

The slogan "tough but caring" that Dianne Feinstein coined for the 1990 election catches the bipolar ideal she envisaged from the outset of her political career. She came of age in San Francisco's elegant Presidio Terrace, the eldest child of a Jewish doctor and professor and a mother whose roots were in the Russian Orthodox church. If she grew up balancing her father's politics on one hand and her uncle's on the other, she did the same with the profoundly different religious and cultural traditions of her parents.

She went to Jewish religious school to please her father but at her mother's insistence became the first Jew to attend the exclusive Convent of the Sacred Heart. And there she made a friend who turned out to have a powerful father. Attorney General Edmund G. ("Pat") Brown met Dianne Goldman when she came home from time to time with his daughter, and she made a lasting impression.

Her interest in politics revealed itself by way of an A+ in American political thought at Stanford University, while a D in genetics undermined her father's hope that she would be a doctor. Her appetite for politics surfaced as early as 1954, during her junior year, when she took a poll to find out whether a woman who ran for student government office would find any support. To her chagrin, though probably not to her surprise, she discovered that students would prefer an orangutan, a giraffe, or a donkey.

Deciding that she had a chance if she ran for vice-president, she began the requisite speaking tour of campus lodgings, and at the Delta Kappa Epsilon fraternity house she got her first political come-uppance: a man lobbed a spoonful of mashed potatoes from the back of the dining hall and hit her smack in the face. Then the brothers carried her off to the shower. (Many years later, when one of them apologized, Feinstein stared him down.) She was elected.

The year after she graduated from Stanford, Feinstein sidestepped the Hadassah, B'nai Brith Women, and the Ladies' Altar Guild world of private good works in which women of her class typically answered their need to be socially useful. On a public policy–oriented Coro fellowship, she did a study of the criminal justice system, and as an intern in the state Industrial Welfare Commission, a daughter of privilege came up hard against the world of crime and social dysfunction. It was also there that she met Jack Berman, a prosecutor eleven years her senior with whom she eloped. The marriage, however, was doomed, if for no other reason than that she did not believe he took her seriously as a professional woman.

In 1960, fate in the guise of Governor Pat Brown intervened to keep her professionally engaged with the world of the outcast. After being elected governor of California, Brown had occasion to recall the sharp and appealing Dianne Goldman. At a meeting of the Women's Board of Prisons and Paroles, he was chagrined to find the directors "awfully tough and mean to the women prisoners," the length of whose terms they had the power to fix. He decided to appoint some younger women who "might be more charitable." As Brown remembers it, he sought Goldman out: "I don't think she knew anything much about it, or was especially interested in it before I appointed her." She spent the next five years in California prisons listening to one wrenching tale after another and deciding who would stay and who would go.

In 1962, she met and married Bertram Feinstein, a top neuro-surgeon nineteen years her senior, and the saga of Dianne Feinstein began—the saga of a woman who grew to power in the raucous, multi-ethnic Democratic party by virtue of guts, brass, resilience, charm, brains, and fanatic attention to detail.

As Harrison Hickman would put it, Feinstein has always run against type. From the time she started in politics, she caught people's attention by being fresh and open. But she was also shrewd. Refusing to rely simply on making a good impression when she ran for su-pervisor in 1969, she was the first San Francisco politician to use television for campaigning. A judge as unsentimental as Assembly-man Willie Brown spotted a comer: "She was bright and attractive, with a naïveté that made her very appealing to voters."

The Board of Supervisors had begun to dabble in "things beyond debris collecting and streetlights and dog dues," Brown remembers, and he had decided that "they could not remain uninfluenced by the real political process." Although Feinstein seemed more conservative than moderate, he supported her because he found her "responsive to the kinds of issues, advocacy, and people I wanted to see in gov-ernment." The only elected official who *did* support her, Brown decided that since she was "on base" on child care centers, as well as fair breaks at jobs and business opportunities, he could leave "the tree-huggers to take care of the other stuff."

The naïveté that beguiled Brown may have been more apparent than real, but there is no doubt that it obscured a very strong will that would lead to more than one battle royal between them. Willie Brown would become a power center in California Democratic pol-itics, and his support in Feinstein's first run for supervisor marked the beginning of a fateful political alliance. Without it, she would have been far less effective and may even have failed in her San Francisco races—especially in 1979, when he brought key political operatives into her campaign for mayor and got hundreds of vol-unteers out working the streets for her. With his help, especially in her 1990 race for governor, she became vulnerable not only to the rising sentiment against incumbency but to the burgeoning distrust of one man: the brilliant, caustic, high-living black Speaker of the assembly.

But that was later. In 1969, Dianne Feinstein was learning how to woo an audience as diverse as any in the United States of America, although at first she did not even know how to work a room polit-ically; as one of her early advisers put it, she would sit down and plunge deep into conversation. Still, she proved teachable. Michael Schneider of the electrical workers' union remembers "her energy and vitality" as she made her way around the Jewish community and through the black precincts. Mattie Jackson, a black woman who became a vice-president of the International Ladies' Garment Work-ers Union, gave one of the first Feinstein coffee parties and "fell in love with her." Elected with more votes than any other candidate, Feinstein automatically became president of the board.

The Reverend Cecil Williams, who would become a kind of father confessor, tells about the first time he heard her voice. It was during the traumatic months after Patty Hearst was kidnapped and the Symbionese Liberation Army was terrorizing California when Feinstein called to ask, "What can I do to help?" A black man who ministers to the poor and the outcast is likely to think such a call under the circumstances misguided, and he admits that Feinstein in days gone by has been "an uptight Jewish lady." He is not a man to reject others out of hand, however, and he would discover that she had the capacity to ask for help herself.

Williams made his reputation in the 1960s by taking a staid Methodist church and turning it into a community haven where the walls metaphorically came tumbling down and all were welcome. Though others have abandoned their 1960s enthusiasms, his have held—more complex, perhaps, but no less compelling.

Glide Memorial Church sits across the street from the San Francisco Hilton, no more than two blocks from some of the fanciest stores downtown but on the border, nevertheless, of the Tenderloin district, where transvestites and prostitutes solicit at half past eight on Sunday morning. In preparation for the nine o'clock service, people wander in and out of the second-floor sanctuary: a woman with a Santa Claus belly and a tattered Mexican multicolored blouse, whose purposes remain obscure; a guy in a black leather jacket, whose straight, combed-back, oily hair makes him look like the standard rock groupie and who seems to be adjusting the microphones. Two men sit in the pews discussing Scripture.

At ten minutes to nine, and with no special ado, four men at the back of the stage start playing jazz: two on electric guitar, one on a shiny, white set of drums, another at an electronic keyboard. A big screen above the stage comes suddenly alive with flashing pictures of Glide Church, and the choir begins to file in, clapping. They're in long skirts, short skirts, pants, T-shirts, spiked heels, sneakers, tuxedo jackets. One woman seems to be wearing a pink and purple fluorescent pajama set. Some are humdrum. Others are outrageous.

By the time they've arranged themselves on a three-step riser, they add up to a score, though for the next half hour stragglers keep joining. They number seven white and five black women, one male dwarf, two ordinary white men, and a fluctuating number of black men. Several look as though they could go either way—black or white, male or female. The choir director is a black woman with a grizzled Afro who wears a black pants suit, a woman whose commanding purpose binds so disparate a group together. They're singing "Lord, Help us to stop running."

Williams' dramatically beautiful Asian wife whips on and off the stage, whispering instructions here, adjusting something there, a great pair of legs shown off by a skirt that ends several inches above her knees. She is wearing a black matador's hat, large dangling silver earrings, and a tight black suit jacket with large silver buttons all down the front and up the sleeves. Cecil Williams' church does not repress eros.

By the time Williams walks up to the stage, a motley audience is in place, a guy in shades standing to one side who looks like a leftover Black Panther and tourists from abroad who must have gotten the word in Leipzig and Cannes that on Sunday morning this was by far the best show in town. Williams is wearing dark gray trousers and a full-sleeved white shirt with a prayer shawl draped around his neck emblazoned with the word AFRICA and colorful symbols. He has a *caffe latte* tone, a high-domed forehead, a gray-flecked Afro, and a beard trimmed close. He wears horn-rimmed glasses and an expression that insists on being called benign, however corny the phrase.

Loping up and down the stairs and across the stage, he holds the microphone with one hand and gestures with the other, calling "Say Yes to your life. . . . Been sayin' No too long!" When he faces the congregation and raises both arms, almost singing "Embrace your neighbors," people turn to lean over the pews, hugging each other and grinning—the human community, of a Sunday midmorning, having a wonderful time.

On the big screen a picture will flash for a few seconds and then change: first, a man holding a big "Free South Africa" sign; next, the words "Come for Recovery"; then a series of demonstrations, people holding hands, men and women dancing, shouting, throwing up their arms. A black man with mournful eyes and a chartreuse shirt emerges from the choir to sing a solo, and people rise up here and there in the pews, clapping in rhythm, gyrating, some of them as though they were on a dance floor.

It is National Children's Day, and a handful of the youngest in the congregation come to the front and tell what they want to be when they grow up. One tiny little girl says "doctor"; a boy who may grow tall says "basketball star"; another almost whispers, "I want to be a helper in this church"; the last rings out: "I want to grow up in a clean, drug-free world" and brings down the house.

When it comes time for Williams' sermon, he looks briefly at some notes on a yellow pad and then starts talking in tones far more conversational than those ringing rhetorical phrases for which black ministers are famous. Although he refers to Christ and the lawyers ("They really did not want him to be a healer . . . to be righteous and just"), anyone, it is clear—Christian, pagan, Jew—could listen without offense to his or her particular creed or absence thereof and come away refreshed. Everyone calls him Cecil, and he is said to make you feel good all day. A man whose twenty-six-year ministry has been spent with people as beaten down as they come, he nevertheless projects sanity and calm.

He speaks about masks—the kinds people put on to keep from knowing each other and from taking the risks of intimacy. The church, he says, promotes pseudo-relationships: we are heavenly addicted, which means, to Cecil Williams' mind, that we neglect what we can do on earth for those with whom we share it. ("What you gonna do up there if all that's true, and I don't know that it is? You been restin' down here. You gonna go up there lookin' for peace? Oh Lawd!") A clanging siren through the open back door makes him pause for a few moments, and when it has passed, he says, "They probably called the fire department and told 'em: at 9:55 A.M., go by Cecil's church 'cause he's gonna be sayin' something."

He is confessional: "I'm baring my soul now. I'm noticing me." Standing at the end of one pew, he points: "That man—he said: 'Cecil, you gotta take care of yourself, you gotta understand that you can't do everything.' " He is speaking not about ego but about admitting one's own frailty and need.

When he has finished, the screen comes alive again with lines varying the old traditional hymn and everybody sings: "We shall free the lonely ones, Hallelujah! We shall free the lonely ones, Hallelujah!" And then "lonely" becomes "phony," becomes "uptight," and so on. A dimpled white man in his forties gives the response, telling the congregation he drives an hour and a half each way every Sunday from Santa Cruz because Glide Church helps him take off the mask he has worn all his life, the mask he wears as a lawyer, so he can feel the human being inside.

To leave the sanctuary, one must first hug Cecil Williams. A man who looks not unlike Bishop Desmond Tutu, whose ebullience he shares, he stands at the foot of the stairs as the congregation descends. "Good morning, Sister!" He pats everyone on the back. The traditional blessing has been irrevocably changed, but the spirit lives.

Cecil Williams has taken Dianne Feinstein to his heart, and she has taken him to hers. The latter fact is the more remarkable. Her openness to such a man and her trust in his judgment belie her image as an ice queen.

Once, after a black official's funeral, Feinstein beckoned Williams over to her car and asked insistently, "How do you ministers speak so extemporaneously? How do you create that cadence, that rhythm?" Williams answered, "You gotta feel it, you gotta experience it, you gotta believe in yourself!" When she said, "I want you to help me," he did.

Since such lessons are a lifetime in the learning, this is one she has mastered imperfectly, but if candor hurts her, she nevertheless asks for it. When Williams and his wife, Jan, read the speech she intended to give at the Democratic convention in 1984, for instance, they decided "it was awful," volunteered to write something, and after three days, "that speech was hot."

Now, when Feinstein is on, she can speak so engagingly that Willie Brown calls her "Ronald Reagan without the bullshit, the Chamber of Commerce jokes, or the props." When she is not, she is wooden and boring; according to *The Economist*, a lunchtime speech on the California economy to a roomful of Los Angeles executives put some to sleep.

By all accounts, Feinstein hangs in there. "No matter what Dianne goes through," Williams says, "she tends to come out stronger. When she gets angry, she can be at her best. When you push her against the wall, she's really terrific!"

Others have been less patient with Feinstein's political evolution. When she used her office as supervisor to go after San Francisco's girlie shows and porno palaces, for instance, she got into pitched battles with civil libertarians who accused her of trying to censor what consenting adults could see and do. As Willie Brown puts it, "She had serious problems with nudity, with encounter studios, with people watching dirty movies," and a good many thought she should keep those problems to herself.

In 1977, the writer Herbert Gold published a novel called *Waiting for Cordelia* that carried on the civil liberties war in a form to which Feinstein was unaccustomed. Widely thought to satirize Feinstein, Gold's book featured a character named Marietta Kirwin, a San Francisco supervisor who aspires to be elected the city's first woman mayor by running against sin. Sin, as Marietta defines it, is embodied in the person of one Cordelia, a high-spirited hooker who aims to create a union of whores.

The author's sympathies are entirely with the madam. He writes that Marietta's image includes "a touch of the old-fashioned Puritan values, plus care for the ethnics, the downtrodden, the plain economical," and what he most laments is that she really means it: "As I recalled that pinched, pretty, tea-party face, I was sure she had another powerful emotional weapon in her anti-prostitution campaign: sincerity."

At once smart and articulate, Marietta is also grim with sexual frustration: "She was clenched and clotted with desire. She was dangerous." She can talk of herself in the third person, as though she were an institution—"Marietta too has a dream!"—and she is stubborn: "I am very determined. . . . I am thinking of what will help this community. And with the cooperation of your good will and that of others, I will—impose is not my style—I will make my dream real." Officious, humorless, and self-deluded, she works at cross-purposes with the life force.

Years later, an arts council Feinstein had appointed gave Gold an award which she had to present, and many people, including the author, wondered how she would react. To his delight, she began by saying, "Herb and I have had our differences." The audience laughed, and Gold remembers appreciatively, "She was wonderful!"

In 1978, when Feinstein became mayor of San Francisco after George Moscone's murder, she took over a city notoriously difficult to run because its divergent constituency groups were for the most part well organized and articulate. Downtown developers were pitted against neighborhood groups that wanted the city's charm preserved exactly as they had found it. Newly arrived ethnic minorities were ranged against those who were better established. Gays and straights often had prickly relations. Law-and-order forces clashed with civil libertarians, who sided with what remained of the counterculture that had found San Francisco a haven in the 1960s.

Feinstein had no intention of being the laid-back mayor her predecessor had been. She instituted a new dress code at City Hall forbidding anyone to come to work in jeans and sandals. And she knew whom she wanted to hire. The Commission on Aging, for instance, had had eleven directors in eight years, and Feinstein was determined to close the revolving door. Joyce Ream, whom she had known through the Coro Foundation, applied for the job, but the list of finalists the three members of the commission handed Feinstein did not include Ream, who did not have a Ph.D. in gerontology. Ream *did* know San Francisco, however, and had experience with nonprofit organizations. Feinstein asked the three commission members to resign and appointed three others, making her own preference clear. Ream was then appointed unanimously and has served in that position ever since.

Most problems were not solved so easily, and if many of Feinstein's friends and supporters have been with her from the beginning, so have many of her enemies. As Ream puts it, "There are all sorts of ways you can cut this city, and each one has the potential for a different dispute." To a degree that may have been impolitic, Feinstein leaped into the middle of many a crisis, always trying to discover what she needed to do to get the discussions going. "She insisted," says Ream, "that they mediate! mediate! mediate!"

San Franciscoans tell many a tale of Feinstein as a "hands-on mayor," and she is almost ritually criticized for her obsession with detail. The fifty-eight department heads who took part in what reporter Susan Yoachum would call her "infamous" Monday morning staff meetings joked that they had to check the newspaper headlines and Herb Caen's column, and if they were mentioned in neither, they were reasonably safe. But they were in trouble if they missed something that had happened on their watch and in their department because the mayor would have been up since 6 A.M. gathering information and would be sitting there with a checklist.

"She was so entranced with her job," Ream says, "with every detail of it, that it transcended the idea of work. She'd come in with her eyes sparkling." Accounts of her style are unanimous on two points: one, that if she was angry, she let people know it; two, that her need for control was unremitting. They disagree, however, on the tone. Ream felt that it was all done in good spirits and that Feinstein did not bully. Others have called her imperious, hectoring, and even abusive, claiming that she would dress down a hapless victim in front of others and would neither apologize nor admit it if she proved to be mistaken. She continually intruded on staff members' private time, calling them as early as dawn and as late as midnight and prompting one to say, "I'm not sure she ever fully comprehended that we were working because we had to make a living." When she described merit pay as "extra pay for extra work," Yoachum commented, "Most nonsalaried people call that overtime."

As early as 1980, the *San Francisco Examiner* wrote that when Feinstein felt overwhelmed by competing demands, she snapped at her staff and created an atmosphere of such anxiety that the tension could last for a couple of hours or stretch out to a couple of days. "I am a perfectionist," she admitted to the reporter, "and I drive myself hard and the people around me hard, and if it's a problem for anybody, they're welcome to resign." She had resolved to be "an ulcer-giver, not an ulcer-taker," and she counted on getting irritated now and again to spark a top-notch performance from her staff. "I want to be a good mayor," she said, "and there's only one way to do it: that's to keep things in control, under control, the constant daily dripping away at the stone." Yoachum would subsequently call her performance as mayor "a solo dance."

When confronted with her reputation as an autocrat, Feinstein has insisted that she surrounds herself with strong people, encourages discussion and even dispute, and then expects her appointees to carry out her decisions. But several people who have worked for her over the years have admitted that there was a solidarity among members of her staff because, as one put it, "we felt in our midst a person who might explode at any minute, and might be unfair, so we supported one another." They stayed because they believed she was a well-meaning person trying incredibly hard, because they were drawn by her charisma, and because they needed the job.

As mayor, Feinstein had a far better opportunity than she had had as president of the Board of Supervisors to live out her fascination with crime. If her anti-vice campaign stirred up the liberals, so did the fact that as mayor, she kept a police and fire scanner in her car, and as Susan Yoachum put it, "four alarms or above, and she's out there!" Willie Brown called her positions on crime not only "bizarre" but "a little crazy."

Rotea Gilford, the executive director of Moscone's criminal justice council, had met Feinstein in the mid-1950s. Gilford is black, and he remembers that during that time people of all races got together more easily than they do today in San Francisco to discuss politics and civil rights. He canvassed the neighborhoods for Feinstein in her first race for supervisor, and she in turn worked closely with him when he was a homicide investigator in the police department, notably on a case that involved tracking a white man suspected of killing twenty-three young black girls. When she took over as mayor, she reappointed Gilford to the position and then elevated it to the status of deputy mayor.

She put 350 more police on the streets, supported strict controls on handguns, and presented an exhaustively researched package on crime to the state legislature in Sacramento. Her Monday morning staff meetings invariably began with the police chief comparing the crime statistics with those of the same period the year before, and if they were up, she agonized over them. Once when she ran into the chief on the street, she said: "I've been hearing too many 211's [robberies] recently. What can we do?" He responded in exasperation, "Turn off your radio!"

He was only miffed by Feinstein. A group called the White Panthers was furious, ostensibly over her support for gun control, and in 1983, they began campaigning for a recall election. According to

Gilford, when Feinstein got word that enough signatures had been gathered to force the recall, she fell into his arms in tears. "She felt really betrayed," he remembered, "and she took it personally. She said, 'If I had done something dishonest, if I were guilty of malfeasance, I could understand it.' "

Willie Brown pitched in again to help her. She hired Clinton Reilly, a local campaign consultant. And intimates noticed that she had never campaigned better. "She internalized the challenge," Joyce Ream recalled. "She'd say, 'This is why I should be mayor!' " Like Cecil Williams, Ream saw that Feinstein was terrific "when her back is against the wall." She won with over 80 percent of the vote.

During her tenure as mayor, Feinstein was so obsessed with her city's functioning that *Los Angeles Times* columnist Bill Boyarsky observed dismissively that she found issues of sewage disposal and traffic lights not only necessary but interesting. (He said the same of her opponent, Pete Wilson.) She improved garbage pickup and public transportation, as well as authorizing a substantial increase in the city's housing stock.

Other aspects of her administration were far more controversial. In the early days, she replaced two men on the planning commission who were critical of high-rise development and, in the course of eight years, presided over the addition of almost 30 million square feet of new commercial office space—more than half again as much as existed before she became mayor. At the same time, she forced development onto the other side of Market Street, away from Union Square, and preserved a record number of historic city buildings.

By 1980, in the face of the gay community's outrage, she had fired her director of health, who favored less extreme measures, and closed down the gay bathhouses as menaces. In 1982, when she vetoed domestic partners' legislation, the gays were outraged again. And when she subsequently vetoed comparable worth, an attempt to raise women's wages to the level that men got in jobs of comparable value, she put herself at odds with women and some parts of labor.*

*Although in the 1970s, San Jose and other cities in the surrounding area had worked out comparable worth arrangements, Feinstein objected to the expense. As Joyce Ream explained, she had to decide when and in what order to take on various additional drains on the city treasury: "She prided herself on being a responsible manager, so she was careful not to overextend herself in terms of available resources." At the same time, the San Francisco

In none of this was Feinstein seriously accused of prejudice against homosexuals. Quite the contrary: in 1969, according to consultant Pacy Markman, she introduced the first legislation in America that prohibited discrimination against gays. In fact, a favorite quip around town was that Feinstein didn't care whom you went to bed with, so long as you were in bed by eleven. Gay friends celebrated their weddings in her garden, to the consternation of Southern Democrats, who told presidential nominee Walter Mondale in 1984 that they could *never* explain that to their constituents. When homelessness burgeoned and the AIDS epidemic swept through San Francisco, Feinstein raised taxes to get the necessary money, and, insisting that city government *had* to respond to human need, she created the political resolve within the city to fight them.

Mark Stein, a reporter in the San Francisco bureau of the *Los Angeles Times*, believes that people have refused to give Feinstein the credit she deserves as mayor: "She can be compassionate and at the same time keep an eye on the bottom line. . . . She somehow rescued her city at the time Prop 13 [restricting government's ability to tax] passed—a city that's also a county—[and so she had to] provide all these services while the money was being sucked dry. At the same time, she was able to keep the loyalty of a man [the Reverend Cecil Williams] who ministers primarily to the poor. It would have been real easy for her to say, 'Hey, the money's not there any more; the poor are on their own.' But she didn't do that."

In the face of the most difficult, even deadly, problems, Dianne Feinstein gloried in the job. Baseball players say that anybody who is going to be a star wants every ball to come flying his way. When Feinstein was playing first, she *never* wanted the ball to go to the shortstop, and when she was at bat, she did *not* want the pitcher throwing balls. She had an appetite for politics so voracious that when her second term as mayor ended in 1988, she wanted more.

Much more!

---

civil service was so archaic that employees were suspected of using quill pens, and it was arguably too inept to negotiate the complexities of comparable worth: its recent court-forced absorption of four thousand employees, a sizable number of whom had been working for the city as "temporaries" since World War II, seemed to have exhausted its capacities.

CHAPTER 10

> *Which is worse—ignorance or apathy?*
> —Man on a Barstool
>
> *I don't know, and I don't care!*
> —Bartender
>
> (quoted by columnist Herb Fredman)

Dianne Feinstein would win the Democratic nomination for governor of California because she was a woman with a rich husband and because the television camera loved her. True, she was a viable candidate because she was smart, hard-driving, ambitious, and compassionate. But as a bright red splash against a background of battleship gray, she appealed to voters in a state in which political power has become balkanized.

The challenge Feinstein confronted fueled the widely held suspicion that women get their chance at office only after men have mucked up politics so badly it is hardly worth trying and may indeed be impossible. By 1990, the great golden promise of California had begun to dull, and voters who bothered to pay attention were both confused and angry. (The majority had given up on the political process altogether.)

The cry that had emboldened adventurers for over a century—"Go West, young man!"—had brought more people to California in the 1980s than at any time in its history, but nobody knew quite what to do with them, or more precisely, how to pay for them. The infrastructures of the state were falling apart, and the mechanisms that people had used to address and solve their collective problems had broken down. The erosion of political order, ironically, gave Feinstein a chance to win high office that she exploited with a stalwart competitor's glee.

In his Pulitzer Prize–winning book *The Making of the President:*

1960, Theodore White described the Texas political culture as among "the most squalid, corrupt and despicable" in the United States, while he ranked California with "those American states whose politics are probably the most decent and worthy of respect." Robert Caro's biography of Lyndon Johnson helped the nation understand why White used terms so harsh to describe Texas politics, and the 1990 gubernatorial election demonstrated that nothing much had changed.

Things *had* changed in California, however, though the rate of decay had been slow: at the end of the 1960s, the National Council on State Legislatures had called California's by far the best in the country. But by 1990, when it had an economy that ranked sixth in the world and almost 13 million more people than the next most populous state, few were bragging that it deserved to rank with Wisconsin and Minnesota as a "good government" state. Still, if Dianne Feinstein was game to take on a challenge as daunting as Hercules' twelve labors, California's demographics and political history showed that she had a chance to be elected governor, even if the odds were against her.

She had a chance in part because she was not a mainstream Democrat, and in top-of-the-ticket races, California has been essentially a Republican state. Since 1948, it has voted only once for the winning Democratic presidential candidate, and that was for Lyndon Johnson in his 1964 landslide. It has elected only three Democratic governors in the twentieth century—two of them Edmund G. Browns—while the third, Culbert L. Olson (1939–43), left so little impression that Pat Brown, when queried, could not remember his name.

In the July–August 1990 issue of the influential *American Enterprise* magazine, demographers William Schneider and Patrick Reddy suggested that the Democrats' chances might have improved marginally by contrasting northern and southern California—comparing the politics of Marin County, across the bay from San Francisco, with Orange County, just south of Los Angeles. Both are essentially white, suburban, upper-middle-class counties, and in the 1950s, both voted roughly two-to-one Republican. But during the 1960s, the former supported Democratic liberals Eugene McCarthy and George McGovern, while the latter became the breeding ground

for the New Right of Barry Goldwater and Ronald Reagan. As a
bastion of cultural liberalism, the Bay Area voted about 20 percent
more Democratic than southern California.

As *Los Angeles Times* columnist Bill Boyarsky pointed out, however, the major growth in California has been in the suburbs and, as
in Texas, suburban voters tend to vote Republican. Even in northern
California, the movement of population has been out from the cities
into the valleys. Oakland, for instance, is predominantly black and
securely Democratic, but the area over the hills to the east and up
to Sacramento is essentially Republican, and so is the area south to
San Jose. The San Joaquin Valley has been filling with Republicans—"working people who can't afford the homes in the East Bay
any more . . . [and] leave to get away from blacks or Mexican-
Americans." In a gubernatorial election, then, even San Francisco is
ringed with votes for Republicans—many of them angry.

Los Angeles, which has a slightly larger percentage of the total
California vote than the Bay Area, is the second most Democratic
area of the state, although its share of the southern California vote
has diminished because the suburbs around it have grown so spec-
tacularly. In fact, the five counties of southern California have not
only grown more Republican but have become as conservative as
Arizona.*

Since roughly two-thirds of the 1990 vote would come from the
southern part of the state, Feinstein took an apartment in Los Angeles
in the fall of 1989 to begin building her support there. She had to
counter a powerful disadvantage: as Schneider and Reddy put it,
"For the past thirty years, southern California has been a burial
ground for Democrats." In statewide elections during the 1980s, it
had given Republicans close to a half-million-vote lead that overwhelmed the Democratic advantage elsewhere.

But the key word for California politics was *volatile*. Its phenomenal growth meant that even Republicans, though dominant historically, could take nothing for granted. Over the course of the 1980s,
more than 1,500 people a day moved to California. That adds up to

*In nonpresidential elections during the 1980s, the Bay Area had 25 percent of the total
vote; Los Angeles County had 28 percent; southern California, 26 percent; and rural California,
21 percent. The last category includes the agricultural valley, the desert, the mountains, the
coast, and cities like Bakersfield and Sacramento.

almost 550,000 people every year, or enough citizens to fill a city approaching the size of San Francisco. Since the 1980 census, in other words, the state had added the equivalent of ten new cities.

One-third of these new Californians had moved south and west from other states; two-thirds were Asians and Hispanics. Many in the former category were likely to be individualists who came in part because they wanted government off their backs. As San Diego columnist Herb Fredman put it, "People who leave their families and friends are much more risk-taking and perhaps more selfish. And maybe they resent government interference more than others." Many in the latter category were wretchedly poor, arrived with a tenuous grasp of English or none at all, and came from countries with terrorist regimes opposed to democratic participation. Immigrants tended to be young, and although the state would soon be majority minority, its voting population was 80 percent Anglo.

In shorthand, this meant that the two-thirds of the new Californians unlikely to vote would probably add to the state's burdens, while the remaining one-third would insist that it was not their responsibility to help shoulder those burdens.

Costs were skyrocketing, and it was unclear who would pay them. The enormous growth had fattened developers, who paid some tax money for city roads, schools, libraries, and fire stations but virtually nothing for the regional infrastructure: the freeway system, the sewer systems, water, and bridges. Longtime city dwellers were incensed that they might have to foot the newcomers' bills. And since Proposition 13 required a two-thirds vote to approve bond issues, most failed and nobody paid for anything. Little new infrastructure got built and nothing got done.

Meanwhile, those who taught the young faced linguistic challenges unparalleled in world history. Fresno, for instance, had the greatest concentration of Hmong outside Vietnam, and at least 117 languages and dialects were spoken by children in the public schools.

Drug-inspired gang warfare among teenagers terrorized Los Angeles, and California had become the amphetamine-producing capital of the world. Even proper, conservative San Diego had become a center of the drug trade, with marijuana plantations back in the hills and criminals with a 95 percent user rate—as high as in New York City or Washington, D.C. According to Fredman: "In southeast San

Diego, there are drug dealers on every corner. Little ten-year-old kids are used as runners. They get $100 a week. The drug dealers themselves are making between $20,000 and $40,000 a year, and when they get arrested, they don't get thrown in jail because there aren't enough jails to hold them." The criminal justice system, he said glumly, had become an oxymoron.

Once a leader in children's issues, by 1990 California had the highest teen pregnancy rate, the highest rate of juveniles in protective custody, and the second worst classroom overcrowding in the nation. Close to one-third of its students dropped out or did not finish high school on schedule, and one-fifth of its children were growing up in poverty. More than half were not fully immunized against disease, and half the meager child support payments that the courts had ordered were going unpaid.

The story gets even worse. Through a convergence of trends no one had anticipated, political power had become balkanized, and the operative term to describe the consequence was "gridlock." The common word is "stuck." Cars were stuck on freeways; bills were stuck in committees; legislators were stuck in office.

A woman with an appetite for governing—for making things work and watching people strive—saw, for all practical purposes, a vast field with no horizon. And nobody could say No to her running for governor. The breakdown of political order meant, among other things, that there was no recognized succession of political power and authority and therefore no one who could give or withhold permission when Dianne Feinstein began thinking about running for governor. But if nobody was in a position to hinder, no one was sure to help either.

Compared to Ann Richards, for instance, Feinstein was essentially a political loner, and the contrast between the two women helps focus the picture. After Lloyd Bentsen defeated liberal folk hero Ralph Yarborough in 1970 for the United States Senate, Richards adjusted her loyalties and spent two decades as a Bentsen partisan. When the other women Walter Mondale summoned to advise him on his vice-presidential choice in 1984 pushed him to select a woman, Richards argued that he should put Bentsen on the ticket. So closely had she worked with Lieutenant Governor Bill Hobby that both described their friendship as special. If former San Antonio Mayor Henry Cisneros had decided to run for governor in 1990, she might well have stepped aside. Richards checked with these crucial people before she ran for governor—she *had* to check—and then, when she was running, they were *there* for her.

But if Ann Richards was a team player in Texas, California did not even have a team. And since Feinstein was not an obvious choice for governor, she would have to make a virtue of necessity by running openly as an outsider.

Though she had been considered for the Democratic vice-presidential nomination, she had held no position higher than mayor of a medium-sized city, and City Hall does not ordinarily have the power necessary to catapult someone to the highest office in the state. She had no ties other than to the Democratic party that would provide a statewide political infrastructure. She was not a labor Democrat, nor a club Democrat, nor an ethnic Democrat—and she had never been involved in the California women's movement.

But television had changed American politics forever—especially in California, which might as well have invented media—and Dianne Feinstein was a candidate who showed to advantage on television. The state had long since taught the rest of the country to expect unusual things: since the early 1960s, California had dumbfounded observers by electing a tap dancer and a sleepy linguist to the United States Senate and giving an affable if mediocre actor a platform from which to rise to the presidency. In so mercurial an atmosphere, a woman governor whose only apprenticeship had been as mayor would not seem wholly out of line.

Nor would anything in California's political party structure work against Feinstein. Since parties are relatively weak there, the Democratic party is not a principal vehicle for setting the policy agenda, for fund-raising, for recruiting new and promising candidates, or for appealing to new voters.

In 1990, there *was* no Democratic center of power in the singular. It resided in centers, which is to say, Willie Brown, the Speaker of the assembly, was a power. David Roberti, the president of the senate, was a power. Before the savings and loan scandal and his precarious health forced him to announce his impending retirement, United States Senator Alan Cranston was a power. Sometimes these men worked in concert and sometimes they did not. And in addition to these major officeholders, the men who ran the professional campaign organizations—who had voter lists and the communications technology to mount big-time campaigns—were described as running machines in the old-fashioned sense, the Berman/Waxman/d'Agostino machine being only the most familiar. These men were the power brokers—in short, the barons in a state without a king.

Los Angeles City Councilman Michael Woo saw the legislative barons as the only force that kept the California governing process from flying into space: "The political parties are weaker here than in most parts of the country, so just about the only hope for effective action comes from the Speaker of the assembly or the president of the senate cracking the whip and getting his members to line up." As a city councilman operating in a political environment without strong party leadership, Woo enjoyed his autonomy but knew that the people of Los Angeles suffered from the city council's tendency toward anarchy—"its inability to hold itself together and to bite the bullet, to make tough decisions."

Woo saw, furthermore, that this same centrifugal characteristic had a marked effect on statewide politics: "In the absence of strong organization, we end up going through these quadrennial cults of personality. Each candidate has to try to put it together for himself and herself."

In the absence of strong party leadership, even the Republicans indulged in quadrennial cults of personality. Two crucial names— Nixon and Reagan—told the same story in a slightly different key. Both had used the California Republican party as a base to capture as much power as a man ever gets in American politics, but they spoke such a different language politically that one might as well have come from Iceland and the other from Crete. One was a moderate who believed in an activist government. The other was a radical who believed in dismantling as much of it as he could. They were hardly products of the same political culture.

When she ran for governor, then, Dianne Feinstein would be engaging in what was essentially a popularity contest—a media-driven assault designed to convince voters that she was a more compelling personality than her opponent. Being a regal woman with a pretty face and a wardrobe full of bold-colored, exquisitely tailored clothes gave her an advantage a Medici might have envied.

Nor did Feinstein misread California history when she decided that 1990 could be a Democratic gubernatorial year. Until 1958, the Republicans had held the governorship almost without interruption, but since then it had alternated between the two parties in four eight-year cycles. Democrat Pat Brown (1959–67) had been a liberal who believed in an activist role for government. Republican Ronald Reagan (1967–75) had been a conservative who distrusted it. Democrat Jerry Brown (1975–83), known as Governor "Moonbeam" because he practiced what one writer called "experimental futurism" and gave new meaning to the term "unconventional," was liberal on social issues. But because of what his father dubbed his "economical" streak, he had allowed the problem created by escalating property tax rates to fester into a crisis that produced Proposition 13, limiting the amounts of money governments can raise. And perhaps in response to that taxpayer rebellion, Republican Governor George Deukmejian (1983–91) had been so intent on *not* raising taxes that he had expressed himself primarily through the veto. Clearly, if these almost dialectical cycles held, in 1990 Sacramento was waiting for an activist Democrat.

Paradoxically, the man largely responsible for balkanizing and polarizing California politics and thereby giving Dianne Feinstein a chance to be governor had disdained her politics. Feinstein was not Congressman Phillip Burton's kind of Democrat, and she lost so badly when she ran for mayor of San Francisco in the 1970s in part because she was running against the Burton machine.

Burton, whom Assembly Speaker Willie Brown calls "the Master," was obsessed with politics—not as an end in itself but as a tool for advancing a liberal policy agenda. He used redistricting to enhance the likelihood that people who cared about working people would dominate the legislature in Sacramento and the California delegation to the United States Congress. And it is an irony of almost tragic dimensions that because of what Burton did, politics in California has become so nearly about power itself.

By maneuvering the Republicans out of legislative seats they considered their due because of their percentage of the registered vote, Burton infuriated them into turning California politics into warring camps. Because he and his disciples had been brilliant and ruthless in redrawing district lines, the Democrats had dominated both houses of the legislature since 1970, even though Republicans polled as much as 49 percent of the total congressional vote in the last decade.

In 1980, for instance, the Democrats had held a one-seat margin in the United States House of Representatives. In 1982, after redistricting, the Democrats had gained an eleven-seat margin. What Burton did so distorted representative politics in California that Bill Boyarsky of the *Los Angeles Times* is convinced that "if it hadn't been for the Burton gerrymandering, we would have had a Republican legislature."

The gerrymanders had furthermore left legislative districts essentially noncompetitive. A Democratic district in California was *really* Democratic, and a Republican district was *really* Republican—and once somebody won a seat, he or she was likely to keep it. Legislators had no incentive to undertake voter-registration or Get-Out-the-Vote campaigns that would benefit Democratic candidates running statewide. Even minority officeholders had to worry that a wealth of newly registered voters might change the composition of their own electorate and make it easier for a challenger to take their seats.

During the 1980s, then, no more than a couple of legislative seats had fallen to the opposite side. And since primaries are dominated by activists who are more ideological than the party as a whole, each party was represented in the legislature by its more extreme members.

In 1978, the taxpayer rebellion that produced Proposition 13 had also brought in a group of very conservative Republicans known as the "cave men." They had arrived on what Jane Wellman, the chief staff person in the early 1980s on the Assembly Ways and Means Committee, called essentially a kamikaze mission to bring down the majority. Their nemesis in the legislature became a group of ultraliberals called the "grizzlies." And California politics had become more polarized and acrimonious.

The people in the middle who were less ideological had been left with the burden of reconciliation and compromise ordinarily at the heart of the legislative process. But since important legislation like the budget required a two-thirds vote, agreement had become exceedingly hard to reach. The minority had been able to block virtually anything, and stalemate had satisfied those Republicans who believed that government should stay out of people's affairs.

Because the advent of television politics had made the electoral process stunningly expensive, such new legislators as there were tended to come from the ranks of Sacramento staff who had mastered that process and cozied up to the power structure and the lobby, rather than community activists who were fighting for causes like the environment. The political game had become self-referential: electoral politics was now merely about electoral politics. Voters had grown disgusted with the typical California politician because they thought he or she was merely holding on to power—not to do anything with it but simply to have it.

The legislature had come to seem a battleground for special interests. The insurance industry and the trial lawyers, for instance, had used campaign contributions to influence legislators to fight each other to a standstill over bills regulating insurance coverage so that no such bills were likely to emerge in the foreseeable future.*

This unpleasant and unproductive situation, if it did little else, gave Dianne Feinstein the chance to go before the voters and insist that she was different: she represented change. If she knew very little about state government, she nevertheless was not tainted with Sacramento. She was *not* the typical California politician.

But Feinstein faced an even more complex situation because in response to what they saw as legislative gridlock, voters had turned to the initiative. Instituted in 1911 as a "good government" reform, the initiative process had been designed to get state politics out of the suffocating hands of the Southern Pacific Railroad, which had literally bought the legislature. The success of Proposition 13 in 1978 had emboldened those who despaired of getting anything they wanted or needed through the legislature, and since that time, more than half the propositions that had ever been put on the ballot had appeared.

---

*To imagine the legislature as simply a wasteland would be a mistake, however. California had already passed legislation that other states had not even considered. Its residents cannot own a semiautomatic weapon, for instance, nor can an employer force an employee to retire. People must use seat belts. The bills that established these rights and responsibilities were hard-fought, and they have contributed to decencies Californians take for granted.

If legislators did not establish policy, citizens would establish policy—
or so the theory went.

Like Phil Burton's gerrymanders, however, the initiative process
had unintended consequences: by 1990, the process had boomer-
anged and become a parody of its original populist intent. Special
interests had turned from buying individual legislators to paying for
initiative campaigns, and professional organizations specialized in
running them. Huge amounts of money were involved: in the fall of
1988, $129 million had been spent to pass or defeat the propositions,
while $40.2 million had gone into all the state legislative campaigns.

The initiatives in 1990 would affect Dianne Feinstein primarily
in three ways. The first was financial: both in the spring and fall
elections, they took substantial amounts of Democratic money that
might otherwise have gone to her campaign. The second was political
in the narrow sense: at least two of the twenty-eight initiatives on
the November ballot were so controversial they became dynamite
that Feinstein *had* to handle. The third was political in the broader
sense: so many and so complex were the propositions that the secretary of state mailed every registered voter two volumes that totaled
almost 230 pages to explain them. Collectively, they ran the risk of
turning people off the electoral process altogether. By September,
more than three-quarters of California's voters, according to an
LA Times poll, thought there were so many initiatives that were "so
involved" that the average voter couldn't make "an intelligent
choice."*

Nobody in California was more frustrated than Speaker Willie
Brown by the voters' resort to the initiative, which he saw, very
properly, as the repudiation of representative government. And nothing illustrated the absurdity of the initiative process better than the
"Save the mountain lion!" campaign on which Brown lavished his
ire. In June 1990, Californians had voted a $30 million annual ap-

*Peter Schrag, editorial page editor of the *Sacramento Bee*, wrote about the conflicts and
contradictions between and among the propositions: "Whichever of Propositions 134 (nickel-
a-drink) and 126 (the lesser alcohol tax) passes with more votes will cancel the other—unless
Proposition 136 (Gann) passes, no matter by how many votes, in which case, even if Proposition
134 gets more votes than Proposition 126, Proposition 126 will prevail." After eight paragraphs
like this one, Schrag ended by saying, "Got it?"

propriation for a wildlife habitat to preserve the mountain lion. "When you have all these homeless people," Brown fumed, "and all these problems involving drugs, a 50 percent dropout rate [in certain school districts] . . . legions of disheveled, mentally ill people clogging the doorways of our towns, looking like they're homeless." He threw up his hands: "Forget schools! There's not a sufficient amount of money even to house the people you've got in jails for breaking the law. And you're talking about dedicating, on a priority basis, $30 million to the mountain lion. Give me a break!"

But the citizens of California had passed the initiative, and now every year, when the legislature began to work on the budget, off the top would have to come $30 million. "You wouldn't get that through the legislature," Brown said emphatically. "There are maybe *two* mountain lion people in the whole place. Legislators wouldn't choose to spend $30 million on the mountain lion instead of spending it on the homeless or on child care." The whole process had grown unsafe and unstable, and now people as different as Brown and Coro director Martha Bredon automatically voted no on every proposition, while former Governor Pat Brown thought the process itself should be abolished.

One problem the initiatives posed for Feinstein centered in the fact that competing interest groups got enough signatures to put their own initiatives on the ballot, and if for no other reason than that her opponents made issues of one or more of them, she felt compelled to take positions that might win some voters but would just as surely alienate others. Each initiative was written primarily to satisfy one interest group: the balancing and reconciling functions basic to the legislative process had not been brought into play. In 1990, for instance, environmental groups were pushing Prop 128, or "Big Green," while the farmers supported Prop 135, or "Big Brown."

"There's no way representative government would go for either of those," Speaker Brown insisted. "You'd balance the equities in between. You'd ask, 'What do we need as a society to survive?' It's crazy to eliminate the ability to produce food to feed all these people. But it's equally crazy to poison the earth in the process. So you make an intelligent decision about how to produce the food you need to feed the folks, at the same time you restrict the resources and the uses of the system so that you don't do irreparable harm to the soil."

Two initiatives in particular presented Feinstein with an acutely difficult political juggling act. One was Prop 128, which had been introduced by her primary opponent, Attorney General John Van de Kamp. Big Green was an environmental initiative that, as columnist George Will put it, took up "thirty-nine single-spaced typewritten pages clotted with sixteen thousand words, many of them technical terms." The other was Prop 140, which would limit the number of terms a legislator could stay in office. It was targeted at one of Feinstein's principal supporters, Speaker Willie Brown.

In 1990, Brown posed an almost intractable problem for Feinstein. In a political world where there was no king, she obviously needed the support of at least some of the barons, and Brown had been with her from the beginning. Without him, her career, if it had gone anywhere at all, would have looked very different. But so much voter hostility at the perceived gridlock in Sacramento focused on the natty Speaker that his support was now a mixed blessing.

Brown is a man whose abundant gifts—of intelligence, energy, ambition, and charm—make him one of a kind in California politics. Sent to the assembly in 1964 from a predominantly white district, he was elected Speaker in 1980, the first black in the country to win that office. A sharecropper's kid who grew up in Mineola, Texas, he has an insouciance that is breathtaking in a man who has to stand for office: he has referred, for instance, to the Berman/d'Agostino campaign that defeated a proposition on reapportionment as "a great con job put over on the voters" and to former California Chief Justice Rose Bird and her court as "Sister Rose and the Supremes."

In the 1960s, the positions he favored were more viable than they would become a quarter-century later. By 1990, decriminalizing prostitution, abolishing the death penalty, lightening sentences for victimless crimes, easing penalties for the possession of certain drugs—all these had been taken off the political table. Brown seemed like a man primed for the lead in *Don Giovanni* who found himself stuck in a road show playing the stage manager in *Our Town*.

Consequently, *Los Angeles Times* columnist Bill Boyarsky could say of Brown that he is brilliant but he does not want to *do* anything. Compared to Phil Burton, who always had a goal in mind that had to do with social welfare and who used reapportionment as a means of furthering that goal, Willie Brown is "a power guy." According to Boyarsky, Brown is interested in getting drug dealers off in the courts and in helping his clients. "He doesn't really care about black issues. Maxine Waters [the newly elected member of Congress from Los Angeles] cares about them: she's destined for the top rung in politics, and she's been Willie's conscience. So without her in Sacramento, there's a terrible loss."

Nor, by most accounts, was Brown a man whom power had improved. He dominated any conversation because he was so much smarter than most other people and much quicker to deal. But his flaws had been magnified because very few people could say, "Bullshit!" to Willie Brown. "Increasingly, there are too many people around him who just want to get along, who don't want to get yelled at," said a Sacramento observer who asked for anonymity. "Any argument with Willie is a risk because he is vengeful and spiteful."

By 1990, the common perception among the electorate was that Willie Brown's legislature was corrupt. (According to the September 1990 LA Times poll, 48 percent disapproved of the Sacramento legislature, and Brown's negatives were just under 40 percent.) The money did not necessarily go into people's pockets for standard luxuries like fancy cars and clothes and first-class trips to Puerto Vallarta, although many resented Brown for being a flip, imperious, high-living black man who said whatever struck his fancy. No, the money seemed to go primarily into politics itself, and it came in the form of contributions for campaigns that never ended.

"I think legislators take legalized bribes, quid pro quo contributions," says Los Angeles Times San Francisco correspondent Mark Stein. "I don't think it's very uncommon for legislators or their staff people to imply that if you want to talk to so-and-so, you've got to pony up the money. That's happened under Willie's administration, and it's distressing to those of us who want to like the guy. But he seems to take pride in saying it's his assembly!"

"Politics have become very much a professional business in California," according to Richard Zeiger and A. G. Block of the California Journal. "We have legislators who are third-generation politicians. They've worked on the staffs of someone in the legislature, and that's all they've ever done in their lives. They're enormously good politicians, though they may be lousy at doing public policy.

They're very good at getting themselves elected and knowing how to deal with political groups. The secret is raising money, and that's been the key for the last ten or fifteen years."

By and large, then, the corruption was institutional. By 1990, it could cost $1 million to run successfully for an assembly seat that paid $45,000 a year, and a run for governor was almost literally out of sight. As Zeiger and Block put it: "The only place you're going to get money like that is from people who basically have something to gain or lose by the outcome, which is to say, people who do business with the legislature. If you get $100,000 from somebody, maybe you can buck 'em on the big ones, but somewhere along the line you're going to have to come through—or the next $100,000 is going to the other side."

Even an uncontested election could swallow half a million dollars for a bravura display that kept the political consultants happy and scared away future opposition. (A candidate who did not hire one of the big consultants to run his show might find that consultant running his opponent's in the next election.)

And the phenomenal expense of the campaigns had insidious consequences beyond the obvious: it put a premium on a certain kind of candidate. Contributors were not likely to give $100,000 to someone who was not perceived as safe and predictable, and as a result, the major races had grown more and more bland.

Exaggerating only slightly, consultant Bill Zimmerman said succinctly, "Colorful people don't go into politics." Not only wealthy donors but campaign professionals were uneasy with colorful people because they are harder to control, and when consultant Gina Glantz moved to Marin County from New Jersey, she was astonished to discover how much clout the pros had in California: "It seemed to be less relevant who the candidate was than who the consultant was."

Consequently, in 1988, the major race in California had been a Senate race which, according to Zimmerman, "no one remembers." It was between Pete Wilson and Leo McCarthy—"two gray men in gray suits, with gray politics and gray ideas and gray personalities." In 1986, the major race had been between George Deukmejian and Tom Bradley, a repeat match that "was also Dullsville." Electoral politics had come to seem like Jell-O fighting pudding.

Worried about the future of the California Democratic party,

Darry Sragow, who had run McCarthy's campaign in 1988, agreed. "Voters were desperate for change and vision and new direction," Sragow says. "They didn't want stratospheric stuff, we're not talking flako. . . . But I'd been looking at polls. I'd been watching focus groups. I'd been listening to voters for four years. They wanted measured, responsible vision—but nonetheless vision. And a change of direction."

John Van de Kamp, a Democrat and the attorney general, had made it known more than a year earlier that he would run for governor in 1990, but to Sragow, "that's a rerun of all those other races, and it's just going to frustrate the electorate even more." Van de Kamp was a fine man with a good record. But even his strongest supporters wished that his wife, Andrea, an ebullient, capable woman who made a vivid impression, could be the candidate.

Enter Dianne Feinstein.

For Sragow, "Dianne is obviously change. She's very independent. She's the outsider. Just on the surface, a Feinstein/Wilson race, if both sides are run competently, is going to be much closer than a Van de Kamp/Wilson race. At least [the Democrats] will have served up a candidate who was an alternative."

And therein lies both a story and a question.

CHAPTER 11

*We never realized that we'd go from 19 per-
cent down to 19 percent up in only six
weeks. . . . I did not expect a sea change."*
—BILL CARRICK

Hadley Roff is a burly, rumpled guy who looks like a character
in a Damon Runyon story—a reporter cum political junkie whose
calming influence was called upon repeatedly during his years as
Dianne Feinstein's chief of staff in San Francisco. A woman who
blanched when she remembered the Monday morning staff meetings
reported that Hadley absorbed a lot of the flak and guff but never
took it out on anyone else. "He just took it out on the machinery,"
she said with a tight-lipped grin. "Once he threw a typewriter."
Observers ranging from Bill Boyarsky, the *Los Angeles Times* columnist, to Pacy Markman, an incisive, puckish media consultant, use
the same word for Roff: "terrific."

He and Feinstein were at Stanford together, and before he came
to work for her in the mayor's office, he had served as press secretary
in John Tunney's 1970 winning campaign for the United States Senate
and then for six years had acted as Tunney's administrative assistant
in Washington. Subsequently, he spent a year as Ted Kennedy's press
secretary and two more as a subcommittee staff director before going
home to California.

In 1990, he had a corner room in Feinstein's bright, airy San
Francisco office from which he would emerge if a noisy dispute called
for his mediation, but most of his time was spent on the telephone.
He played a major role in assembling and coordinating the team that
would take her as far as the voters were willing for her to go, and
a big part of the challenge was to keep northern and southern California working in tandem.

By January 1989, when Governor George Deukmejian announced
that he would not run for reelection and Feinstein decided to enter

the race, John Van de Kamp had already garnered $1.5 million and, according to Roff, "vast numbers of endorsements" in his bid for the Democratic nomination. "Dianne came into the campaign late because of the demanding system of raising money," Roff explains, and because "Deukmejian was expected to run again." Nevertheless, even Van de Kamp's polls put Feinstein eight points ahead of him that January, and once the decision was made, the Feinstein core group began looking for good people to join them.

Duane Garrett, a forty-three-year-old San Francisco lawyer, signed on in February to be the campaign chairman, or titular head. His primary responsibility would be to raise money—the same job he had undertaken in 1982 for Los Angeles Mayor Tom Bradley in his run for governor. Garrett's credentials as a national Democrat were impeccable: in 1984, he had been the co-chair for presidential nominee Walter Mondale and in 1988 had held a similar post for former Arizona Governor Bruce Babbitt in his campaign for the Democratic nomination for president.

In both Alan Cranston's 1986 campaign for reelection to the United States Senate and Leo McCarthy's 1988 campaign against Pete Wilson, Darry Sragow had worked with consultants David Doak and Robert Shrum, who had designed the media. Now Doak and Shrum were asked to write a strategy memo for Feinstein.

"They did that," says Sragow, "but they came away . . . having decided that Dianne was not really a viable candidate. She's outside of the political establishment." Along with the pollster Paul Maslin, Doak and Shrum went over to Van de Kamp, whose campaign clearly became "the establishment place to be," and 1990 was declared to be "John's turn" at running for governor. (Doak and Shrum were also Jim Mattox's media advisers for his campaign in the Texas Democratic primary against Ann Richards.)

Sragow, on the contrary, thought Van de Kamp a nice man who was wrong for California and the Democratic party in 1990, and he signed on with Feinstein in April to help her develop a presence in southern California. In the circles in which he travels, this was tantamount to heresy, and although he didn't come cheaply, getting Sragow was such a coup that Garrett exultantly dubbed him their General Patton.

Clinton Reilly, with whom Feinstein had negotiated for months in 1988 and finally hired to manage the race, had gone through three campaigns with her already, working first in the 1983 recall and then the regular mayoral election that followed hard on it. Never before had he run a statewide campaign, but both Garrett and Dick Blum "wanted him in the worst way." Reilly, furthermore, was keen to do it. To Sragow he seemed a "brilliant strategist and campaign manager" who'd done a good job electing candidates to local offices and the assembly but hadn't yet had a chance at the state level. "He bristles at outsiders coming in and doing what he thinks he ought to be doing," Sragow says, and "Dianne was the horse he was going to ride: he was grooming her for a statewide race."

Reilly, it turned out, bristled at a good many things, including his candidate, who spent the early period of the campaign badly anemic. She is also a boss whom one person after another would describe as "a holy terror" to work for and a woman whose obsession with detail exhausted a good deal of the available time.

Consequently, over the next five months, Feinstein and Reilly frequently disagreed about what to do and how to do it. Suffering from a lack of energy that exacerbated her physical problems, Feinstein finally decided to undergo major surgery in July, when she had a hysterectomy. Chief adviser Hadley Roff also had surgery about the same time, and so they were calling each other from their respective hospital rooms to plot and commiserate. During the six weeks of Feinstein's recovery, it became clear that her arrangement with Clint Reilly was not working out.

Each side has his and her interpretations of their dilemma. Reilly complained that Feinstein would not commit herself to either a schedule or a budget that made a big race tenable and refused even to let him spend money for telephone calls while she was recovering. Roff, on the other hand, guessed that "by July, four or five months into the campaign, Reilly had really not devised a workable strategy."

They disagreed about fund-raising: "[Reilly] wanted to do what Van de Kamp had done—to put initiatives on the ballot and use those as a surrogate way of campaigning. Dianne was opposed to that." He wanted to go with an initiative on women's right to choose that Roff thought women's groups opposed. ("They didn't want to make it that much of a yes-or-no issue," he said.) "We were having difficulty raising money for the campaign," Roff recalled with exasperation. "I couldn't see raising money separately for another campaign. To diffuse our efforts seemed a mistake."

On the very day Feinstein got back to her office, Reilly quit, faxing his resignation to newspapers throughout the state before telling Feinstein. As Roff remembered, "We're getting calls from the *San Diego Union* before we hear from a campaign manager whose office is only a block away." For Duane Garrett it was the worst day of the campaign. "We were really on the ropes," he recalled. "The *San Jose Mercury* used a headline font that hadn't been used since the *Hindenburg* went down." The bad manners rankled, and so did the phrasing: Reilly had accused Feinstein of not having the "fire in the belly" a candidate must have to win—remarks particularly insensitive to a woman who had just undergone a hysterectomy.

The insult had the virtue of making Feinstein furious. She went up to Sacramento—"right to the heart of the most skeptical part of the establishment, both party and press," as Duane Garrett put it—and "weathered a press conference" rather than taking advantage of "the fact that it was summertime and perhaps it would just sort of disappear." When someone asked if she had "the fire in the belly" for the campaign, she responded tartly, "I thought I had that removed." Standing on the fringes of the crowd, Richie Ross, Van de Kamp's campaign manager, saw that Feinstein was back in the race.

The press, however, seemed more damaging to Feinstein than to Reilly, especially since he was not running for office, and now, in August, her electoral prospects were discouraging. On top of starting behind financially, she had not been on the stump for months. At a time when John Van de Kamp was in high gear, Feinstein was invisible and her campaign badly in disarray.

Nor can the news Reilly gave Feinstein before he quit have been encouraging. Knowing that eight hundred thousand more women than men were likely to vote in the Democratic primary, Reilly had asked consultant Gina Glantz to work in the Feinstein campaign and take on the special assignment of reaching them. A crack organizer with superb ties to the women's movement, Glantz had been a key staff person in the Mondale campaign, and although she had promised her business partner that she would no longer do candidate politics, she decided to sound out their clients.

Every one of them had been appalled. The Service Employees

International Union had been one of the chief protagonists in the comparable worth fight in San Francisco, and Feinstein's veto of that legislation had left them bitter. The California League of Conservation Voters said that Feinstein was pro-development, whereas Van de Kamp was "great" on their issues. The California Abortion Rights Action League (CARAL), in both its northern and southern branches, had taken essentially the same stand. "Everywhere I turned," Glantz said, "people were saying, 'How could you do this?' "

Sragow took over for the time being as campaign manager, while Feinstein spent the next three months deciding on a new media team from among the consultants who sent their résumés after Reilly quit. "I took my time," she said, "because it was very important that I make a right decision. This is expensive, so I wanted to be sure."

She wanted someone who knew California: "It makes a big difference if you're running a campaign and you have a real knowledge of the state. A number of [political operatives], even during the campaign, are not in the state. They may come once or twice a week, but basically they operate out of other states." So she was captivated for a while by the Berman/d'Agostino team, with whom Garrett said "we entered a series of negotiations" he whimsically called "the dance of a thousand veils." They had powerful fund-raising ties and notable organizational strength in southern California, but according to Garrett, the "entry price" they named was $3 million and Feinstein was not yet prepared to make such an irrevocable commitment.

The negotiations were so discouraging that in mid-November Garrett took it upon himself to call Barbara Johnson, his counterpart in the Van de Kamp campaign, to explore the possibility of a graceful exit. In the event that Feinstein decided to get out, he wanted to know whether they would "confront gloating, were we going to confront the kind of graciousness that John brought after the primary, were we going to be able to rein Richie in, or were we going to be blasted by him even if John was saying nice things?" In other words, he wanted to know what Feinstein's "image" was likely to be if she conceded a Van de Kamp victory.

In the meantime, Hadley Roff worried about the big California picture. "I'd been essentially involved in city government," he said. "I could tell you a lot about the city, but I had not been involved in a statewide campaign in California since 1976." Both the technology and the demographics had changed fundamentally since then.

So they looked at a number of New York–based consultants, all of whom were good, but all of whom had other clients. Still, "fortune has a way of smiling on Dianne," Roff remarked appreciatively, and it turned out that Bill Carrick, who had been Ted Kennedy's political director for five years and had run Richard Gephardt's presidential campaign in 1988, was interested in the job.

Carrick, a big, beady-eyed man in his early forties with a bushy auburn beard that makes him look like a lumberjack, had moved to California two years earlier to work for an Australian firm in the entertainment business. When the company was sold, he took "a platinum parachute" out, and now he wanted to get back into politics. He and Hank Morris, who was based in New York, had decided to start a business together doing campaigns "from the media production end."

To Roff, Carrick seemed attractive not only because he could be in the Los Angeles headquarters full time but because he appeared to have "an absolutely sure political judgment." Duane Garrett was more restrained. Campaign managers, he thought, tended to be "too creative by half." Carrick, though "incredibly creative," at the same time had the virtue of "mumbl[ing] so much that it's hard to hear him." The combination proved irresistible.

On the Gephardt campaign, Carrick had been one of a five-part inner circle, with David Doak and Bob Shrum making up another two-fifths. Since Doak and Shrum were doing Van de Kamp's media, Feinstein could be confident that Carrick knew her enemy, and there is no evidence that she saw his advent as anything but a plus.

In a postmortem on the Gephardt campaign, however, a team of three *St. Louis Post-Dispatch* writers hinted that his inner circle had created at least as many problems for Gephardt as they had solved. Referring to them as "The Boys" and even "The White Boys," the *Post-Dispatch* noted that other insiders had found them "frequently arrogant, occasionally myopic and sometimes counterproductive." Their "attitude of exclusivity," according to the writers, had particularly galled those who found Gephardt himself unusually accessible, and Missouri Lieutenant Governor Harriett Woods had cited them as "an example of a pervasive problem—the inordinate influence of professional political consultants." Woods believed that they tended to lose sight of the big picture in their lust for winning games with one another and said they often failed to return phone calls even to key insiders. For Feinstein, who was already suspect because she insisted on doing things her own way, Carrick could mean trouble.

But in the late fall of 1989, the question was whether Feinstein would even survive as a candidate. About the time Carrick and Morris took over, she was 18 percent down, according to the Field poll, and underfunded to boot, while John Van de Kamp had close to $2 million in the bank. Every year for the preceding three or four, a group of 135 donors had each contributed $5,000 to his campaign, and more recently they had become a working committee obligated to raise $10,000 each. Because this group did not even include Van de Kamp's "superstar fund-raisers," his campaign team, lulled by the negative publicity into dismissing Feinstein as a serious candidate, was feeling cocky. According to pollster Paul Maslin, their comforting illusion prompted them to "just be kind about [the Feinstein debacle], just let it happen, it's going to drift away, we're not going to have a problem, we're not going to have a primary!" Campaign chair Barbara Johnson expected that when the filing deadline for the primary passed, "the general [election] would start for all practical purposes, and the jockeying would start between the two parties."

Willie Brown and senate leader David Roberti, however, had both leaned hard on Feinstein not to quit. "They were making commitments about money," Carrick revealed after the election, "none of which ever came to pass." With two key members of the Democratic establishment treating Feinstein to a "constant bucking up in support," the new team saw that it needed to turn the campaign around and, as Roff put it, "capitalize on [Feinstein's] strengths, her personality, her ability to communicate effectively, her star quality."

The new men melded into the old team, on which a key player was Dee Dee Myers, Feinstein's twenty-nine-year-old press secretary, who had signed on before Reilly quit. Although young, she was a cool, accomplished veteran of Democratic campaigns and a favorite of the press. As Los Angeles Mayor Tom Bradley's press secretary, she had worked on his 1986 campaign for governor, as well as for

Democratic presidential nominees Walter Mondale in 1984 and Michael Dukakis in 1988. She made an appealing, no-nonsense spokeswoman for Feinstein.

Carrick and Morris then broke the challenge into two components. The first was money. "There wasn't time to raise the money through the traditional Democratic sources," Carrick acknowledged. "If we needed $6 million, which we collectively agreed we needed to win the primary," Feinstein and her husband, Richard Blum, would have to provide half of it. Although Feinstein had refused to commit a comparable sum several months before to Berman/d'Agostino, she agreed to it now.

Second, in December, they held focus groups in Los Angeles, San Francisco, Sacramento, and the Valley, "and we concluded from that that the race was wide open. [The voters] didn't have any sense who John Van de Kamp was! The conventional wisdom about the Van de Kamp candidacy was that there was a kind of Mondalesque inevitability about it, which was all hogwash. Even in Los Angeles, where he'd been district attorney and there's been a family bakery in his uncle's name, Van de Kamp Bakeries, people didn't have a clue. . . . There was no evidence or history that this candidate was invincible." In the Los Angeles focus groups, furthermore, it was obvious after the first five minutes that "there was no [Van de Kamp] campaign for real people." Although the participants considered themselves "at least somewhat active" politically, most couldn't tell one from another when pictures of Pete Wilson, John Van de Kamp, and Leo McCarthy were held before them.

Since the conventional wisdom, even if it's hogwash, has an impact on fund-raising, and since, when a woman is making the race, donors are less likely to raise or give big money, the financial problem had to be addressed first. If "Dianne and Dick" were prepared to put up the money, Carrick and Morris were convinced "the race was wide open." As Carrick puts it, "If we defined for people who Dianne was, in a positive context, we'd catch up."

The evidence to make the case for Feinstein was all there, and it was strong. "People needed to understand that she'd been named the most effective mayor in the country. She'd managed a tough city and done it well. And that was the way to turn San Francisco from a negative into a positive. We had no disagreement over strategy early on, or at any level of the campaign." For a campaign riven with discord for almost eight months, this new condition was the political equivalent of attaining a state of heavenly grace.

"The first research we did," Hank Morris remembered, "showed enormous interest in Dianne Feinstein, so people were going to pay attention to information about her. Once they got it, they would move to her. When we did the focus groups, as the moderator read facts about her, people would say, 'That's interesting!'"

Neither Carrick nor Morris—nor Ed Reilly, whom they brought in to do the polling—could see a problem in Feinstein's gender, although in December 1989, the candidate herself had been quoted as saying, "Being a woman is not a great help." Determined to convince voters that she was a tough manager, Garrett in fact wanted to run her "as a better-looking, better-spoken version of Margaret Thatcher." "The biggest problem with a stereotype," Morris says, "was with her being mayor of San Francisco."

Meanwhile, Sragow and John Plaxco, who had signed on to raise money, were explaining the hard financial realities to the candidate, rooted as they were in Proposition 73—a campaign reform that had passed in 1988 limiting to $1,000 the amount that any individual could give and putting a $5,000 ceiling on contributions from groups. Ironically, the reform gave an advantage to the wealthier party because there were many more Republicans than Democrats who could easily write a check for $1,000.

The financial facts of life were more than sobering. If Feinstein won the primary and came up against United States Senator Pete Wilson in the general election, she would have to raise upward of $15 million, since it was widely believed that the Republicans had promised Wilson $20 million to enter the race and she would have to raise three-quarters of that amount to be competitive. "The math on that," Sragow points out, "$15 or 20 million, divided by $1,000, means reaching out to an obscene number of people.... You beg and plead, and you do all kinds of things you'd never thought you'd do for *endless* hours. Because if you don't, you never reach that aggregate figure you need!"

As Ann Richards knew, some things can be learned only by doing, and now Feinstein was up against one of those things. "You can talk to Dianne about something," Sragow says, and "give her things to read, but she has to experience it." Eight months later, he was impressed by how much she had grown: "She dismissed things she now understands about running statewide. When you tell somebody that under the rules established by Prop 73 [which were suspended in September 1990 by Federal District Judge Lawrence K. Karlton] they're going to spend 80 to 90 percent of their time as a candidate raising money, and doing nothing else, *they think you're just mean.* They don't understand, until they've lived through it, that when you have to raise the obscene amount of money we have to raise to run statewide in California, and at no more than $1,000 a check. . . ." Sragow's voice trailed off in memory of the ordeal.

Plaxco explained to Feinstein that a certain amount of money could be raised from her traditional sources in San Francisco, but any more would have to come from Los Angeles. So he took the schedule and put in whatever he thought he needed to recruit fundraisers and more money, and then Carrick "built all this political stuff around it."

As *Washington Post* columnist George Will points out, the Los Angeles basin's 14.5 million residents exceed the total population of any state other than New York and Texas. Plaxco put it starkly to Feinstein: "LA is the biggest financial market as well as media market in the state." Although they began their Los Angeles "prospecting" in November 1989, by January, they had gotten "nowhere." "We spent a lot of time just going around meeting people," Plaxco says. "In the early days, I'd go with her and we'd have lunch with somebody, have these one-on-one meetings to expose her to more people." It was tedious and discouraging until her first dramatic television ad, when "all of a sudden there was a lot of interest in her."

"Dianne has a tremendous appeal to nonconventional sources of money," Plaxco discovered, "but nonconventional sources of money take time to dig out. We accepted every dogshit invitation we got, whether it was women in real estate or Stanford women's alumnae. Some of the things she went to were unbelievable—it was almost embarrassing.

"So we needed a few months of prospecting and exposing her to people. But the interesting thing was that after these meetings—at some political event, at churches, temples, or whatever—people who had never been involved in politics before would come out and hand us their cards. By the end of the primary, we had people giving fund-raisers for us who would stand up there and say, basically, that not only had they never given to a politician before, they'd *certainly* never asked their friends and families for money. There was a lot of that!"

In the course of trying everything, they even went directly to John Van de Kamp's supporters, although they expected little for their pains. Again they were pleasantly surprised. By May, people who had been Van de Kamp fund-raisers for years had become Feinstein partisans. "It took a while," Plaxco says, "because they didn't think we were going to win. Then all of a sudden, it became obvious that we could. And the more people saw her, the more they liked her."

Virtually everyone involved in Feinstein's gubernatorial race not only calls her a quick study but says she grew over the course of a year. As Plaxco put it, "She went from being a fairly parochial can-didate used to doing things that were effective in a tiny geographical area to a candidate comfortable in a huge state." In raising the record-shattering amount of money she needed to be a viable candidate for governor of California, Feinstein mastered a challenge even more formidable than Ann Richards'—because California has almost twice Texas' population and she had none of the ties Richards had secured in the financial community while serving as state treasurer.

When Bill Carrick said of Dianne Feinstein that she is "the most complex candidate I've ever worked for," he echoed many others. "She has a strong sense of who she is," Carrick discovered, and "what she wants to do." Like others, he used the word "mission" to describe her purposefulness. "We may be hired guns in the cam-paign," Carrick said, "but she's not a political professional in the standard sense. If she's for something, she's for it: it's pretty hard to move her with a political argument away from something she's ba-sically decided on."

Willie Brown thought Feinstein was "crazy," for instance, to support either the crime or the environmental initiatives on the ballot but was convinced she did it "because she believes" in them: "She has zero ability to be politically expedient." Though he didn't think that a politician could make it to the big leagues without being expedient and conceded that "that may be her political undoing," he insisted nevertheless that "she can't pull it off. This woman is a rare breed. And that's what makes her attractive to me! If I argue with her, I know she hasn't even *considered* the political benefits or the political downside. You have to be able to convince her *on the merits*."

Carrick said the same thing. John Van de Kamp, for example, had drawn up Big Green, which among other things would phase out potentially hazardous pesticides, and Feinstein "basically spent two months analyzing the thing before she decided to come out for it." In the primary, according to Carrick, the easy approach would have been "to say right away, 'I'm for it too!' *And neutralize it!* [But] we went through this torture where she had every goddamn lawyer, environmentalist, agribusiness person, and scientist [in the state]. We dragged through a parade of maybe twenty meetings. The agony was enough to kill a guy! The press was fixated on 'What's she going to do on Big Green?' Finally she got all her answers, processed them, decided it was a solid thing to do, [and] moved on."*

"The plus side of that," with which Carrick consoled himself, "is that she stands up for what she believes in. She's got an edge to her. She's a leader. She's got conviction."

The downside is that Feinstein has not been a reliable team player. As the Reverend Cecil Williams puts it, "Dianne's always said, 'I don't want to be caught up in the Democratic party as such. . . . [I want] to be seen as independent.' " But a Democrat who expects to run for higher office and, like Feinstein in 1988, does not support the Democratic party's candidate for the United States Senate, has to expect at least a handful of the powerful to look on her candidacy as they might a six-month siege of walking pneumonia. No doubt Feinstein did not see it that way, however, because she thinks of herself as a woman who rejects mere political expediency, convinced of what reporter Susan Yoachum calls "her own sincerity and good intentions."

The issue of expediency became salient in part because of John Van de Kamp. As John Balzar put it in the *Los Angeles Times Mag-*

---

*"In the general election," Carrick went on, "the thing turns out to be less than positive: she goes to the [agricultural] Valley and for two days tells everybody she's for Big Green, giving many of our supporters a heart attack."

azine, for thirty years of public life, Van de Kamp had seemed to be
part of the political landscape. Suddenly, however, he was running
as an outsider and it was unclear what he stood for.

At the prompting of Doak, Shrum, Maslin, and campaign manager Richie Ross, Van de Kamp had linked his candidacy to three
initiatives—one aimed at "draining the ethical swamp" of special
interests in Sacramento, in some measure by limiting the length of
time legislators and statewide officeholders could serve; a second, the
environmental initiative that had earned the sobriquet Big Green;
and a third establishing a superfund to fight drugs and making it
easier to seek the death penalty.*

A longtime team player, Van de Kamp had infuriated the Sacramento establishment, who considered his term-limits initiative a
cynical pandering to public anger at the legislature. (Willie Brown
said with disgust, "I'm against anybody in the political world who's
really, genuinely phony.") Whether or not Van de Kamp had suc-
cumbed in a weak moment to the will to win, he was more conflicted
than most politicians. As a Catholic, he was personally opposed to
abortion, but as a candidate, he supported a woman's right to choose.
In 1974 testimony before the U.S. Senate Judiciary Committee, he
had called the death penalty "barbaric" and "a blot on the American
system of justice," but with his initiative, he proposed to expand the
number of murderers liable for death row and expedite the executions
of three hundred condemned men waiting for the gas chamber.

At the same time, the way Van de Kamp handled the Hillside
Strangler case in 1981, as Los Angeles district attorney, gave Feinstein
ammunition she could use to suggest that he was ambivalent about

*Van de Kamp's initiative strategy turned out to be a fatal mistake because it split his
campaign into warring halves that never fully reunited. According to deputy campaign manager
Vicky Rideout, Van de Kamp wanted "to inject some drama into his candidacy and define
himself . . . as being for change and being an outsider." Campaign chair Barbara Johnson,
however, confessed that on the July 4 weekend, 1989, "the decision makers in the campaign"
deadlocked and even "the phones stopped for three or four days." Those supporting the
initiatives expected them to prove "a great organizing device on all the campuses," as Johnson
put it, where students "were hungry for causes," and to "create a substitute infrastructure
around them that would get out our vote." But the initiative strategy required Van de Kamp,
in effect, to run four different campaigns, and in a postmortem conference at the University
of California at Berkeley, George Gorton, Pete Wilson's campaign manager, confessed that
since the Wilson campaign team was "terrified to death of running two campaigns at the same
time" they had been "absolutely astonished" that Van de Kamp was running four.

prosecuting potential death penalty cases. Ten young women had been murdered and their bodies dumped on the hills around the city. Kenneth Bianchi, a suspect who made a deal with prosecutors and pleaded guilty to five killings in order to escape the death penalty, became the key witness against his cousin Angelo Buono. When Bianchi subsequently began changing his testimony, however, senior prosecutors recommended dropping the murder charges and prosecuting Buono on lesser counts. Van de Kamp supported them in that position, but the superior court judge transferred the case to Attorney General George Deukmejian, who then staged a spectacular trial and got Buono convicted for nine of the ten murders.

Feinstein, then, was facing a worthy opponent who had recently been named "Attorney General of the Year" by his peers in the National Association of Attorneys General. A man whose trademark was civility but whom his most ardent admirers called juiceless; a man whose publicly acknowledged convictions were at odds with positions he had taken as attorney general and was taking in his campaign for governor; a prosecutor who had made what many people considered a colossal mistake in judgment in perhaps the most dramatic case he ever handled.

These contradictions were ripe for political exploitation: they made explaining and presenting John Van de Kamp so complicated that campaign chair Barbara Johnson would admit, ruefully, that "the campaign was not consistent with the campaign." At a gathering of publishers in San Diego, Feinstein skewered him by saying, "You can't be for what you're against and against what you're for." On top of that, the chance to outperform him was irresistible.

Late in the fall of 1989, apart from women's organizations headquartered in Washington like the Caucus, NARAL, and EMILY's List, Feinstein did not have the backing of the traditional components of the Democratic coalition. Carrick ticked them off: "We didn't have labor. We didn't have teachers. We didn't have [state] women's groups. We were fighting and scratching for California NOW [the National Organization for Women]." Most of these groups were backing Attorney General John Van de Kamp.

But Feinstein now enjoyed the advantage of having at the core of her campaign a handful of people who respected each other and got along. As Carrick would say not long before the general election, "There's very little backstabbing or sniping, and Dianne hasn't done anything to undermine us." Sragow put it finely: "We've all been on so many campaigns. We're too experienced and too honorable, frankly, to get involved in big disputes. We've disagreed, surely, but not over big things. It's Dianne's responsibility, ultimately, that such experienced people are running the campaign."

Nevertheless, they did not have a situation that would allow what Ann Richards called "synergy" to happen. Spending their days in a series of uninviting rooms on the third and fourth floors of an anonymous office building on Wilshire Boulevard in downtown Los Angeles, they worked constantly to keep overhead down. And because everybody had so many tasks, the campaign workers were too busy to talk with one another beyond the bare minimum. Two weeks before the general election, Sragow longed for "a larger staff that has the luxury of sitting down and communicating with itself more often." All the resources that might have let them become greater than the sum of their individual parts went into the insatiable maw of the media.

In the winter of 1989, the Feinstein focus groups and polling convinced this tight nucleus of pros that Van de Kamp's support was so shallow he seemed, politically speaking, to have "no moorings at all." So although Feinstein was a northern California candidate, they made the strategic decision "to invest a lot of time in LA, not only in paid media, but scurrying around to retail political [events]—black churches, women's groups, seniors groups, temples." In other words, they treated Los Angeles as if Feinstein were running for the city council and "put together an indigenous political organization."

Rummaging around in Feinstein's library, Morris discovered the videotape footage from the day George Moscone and Harvey Milk were murdered. He put the tape into the VCR, and a few seconds later, he started yelling for Carrick: "Come here! You've got to see this!" They stood watching it with a dizzy sense of its dramatic possibilities.

Wrestling briefly with the question of whether it was too emotional, they decided, as Carrick put it, that "if we were going to get the campaign off the ground at all, we were going to have to take some risks." If it turned people off, so be it. So they cut a commercial that would be dubbed the "grabber ad" that began with Feinstein on the steps of City Hall solemnly announcing that the mayor and supervisor had been shot and killed, using a voice-over that began "Forged from tragedy . . .!" The ad then went on to show her with black children, policemen, and community people and trumpeted the slogan she herself had devised: "Tough and caring." In the last few seconds, the voice-over said: "Named the nation's most effective mayor, and always pro-choice, she's the only Democrat for governor who's for the death penalty."

Morris and Carrick brushed aside the focus groups they ordinarily used to test their ads because they expected people to complain that this one was too emotional and exploited tragedy. Determined to pay no attention to nay-sayers, they bought air time over a five-week period "so it was sort of a slow burn buy." For the first few days, it ran often, and then twice a day.

By the end of February, they had spent nearly $600,000 in the major media markets, except for San Francisco, airing what Carrick called their "surgical strike"—and to brilliant effect. Traveling around the state, Van de Kamp chair Barbara Johnson "saw that blasted ad eleven times." She kept calling her colleagues to say, "This is big stuff: it could take off!" But Van de Kamp's advisers told the campaign staff that the ad wouldn't matter because Feinstein was going nowhere—deciding, in fact, that it was nothing more "than a last expensive noisy gasp." Seldom had they been more mistaken.

After the ad had been running two weeks, 49 percent of those who had had no opinion on Feinstein ranked her favorably. In the major markets in which it had been shown, 22 percent of the audience polled recalled the ad and identified it with her. And her advantage over Van de Kamp soared. As Carrick himself put it, "We never realized that we'd go from 19 percent down to 19 percent up in only six weeks. I thought quite optimistically that we'd get within four or five points, but I did not expect a sea change."

Then Van de Kamp began to hemorrhage in his other principal stronghold, the legislature. His support for Proposition 131, with its term-limits clause and its attack on the "swamp" of Sacramento, had a consequence he had not expected. Barbara Johnson confessed that in their internal discussions "at no time was the impact on the leg-

islature or on the other people running for office ever considered."
But according to George Skelton, the *LA Times* Sacramento bureau
chief, angry legislators used their leverage over bills to persuade his
contributors to dry up the well. The trial lawyers who had been
particularly important to his fund-raising were heavily influenced by
Willie Brown, and at least $1 million Van de Kamp had expected
did not materialize. Johnson ultimately conceded that because they
had not been "wise enough to anticipate the reaction," they hadn't
made "an informed decision" on the campaign reform initiative.

If Van de Kamp had set his own controls on self-destruct, however, the Carrick/Morris team nonetheless had to defuse his support
among women's groups who considered his record on women's issues
outstanding. Unlike Jim Mattox, Van de Kamp was widely respected,
and his popular wife, Andrea, clearly played a crucial role in his
politics: in the *Los Angeles Times Magazine*, veteran reporter John
Balzar admired her "50,000-watt smile" and "a zest that no spouse
in more than a generation has brought to the California campaign
trail." She even got away with teasing her husband publicly when
she introduced him by claiming that his idea of autoeroticism was
using the cruise control in a government car. A successful career
woman, she had been so effective an advocate for women's organizations that San Francisco Congresswoman Barbara Boxer called Van
de Kamp the best feminist in the race.

With the cynicism endemic to political consultants, like city reporters, Carrick scoffed at women who declared their support for
Van de Kamp: "The truth is they were all political hacks who signed
on because the train was leaving the station. . . . They thought he
was an inevitable winner. He'd been running for three years; he'd
been raising a lot of money and had all the inside folks locked up."
Hope Warschaw, who joined Feinstein's staff in March 1990, seemed
almost as contemptuous. According to Warschaw, the litany of hei-
nous crimes that Van de Kamp fans claimed Feinstein had committed
against women included "enforcing a dress code in City Hall so that
women couldn't wear slacks [and] refusing to sign a proclamation
about Reproductive Freedom Day" in San Francisco.

But most people thought Van de Kamp had the "inside folks"
locked up for the good reason that he had come through for them

politically. As Margery Tabankin, executive director of the Hollywood Women's Political Committee, put it, "he's had an incredibly
close working relationship with women's groups in southern California," whereas Feinstein was "unconnected to women's organizations." The Hollywood Women remained officially neutral during
the primary, like many others whose ambivalence kept them on the
sidelines, while some groups strongly supported Van de Kamp. For
instance, *women for:*, a newsletter put out in Beverly Hills, described
Feinstein as "a recent convert to women's issues" and criticized her
as an opportunist who took positions in response to public opinion,
rather than from "deeply held convictions."

Feinstein, in fact, had alienated some women's groups so thor-
oughly that in 1988, when her name appeared on the list of speakers
the National Organization for Women considered acceptable for the
keynote at the Democratic National Convention, the California chapter of NOW had strenuously objected. Consultant Gina Glantz noted
that as mayor, Feinstein "would never sign on to invitations to
CARAL's dinners in San Francisco." In mid-January 1990, Assem-
blywoman Delaine Eastin explained her support for Van de Kamp
by saying that Feinstein "has not really taken the kind of role that
she could have taken. . . . The National Women's Political Caucus
and NOW and other statewide women's organizations many times
invited Dianne to participate in conventions and events and she did
not choose to do so!"

But if the leaders of women's organizations who had worked with
Van de Kamp had learned to appreciate the lengths to which he had
gone to fight their battles, the plain fact was that most women had
not. Many were thrilled at the sight of a strong, dynamic woman
running hard for governor, and since a key goal for the women's
movement had always been getting more women into positions of
power and conspicuous influence, Feinstein's candidacy presented
them an irresistible opportunity.

As Warschaw could see, "you're not going to convince the average
voter out there that the woman running is not a good feminist,
particularly if she's pro-choice." Henri Galina-Rosin, vice-president
of Los Angeles NOW, the largest chapter in the country, thought "it
would be unconscionable for me not to support the woman." And
Elaine Gallinson, who had traveled as Joan Mondale's aide during

the 1984 presidential campaign, switched her vote from Van de Kamp after she saw Feinstein in person and realized that "she would be a much more exciting candidate to run against Pete Wilson."

So when Feinstein called on voters to make history and elect the first woman governor of California, many women followed her lead. In May, Democrats watching her two televised debates with Van de Kamp realized that she could be governor. Like many others, Warschaw saw those spirited appearances as pivotal: "She grew in stature just by debating Van de Kamp." And unlike him, Feinstein was vivid, bold, and dramatic.

Her burgeoning support among women mirrored the groundswell among voters all over California. Carrick recognized a familiar dynamic: "Dianne doesn't do terribly well with the leadership of organizations. They just wake up one morning and find out that half their membership is with her. And then they begin to take a second look." Democrats were beginning to call her their Ronald Reagan, and although Van de Kamp won the party nomination by one vote in a fiercely contested spring convention, his victory did nothing for him in the primary itself. The fight over the nomination simply forced both sides to squander lots of time and money, and as Duane Garrett saw, it planted "the seeds of potential disaster" by showing the Democratic party on record opposing the candidate the Democratic electorate would choose.

In the black community, Feinstein had the leaders as well because Willie Brown, now Van de Kamp's determined enemy, rallied many key ministers and politicians to her cause. To have the foremost black politician in California with a statewide constituency not only in your camp but convinced that his well-being depends on your winning would be like having St. Christopher arrive to hoist you on his shoulders when you hit the banks of the river.

But Feinstein did superbly on her own with blacks. Like *Los Angeles Times* columnist Bill Boyarsky, state senator Diane E. Watson, who is black, recognized that Feinstein "has the same quality Jimmy Carter had: in churches she reaches right out to the people." At the beginning of her campaign, nobody in Los Angeles knew her. As Watson put it, "She might have been just an affluent, snobbish woman from San Francisco, that sophisticated city to the north that looks down on us from up the coast. But when her ads first came on, and they said 'Forged by tragedy!'—you see, we live with tragedy in the neighborhoods every day—everybody stopped and listened. Those ads showed her rising to that challenge! The next scene showed her talking to small black kids, so people bonded with her.

"*And then she came.* Very few candidates will come into the deep ghetto like she did. She talked to the people. She talked to children. And she said, 'I want to know you. I want to work with you.'"

To be sure, Feinstein's moderate politics, and especially her pitch for the death penalty, troubled black leaders like Maxine Waters, the seven-term state legislator from Los Angeles who was running in 1990 to succeed Gus Hawkins in the United States Congress. An outspoken feminist, Waters wanted more women elected to office. In her view, however, Feinstein "did no organizing to speak of in the black community: she got a few elected officials to take her on Sunday morning to the black churches. [But] I don't consider that organizing . . . [and] I don't like that kind of politics." Still, Van de Kamp's initiatives had undermined his standing, and politicians like Waters, who had no place to go, remained neutral.

Gay groups, among others, stayed with Van de Kamp because he had actually *acted* in response to their anxiety about what the Department of Health and Human Services was doing on AIDS testing. Within two weeks after meeting with some of the most powerful people in the LA gay movement in a study group headed by former nun Jean O'Leary, he had drawn up legislation bypassing the Food and Drug Administration and making it possible to test drugs in California—drugs to be given to those who tested HIV positive if they wanted them.

"Van de Kamp then went to Deukmejian," O'Leary remembered, "who promised not to veto it." Subsequently he got two leaders at the opposite ends of the political spectrum to agree to support the bill, and after they stood "in front of the podium with locked arms," the vote was unanimous. Meanwhile, Dianne Feinstein was lobbying publicly against the bill, on the theory that the drugs were dangerous.

San Francisco Mayor Art Agnos also supported Van de Kamp, quarreling publicly with Feinstein about the state of the city's finances when he took over and accusing her of leaving him with a $172 million deficit. To account for the Agnos/Feinstein feud, Mark Stein, of the *Los Angeles Times* San Francisco bureau, cited both his city's treacherous politics and Agnos' personal ambition. Some seven or eight years earlier, when Mayor Feinstein and Senator Pete Wilson had fought together to "homeport" the battleship *Missouri* at Hunter's Point, an impoverished part of the city, they had sparked a battle that split the San Francisco political community. Feinstein had argued that homeporting would bring jobs and money to an economically depressed area. But because the *Missouri* carried nuclear weapons they considered dangerous to nearby populations, many politicians, including Congresswoman Sala Burton, were violently opposed. One of those politicians was Art Agnos, who was then in the assembly.

Wilson had taken their battle to Washington, and Feinstein was so grateful that, in 1988, when he ran for reelection, she had refused to back the Democratic candidate, Lieutenant Governor Leo McCarthy, against him. This made things even worse between Feinstein and Agnos, who had first gone to Sacramento as McCarthy's administrative assistant. Agnos and McCarthy were close friends as well as loyal Democrats.

On top of that, "Art wanted to look like a genius," Stein said, and boast that he had rescued the city from a huge deficit: "Well, it's just not so. There's never been a deficit. The Agnos administration chose to take the worst-case scenario and save the city from that." (Others argued more simply that Agnos hates Feinstein.) Since California cities, like the state itself, are prohibited by law from running deficits, Feinstein's final budget had projected a $16.2 million surplus, and she continued to use the term "shortfall" for what Agnos called a "deficit."

But Agnos had given Van de Kamp material to attack Feinstein as a way of getting back in the race. Although Carrick had hoped "to stay positive all the way along," in March Van de Kamp felt he had no alternative to a negative campaign. "We had to try to bring her down," one staffer insisted, because "it was the only possible hope we had." Accordingly, they spent $1 million on ads in March alone, largely to say that Feinstein had left San Francisco with a budget deficit—prompting the *Los Angeles Times* to set a precedent that newspapers around the country followed in systematically examining television ads to question truth in political advertising.

The Van de Kamp attack did not work. By late spring, the *LA Times* polls were consistently showing Feinstein not only socking it to Van de Kamp but also edging out Pete Wilson. Even in March, for instance, they ranked Feinstein at 30 percent, Wilson at 29 percent, and Van de Kamp at 20 percent.

The *Sacramento Bee*, however, spoke for others who would not be stampeded. Three weeks before the June 5 primary, they endorsed Van de Kamp in an editorial that dismissed Feinstein's claim that she had broader experience as "just flat wrong." "Feinstein tends to glitter, both in personality and in the generalities she dispenses on public issues," they wrote, and "she often seems disturbingly uninformed." The two Democratic candidates "could hardly be more different," and the *Bee* chose Van de Kamp "easily." When she was mayor of San Francisco, Feinstein had "spent down the city's financial reserves and then tried to blame her successor, Art Agnos, for the fiscal problems he inherited." Since her responses to questions about specific problems the next governor would face were so vague she seemed "not to want to think about" them, the *Bee* concluded that "it would be unfortunate if Feinstein, like Ronald Reagan, were to win the primary with smiles, anecdotes, and generalities."

Sherry Bebitch Jeffe, of the Center for Politics and Policy at the Claremont Graduate School, however, wrote in the *LA Times* that "print media [have] become almost superfluous to the campaign process," and another medium proved far more important than any newspaper, no matter how politically astute its readers.

That medium, of course, was television, and after the Van de Kamp budget attack, Bill Carrick decided that "they'd crossed the line and [we] had no choice but to go" negative as well. He and Morris accordingly designed two final thirty-second ads against Van de Kamp, one of them ridiculing his decision, as Los Angeles County district attorney, not to prosecute Angelo Buono for murder in the Hillside Strangler case. Showing a victim's body being carried up a hill on a stretcher, it said that Van de Kamp had taken money from the Hillside Strangler's lawyer and waited ten years to admit he had made a mistake in dropping charges.

Referring to that ad as "the body bag spot," a veteran reporter
in the Berkeley postmortem called it not only "in incredibly bad taste"
but one of the two worst political ads he had ever seen, and Pete
Wilson campaign operatives subsequently collared reporters with the
line that in taking the low road, Feinstein had run the most despicable
ad of the campaign. Good taste, however, was considered no more
relevant a criterion than fairness, and Carrick confessed that he
thought one he and Morris had designed to link Van de Kamp with
Richard Nixon was even worse.

Although Carrick admitted that he "was less than comfortable
doing that spot," he considered Van de Kamp "dead wrong on the
Hillside Strangler" and believed that "if you're going to do it, you'd
better make it emotionally powerful." The campaign bought
$500,000 worth of air time from Thursday to Sunday just before the
primary, which is the functional equivalent of saturation bombing,
so that the average viewer saw either that spot or one calling Van
de Kamp's record into question at least four times. Because the press
reacted so strongly to the Hillside Strangler ad, it "generated enormous free media coverage," and the ad may well have cinched the
election.

Feinstein closed her primary campaign with a songfest at Glide
Memorial Church, where Cecil Williams said she always came to get
in touch with the "real folks." The next day, she won three-fourths
of the black vote against a man who had always run well in the black
community. According to exit polls, she also won a majority of
organized labor, the teachers, self-described feminists, both liberals
and moderates—and Los Angeles County to boot.

"The leaders of all those groups were for John," Bill Carrick said,
but "after the primary we were having one of those makeup sessions
with the building-trades guys, and one of them got into his third
glass of wine and said, 'I'm gonna cut this bullshit: the truth is, we
were the only labor people who were for Van de Kamp, all our
members were for you. I woke up and looked around, and there
wasn't anybody behind me!' "

Feinstein beat John Van de Kamp by almost 13 percent. And if
the Los Angeles Times exit polls could be trusted, the overriding

factor in her victory was that many Democrats decided it was time for California to have a woman governor.

The day before the election, Hope Warschaw had begun calling Democratic bigwigs to arrange what she called a "fly-around" on the day after. She said, "We don't want to be presumptuous, but if we don't put this together now, it won't happen." One of the people she called was Bruce Lee, a Van de Kamp partisan on the executive committee of the DNC. As Warschaw told it, "He's one of the people who'd walk up to Dianne in the spring saying, 'Get out of the race! You're just going to be a spoiler! You're never going to win.' " All through the primary he was "badmouthing" Feinstein everywhere. "So I called him up and said, 'Listen, Bruce, I think we're going to win, and we'd like you on this trip.' He said, 'I'll have to see if I can clear my calendar!' He called me back in ten minutes and said 'Yes!'

"He traveled with us the whole way. He saw that she was a star. She was so impressive: people stopped her all along the way. He was a true believer after that trip. He called everybody he knew and said he'd never seen anybody with that kind of magnetism before. He'd never seen such a transformation. When you win, you develop confidence. And ever since then, she's been just fabulous!"

CHAPTER 12

Separated at Birth?
—JAY MATHEWS of the *Washington Post*

Not long before the fall 1990 election, the *Washington Post* ran a column on the California gubernatorial contenders by its Los Angeles bureau chief, Jay Mathews. He took his title from a phrase popularized by *Spy* magazine referring to twins separated at birth, and ended by saying, "I cannot think of any gubernatorial race in the past thirty years with two candidates better equipped for office by temperament, intellect, and experience. . . . The state will be well led whichever one wins. I just wonder why the act of choosing no longer seems to be much fun."

Two weeks before Californians went to the polls, the *Los Angeles Times Magazine* ran a cover story with caricatures of Ann Richards and Clayton Williams. Under its title, "The Cowboy and the Good Ol' Girl," was the question: "Bored with Pete and Dianne? Try Politics Texas-Style." The awful truth was that people *were* bored. And except for the candidates, the pros, and those with a direct personal investment in the outcome, nobody much believed that it mattered who won.

United States Senator Pete Wilson was to the left of his party, just as Dianne Feinstein was to the right of hers. Like her, he had been mayor of a major port city in tough times (San Diego) and by all accounts a superb one. He had supported choice for women, to the indignation of the very considerable and active fundamentalist wing of his party, just as she had infuriated the progressive wing of hers by supporting the death penalty. (A chief aide to one of the big guns in Sacramento was plainly disgusted by a Feinstein ad that showed her being booed at the Democratic party's state convention when she confirmed that support. Imagine a Democrat, this woman said, who expects to get political mileage out of being booed by the

Democrats in convention assembled! Not only had it come to that, but there was compelling evidence that the Feinstein forces had set up that scene so they could use it precisely the way they did.)

The Mathews column was accompanied by photographs of Feinstein and Wilson with mouths pursed exactly the same way and with eyes slanted and heads tilted at precisely the same angle. As Mathews went on to point out, the two candidates were the same age, the same height, and probably about the same weight. They seemed to agree, furthermore, "on nearly every major national and international issue." The copy editor on two long articles by the best political reporters on the *Los Angeles Times* had clearly struggled to avoid using the same title and the same phrases to describe both—and had failed. One title read "Feinstein's Deliberative Style Tempers Decisions," while the other said, "Deliberate Wilson Relies on Experts, Longtime Aides." Both candidates were obsessed with detail; both believed in hard work; both imagined an ideal day off to be one when they could sleep late and watch movies on the VCR.

A subsequent article by writer Garry Wills made much the same point at greater length and in a tone so patronizing it lapsed now and again into vulgarity. (He referred, for instance, to "the drowsy oratory of two millionaire policy nerds" and to Feinstein's opposition to "gay-marriage benefits despite her moment in the pietà pose over Harvey Milk's body.")

The nation had looked to California to discover the future, and here it was. As Mathews put it, "Perhaps all this money and effort has produced the formula for the ideal candidate—the balanced personality and cautious intellect guaranteed to guide any multilayered economy and multiethnic electorate smoothly and efficiently into the next century."

A lower percentage of eligible voters had come out for the primary than ever before, and no one expected the general election turnout to be much higher. It was the most important gubernatorial race in the country because the 1990 census would give California seven new seats in Congress, but the people on whom the burden of choice rested were having trouble paying attention.

Unlike the contest between Ann Richards and Clayton Williams, then, the one between Dianne Feinstein and Pete Wilson would not rest on fundamental differences about the direction in which the polity should go. But it seemed unfair to blame the candidates, as some writers were inclined to do, for being diligent people who had done their jobs responsibly and well. And it seemed particularly unfair to blame Dianne Feinstein, who had surmounted monumental obstacles in the political culture of her state and nation to run the most ambitious race by a woman since Geraldine Ferraro tried for the vice-presidency in 1984.

Republican Senator Pete Wilson was the most formidable obstacle she had faced. It was widely rumored that GOP leaders had guaranteed Wilson $20 million to take on this race, and his campaign staff, led by a core group that had been working with him and each other for fifteen or twenty years, was adroit, battle-tested, and enormous. As campaign manager George Gorton put it, he and Otto Bos, the campaign director, and several other key campaign operatives were "best friends." "People try to divide us sometimes," he said with a laugh, "and it's a joke . . . you can't. I don't remember since 1982 ever having been angry with any one of these guys for more than about twenty minutes." They considered Wilson "a great guy to work for" who "keeps us together."

Since they were running their fourth statewide campaign, everything they did could be juxtaposed to earlier polls and records to monitor their progress. For instance, they could compare how Wilson was polling three weeks before the election in the 234th precinct in Los Angeles with how he was doing at the same time in 1982, while Bos could say, "Hey, George, do you remember that crap shoot in April of '82?" and put things in perspective.

In addition, Wilson had a thirty-four-person staff in his Senate offices in Washington, D.C., plus five directors of senatorial branch offices spread throughout California. He also had access to the staffs of the Republican National Committee and the five Senate committees on which he served, as well as to twelve subcommittee staffs— the latter of which were backed up by the incomparable resources of the Congressional Research Service.

"If Pete Wilson wakes up one morning," Darry Sragow reflected, "and says, 'I've got an idea,' he's got an extensive staff, probably paid for by the feds, who can do the necessary research to get out the paper." Feinstein, by contrast, had gotten through the primary with only two issues people. "[The Feinstein campaign operation] is not even a PT boat," Sragow said with his palms and impressive eyebrows gesturing to the ceiling, "it's a rowboat. And it gives me a certain amount of satisfaction to think of beating a battleship."

Indexed on Pete Wilson's computers were hundreds of thousands of items so that, according to Gorton, "if you said, 'What did Dianne Feinstein say about fishing in Albrook?' you type in *Albrook* and boom, there her quotes come up!" With all those resources at the ready, Gorton had nevertheless contracted out most of the research, which was believed to be important enough to determine the outcome of the race, especially since "this was like a national campaign."

Furthermore, since the spring of 1989, Wilson's campaign staff had been organizing the Republican party and engaging, as pollster Dick Dressner put it, "in those activities which ultimately were the Get-Out-the-Vote effort and the absentee ballot program." Beginning in September 1989, they had gradually merged the Wilson stalwarts in each county and locality with the Republican party leaders to create a unified field organization. Using the state of California as "a big political laboratory," they had experimented in key legislative districts during special elections with strategies for increasing voter participation. They had put what even they called a huge staff to work in pacifying their right wing, doing what Gorton called "a lot of handholding." Negotiating a deal with television producers that saved them as much as $700,000, they had agreed on their major themes—education, environment, taxes and spending, and criminal justice—and honed their messages.

Taught by their polls that Californians were dedicated to "quality of life issues like the environment," and convinced they had a candidate the environmental movement could support, they had even "hired Michael Dukakis' environmental guy" because people had so much trouble believing that Republicans could be good on that issue.* By the time the election came, the party was united and had *ten thousand paid operatives* working for Wilson's campaign.

---

*In the Berkeley postmortem, a member of the Van de Kamp team admitted that, because they wanted all the credit, they had pressured environmentalists into giving the Wilson campaign only five days to decide whether to support Big Green, which everyone then expected to pass. With a longer lead time and somewhat more flexibility, it was clear that Wilson might have endorsed it, dramatically increasing the odds in its favor. Big Green's ultimate defeat

*   *   *

Faced, then, with an opponent whose resources were virtually unlimited and a massive and largely indifferent electorate, Feinstein was confronted with a key question: how could she catch and hold the voters' attention? The obvious answer was through the media.

Although California is fortunate in having one of the country's world-class newspapers, the *Los Angeles Times*, it reaches fewer than one-third of the households in its region. Its political reportage typically begins on page 3, yet surveys suggest that three-quarters of even *Times* readers seldom make it past page 1. Feinstein staffers were convinced, furthermore, that the *Times* was preoccupied with the mechanics of the race rather than the issues.

Vicky Rideout, for instance, who had moved to Feinstein's campaign from John Van de Kamp's to be issues director and chief speech writer, was well positioned to appreciate her dilemma. "The political reporters around here are ridiculous," Rideout said disdainfully a few days before the election. "They poked fun at Van de Kamp for trying to run an issue-oriented campaign, and now they write that the candidates won't talk about issues. The very next day [after a reporter or columnist has so complained] we'll give a totally issue-oriented, substantive speech, and they won't be there to cover it."

Darry Sragow summarized Feinstein's exasperation with the print media: "The *Times* probably won't cover a press conference, and people probably aren't going to read [a story about] it anyway." If this was true of the *Times*, no other newspaper (with the possible exception of the *Sacramento Bee*, which serves an audience of political junkies) could be expected to do better.

Then there is television. Roughly half of California's 30 million people live within range of the Los Angeles media market and a quarter within range of the San Francisco media market. San Diego and Sacramento split the difference, to make four media markets that reach about 88 percent of the voting public.

So what about television news? According to Sragow, "The budgets of the TV news bureaus have dropped dramatically, [and] there's not a single TV news bureau in Sacramento." Since network television

---

therefore created "lasting animosity by the environmentalists toward the Van de Kamp organization."

is a commercial proposition, "the people who run the news media,
whether electronic or print," as consultant Bill Zimmerman puts it,
"are in the ratings business." Together the network news programs
have a rating of 40 percent—if Zimmerman is correct, MacNeil/
Lehrer "doesn't even register in terms of a percentage of the total
audience"—which means that less than half the voting population
looks to television for news. So instead of dwelling on less sensational
developments, the media report murders, rapes, fires, and natural
disasters that capture people's attention.

Therefore, a man paid to reach the voters, as Sragow was, had
a problem. Concluding that "generating news doesn't work" and
observing that "electronic entertainment, in one form or another, is
[our] main leisure activity," Sragow decided that the best time to
reach California voters was at eleven o'clock at night with thirty-
second television ads interspersed between programs and the segments of programs. "It's the only chance we have," he said, and
"that's the reason we have to raise such obscene amounts of money."

Sragow's consolation was that "anybody who's different breaks
through the information barrier more readily [and] a woman's different. In 1988, with a week to go before the election, Pete Wilson
and Leo McCarthy between them had spent more than $10 million
on TV, and most voters couldn't tell them apart." If Jay Mathews
and Garry Wills had trouble telling Feinstein and Wilson apart, Sragow was confident that the voters would not find the problem so
nearly insurmountable.*

The other way to reach voters is through grass-roots organizing,
but because California has more than 13 million voters and twenty-
six thousand precincts, the conventional wisdom goes against spending money on a field operation. To make it work, it is necessary to
target carefully and find thousands of canvassers who will hit the
streets and dial the phones largely because they have faith in what

---

*Eight people out of ten, however, according to a *Los Angeles Times* poll, think virtually
all advertising is a lie. As Zimmerman says, "There's no need to advertise if you've got the
truth. The only reason you have to advertise your can opener is that it's no different from any
other can opener. So you attach sexuality or power—or whatever—to it in the form of a
commercial that tries to make it more attractive to the consumer." Nevertheless, the available
evidence suggests that TV ads work more effectively for politicians than any other medium.

they are doing. So a candidate needs, on one hand, a political organization that believes that grass-roots efforts matter and is willing to find the money to pay for them, and on the other, organizers who believe that electoral politics matter.*

Feinstein knew that an effective grass-roots operation *can* be mounted in California, however, and can make the difference in a tight election. U.S. Senator Alan Cranston, for instance, had been dedicated to grass-roots organizing—not merely for reasons of political expediency but on principle—and had squeaked by his Republican challenger in his 1986 reelection campaign in part on the strength of his support among newly registered voters. That support had been mobilized by nonpartisan registration drives that targeted voters in minority communities.

As recently as 1988, Bob Lawson and Larry Tramutola had put together an effective Democratic party field organization in only three months: California Campaign '88 had turned out over seven hundred thousand voters on election day and contributed to a total for presidential nominee Michael Dukakis that was 2 percent higher than his national average.

Feinstein knew Tramutola's work because he had designed her 1983 grass-roots effort, which Hadley Roff called "enormously effective." "We had two thousand persons out on weekends with ironing boards," Roff remembered, "to sign up people for absentee ballots and to register them, [and] we went door-to-door canvassing."

In the 1988 presidential campaign, Dukakis had not come close enough to give the field operation a chance to make the winning difference for him. Nevertheless, because of California Campaign '88, three initiatives and several candidates for local and state legislative offices won who otherwise might not have made it. So not only did California have campaign-tested organizers who believed in electoral politics, but one of them had already done critical work in a Feinstein campaign.

---

*Ernesto Cortes, for instance, who won a MacArthur "genius" grant for being what the *Los Angeles Times* called "the most effective Latino organizer in the country," believes that elections are for the most part *not* about real politics. To his mind, the one involving Feinstein and Wilson would have been simply a "quadrennial electronic plebiscite" that provoked very little discourse, meaningful or otherwise—a duel between marketing strategies. His thesis obviously has a lot to recommend it.

Furthermore, Carrick and assembled company could read Lawson and Tramutola's twenty-five-page report explaining what they did and how they did it. Working on the assumption that "Republicans invest their money in slick commercials while the Democrats invest their money in people," Lawson and Tramutola had argued that "the real impact of the field operation was the training and mobilization of the five hundred staff, eleven thousand precinct leaders, and thirty thousand volunteers who participated in the campaign." After suggesting how to make such an operation even more effective, they had concluded that the future could easily belong to the Democrats: "It was just the beginning of building a real political organization in California. . . . We had only scratched the surface of a potential gold mine for the Democratic party."

Enter former Governor Jerry Brown, whom Proposition 73 had made critical to Feinstein's political future. The Cranston and Lawson/Tramutola grass-roots experiences had proved powerful enough evidence to persuade Brown to run for chairman of the California Democratic party on a platform that, according to *Washington Post* reporter Thomas B. Edsall, sounded "like the creation of a Philadelphia ward leader."

Observers suspected that Brown wanted to use the party as a springboard to the United States Senate, but that very ambition could be useful to Feinstein. If he helped elect her governor, she would then be well placed to return the favor.

First, however, he had had to build the party, and his apparent determination to do that had been good news to the DNC. Its new chairman, Ron Brown, and political director, Paul Tully, were insisting that state parties submit written plans for coordinated campaigns like Unity '90 in Texas, to which the major statewide candidates had already given both their formal endorsement and a significant financial contribution. After a state proved it not only intended to mobilize its troops but had persuaded its generals to agree on the battle plan and commit their own resources to it, the DNC would be willing to contribute some of its heavy artillery. Since California, in 1990, was the state that the Democrats most wanted to win, the DNC had promised Jerry Brown national money and technical assistance as soon as it saw a written plan it could approve.

For a time, with his careful attention to detail and his willingness to stay out of the spotlight, Brown had not only amazed people who disparaged him as "Governor Moonbeam," but he told Tom Edsall that he had even surprised himself. Elected chairman in February 1989, Brown had begun raising phenomenal amounts of money and had hired both Marshall Ganz of the United Farm Workers and Cathryn Calfo, who had organized for state representative Tom Hayden, to put together the grass-roots operation that would transform the party's fortunes. Ganz, who had been connected with the 1986 nonpartisan voter registration campaigns, had come to Brown's attention as a man whose commitment to ordinary people made him ideally suited to help shape the party into a force that could fight for them more effectively.

The alchemy had seemed to work: in three special elections, Democratic candidates had trounced their opponents by deploying their ground troops effectively and swamping the Republicans with absentee ballots. In just over a year, Brown had raised almost $4 million in a telemarketing campaign that developed a donor list of 240,000, three-quarters of whom were new contributors. His list was even longer than the DNC's, but telemarketing campaigns are expensive, and for reasons that continue to baffle Sacramento insiders, the party's net gain had been only $600,000.

Whether or not in a belated concern over expenses, when Ganz asked to have his monthly contract raised from $7,500 to $20,000, Brown refused and Ganz and Calfo quit. For the first time since the Depression, Democratic registration then dropped below 50 percent of the total, at the same time Republicans were spending millions on voter registration and planning a massive absentee ballot and Get-Out-the-Vote push. Ganz was furious: "The Republicans seem to be the ones who really learned the lesson from what we did in 1988," he told Tom Edsall.

All this had happened by late March 1990.

Using the carrot of national money and the stick of comparison with other state parties that were getting their respective acts together, the DNC continued to push Brown for solid evidence of a coordinated campaign. For months, there were interminable negotiations between the DNC on the one hand and representatives of various candidates, as well as Jerry Brown, on the other. More than once, the DNC

San Francisco Mayor Dianne Feinstein at a rally commemorating her predecessor, Mayor George Moscone, and Supervisor Harvey Milk, both of whom were murdered by a deranged former member of the Board of Supervisors. Feinstein responded with a dignity and calm that won her unqualified praise. (AP/Wide World Photos)

Feinstein celebrating her election to her first full term as mayor of San Francisco. Willie Brown, speaker of the California assembly, and Feinstein's third husband, Richard Blum, appear beneath her right arm. Both men were at once crucial to her political success and sources of bitter controversy. (AP/Wide World Photos)

Legendary San Francisco congressman and reapportionment genius Philip Burton, standing in Golden Gate Park with his wife, Sala, who won his seat in a special election after his sudden death in 1983. Outspokenly liberal Democrats, the Burtons were skeptical of Feinstein. (John Burton)

Hadley Roff, Feinstein's chief of staff during her tenure as mayor of San Francisco from 1978 to 1988, was often called upon to play the role of peacemaker for his demanding boss. During the 1990 gubernatorial campaign, Roff was a key adviser and ran her San Francisco office. (courtesy Hadley Roff)

Feinstein apparently placating Phil Burton, whose motto was "The only way to deal with exploiters is to terrorize the bastards!" (Gaton Photo Studio)

Feinstein and U.S. Senator Eugene McCarthy flanking the Browns—Edmund G. Brown, Jr. ("Jerry"), Bernice, and Edmund G. Brown, Sr. ("Pat"), California's most prominent Democratic family. Both Jerry and Pat Brown were governor, while many consider Bernice, the matriarch, to be the family's political genius. In 1990 Jerry Brown was the controversial chairman of the California Democratic Party, while his sister Kathleen was elected state treasurer. (Tom Gibbons)

Dianne Feinstein with her daughter Katherine, who took a leave of absence from her law practice to work in her mother's 1990 gubernatorial campaign. (Tom Gibbons)

Feinstein with husband Richard Blum and press secretary Dee Dee Myers at a fundraiser in the summer of 1990. (Tom Gibbons)

Feinstein with Assembly Speaker Willie Brown, who was the primary target for the term-limits legislation embodied in Proposition 140, which passed in 1990. (Tom Gibbons)

Attorney General John Van de Kamp, with his wife, Andrea, and their daughter Diana (center). Van de Kamp was the "establishment" Democratic candidate in 1990, but Feinstein trounced him for the gubernatorial nomination with a margin of 13 percent in the primary. (courtesy John Van de Kamp)

Key Feinstein campaign operative Darry Sragow on the telephone. He spent 90 percent of his time fund-raising. His approach is to reach out "to an obscene number of people. . . . You beg and plead, and you'd do all kinds of things you never thought you'd do for endless hours. Because if you don't, you never reach that aggregate figure you need!" (courtesy of Darry Sragow)

Feinstein and primary campaign manager Darry Sragow at an airport stop during a flying trip around the state the day after her primary victory in June 1990. Los Angeles County Supervisor Kenny Hahn appears in the right foreground; Secretary of State March Fong Eu is in profile on the left. Next to Sragow is Basil Kimbrew, a campaign aide. (Board of Supervisors, County of Los Angeles)

Feinstein with campaign chair Duane Garrett and San Francisco Congresswoman Nancy Pelosi, who won Sala Burton's seat after she died of cancer. A longtime family friend, Pelosi was far more congenial politically to Feinstein than the Burtons had been. (Tom Gibbons)

Feinstein with John Van de Kamp, who displayed such graciousness in defeat that she described him as "a class act." (Tom Gibbons)

Jean O'Leary, a former nun who became executive director of both the National Gay and Lesbian Task Force and Gay Rights Advocates. Originally a Van de Kamp supporter, O'Leary organized the "Feinstein 1000" houseparties, fund-raising events for the general election campaign. (courtesy Jean O'Leary)

Robin Schneider, associate director of the California Abortion Rights Action League (CARAL) (left), with activist and comedienne Tracey Ullman (center) and state senator Lucy Killea, whom CARAL helped elect. (courtesy Robin Schneider)

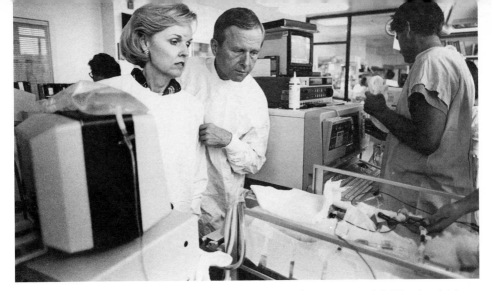

U.S. Senator Pete Wilson, the 1990 Republican candidate for governor of California, visiting a neonatal intensive care unit with his wife, Gail. Wilson campaigned "against type," supporting many issues commonly associated with Democrats; among other things, he was pro-choice and had a strong environmental record. (Pro Wilson '90)

Julie Wright, chair of Pro-Wilson '90, the Republican women's campaign effort designed to counter Feinstein's appeal as a woman candidate. Wright compared Wilson's record on women's issues with Feinstein's and dismissed the latter as mere rhetoric. (Pro Wilson '90)

Feinstein flanked by the Reverend Cecil Williams of Glide Memorial Church and his wife Jan, with Democratic National Committee Chairman Ron Brown on the left. The Williamses were close personal friends of Feinstein and her husband, as well as key political supporters. (Tom Gibbons)

Feinstein with campaign manager Bill Carrick and press secretary Dee Dee Myers. Carrick had run Congressman Richard Gephardt's losing campaign for the 1988 Democratic presidential nomination, and in 1990 he did many of the same things with Feinstein that he had been criticized for doing in the earlier Gephardt campaign. (Tom Gibbons)

Feinstein with the next generation of voters. (Tom Gibbons)

violated its own principles by sending money to California in the absence of an approved written plan.

It was not until the beginning of August 1990, however, that Bob Lawson got a call from Leo McCarthy, who was running for reelection as lieutenant governor, and then another from Speaker Willie Brown, asking him to come talk about the possibility of a field operation in the fall. Tramutola got the same calls. "I said I'd talk," Lawson remembered, "but I didn't want to do [the campaign]."

Included in the meeting was Assemblyman John Burton of San Francisco, Phil's youngest brother, along with Blum and Carrick representing Feinstein. Lawson could recall nothing about the meeting that conveyed either a sense of urgency or a shared conviction that Democrats should put their money into people rather than slick advertising. It gave new dimensions to the phrase "laid back."

"They said, 'We know you don't want to do it,'" Lawson remembered, " 'but would you take some time and think about a plan, given this late date?' " Weeks went by while faxes sped between the DNC and political enclaves in California. Finally, they got together a plan with a $3.7 million budget that would focus on Democrats who voted only sporadically and would deliver four hundred thousand by election day. Nobody much liked it, but it was late and California was a crucial state.

Then the politicians and consultants said to Lawson and Tramutola, "So why don't you guys do it?" Lawson recalled: "We said we didn't want to do it. So they said, 'Why don't you act like consultants and hire the staff?' " On the eve of the election, Lawson credited their capitulation to something that "relates to mental illness on our parts."

Carrick is a true believer in the powers of television, and his experience with one ad that brought Feinstein from 19 percent down in the primary to win with a 13 percent margin only confirmed his belief that in a big state like California, media is all that matters. Cynics view his bias as deriving from the fact that he and Hank Morris got a substantial percent off the top of every media buy. (The standard cut for big-time media consultants is 15 percent. Through a spokesman, Carrick denied that theirs was that high but refused to say what it was.)

But Feinstein was a first-rate grass-roots politician and Carrick knew how to do grass-roots organizing when he thought it necessary to winning. In the 1990 general election campaign, he was basically indifferent: as in the Gephardt campaign for the Democratic presidential nomination, he believed, as the *St. Louis Post-Dispatch* wrote in its postmortem, "that television ads would make up for the absence of organization."

Beegie Truesdale, who ran Feinstein's LA office and has lived with Carrick for almost twenty years, phrased it succinctly: "Dianne has learned that old-time constituent politics probably work against you in statewide politics. Whereas she played those politics deftly as mayor and balanced off those groups, she made a bunch of people mad. In statewide politics, you can't be seen as placating one group or another. Before, she'd have booked herself into every teachers' association, every black group, every gay group. Now she knows it's more important to talk to a broader audience." Lamenting the fact that when media is all-important "you don't get to work with a wide range of people—you don't get a sense of community," Truesdale accepted the loss as a fact of life in modern politics.

Hadley Roff was sadder still that "more money doesn't go into the grass-roots effort." "I may date myself," Roff said, "but I look at campaigning as having two goals: obviously to elect the candidate—but also as an act of empowerment, to bring more people into the process." The hard truth, however, was that "in this age, more people are influenced by television" and "there isn't enough money in most campaigns to do both effectively." The Feinstein campaign staff would therefore use the money they worked so hard to raise almost entirely for media.

In the spring, Jerry Brown had argued fruitlessly with the Feinstein and Van de Kamp campaign teams that they should give money to fuel the party's voter-registration campaign, and by the end of October, he had conceded that since "the collective judgment" of the party "was to go to an 'air war' rather than a 'ground war,' " he could not spend big money on Get-Out-the-Vote efforts. Since his own reputation was on the line, and his sister Kathleen was running for treasurer, Brown had a vested interest in the highest turnout the Democrats could muster. Whatever his reservations, Brown convinced himself that a media campaign was the surest means to that end and assured the press that Feinstein herself wanted every available penny committed to television.

The Lawson/Tramutola effort was not approved until after Labor Day. The final amount offered them was $1.6 million, and because both time and money were short, they cut in half—to two hundred thousand—the number of voters they could get to the polls. A week before the election, they expected to meet their total easily, at a cost of $8 a vote, by focusing on occasional voters in the black community, as well as women between the ages of eighteen and fifty in the twenty-two largest California counties.

Lawson was discouraged. "When I'm being really honest," he said, "I don't see that the Democratic party has anything to offer black people or poor people in this country. I don't see anything on the national agenda—or the California agenda—to give them a reason to care and to work. I know one guy in the Feinstein campaign who's making $11,000 a month, and he's not even a major player." The people in the field operation, on the other hand, were spending fourteen hours a day for piddling wages and "are not really honored by the people who are running the show." Because Lawson felt he was essentially an apologist for "these big-money people," he never wanted to do grass-roots organizing for candidates again.

The Democrats, then, had their belated Victory '90, a coordinated campaign to reach some traditional voters, but at the same time, the Republicans were fighting hard for a larger electoral share of the minority communities. Dick Dressner, Pete Wilson's pollster, had persuaded his colleagues that even if the Hispanic vote was likely to be small in relation to its potential, "you're talking about the difference in this election." In the Berkeley retrospective, he said, "It's the Hispanic vote that's really the crucial one [in a statewide California election], and the Asian vote, because it's bigger."

Since Hispanic leaders knew their votes could mean the difference in a close election, Richard Martinez, the Los Angeles–based executive director of the Southwest Voter Registration Project, was scathing about Victory '90's disregard for the Hispanic male and dubious of the Democrats' electoral chances. As he pointed out, Hispanics make up one-fourth of the population in both Texas and California—

states in which the Democrats have been consistently losing the Anglo vote. In the former, however, they keep winning top-of-the-ticket races because Texas Democrats, although relatively conservative, court and thereby win a substantial majority of the Mexican-American vote. In recent years, California Democrats, by contrast, have lost most top-of-the-ticket races, and Martinez argued that they lose because they are apparently indifferent to Hispanics, despite their liberal rhetoric.*

Feinstein herself did not seem as comfortable with Hispanics as she was with blacks, and they responded in kind. Early in her tenure as mayor, the *San Francisco Examiner* noted that Hispanics were less than enthusiastic about her, and an *LA Times* poll in mid-October 1990 indicated that only half the Hispanic voters would support her.

Nor did Feinstein effectively use the help she was offered. Congressman Esteban Torres, who represents the thirty-fourth district in the heart of Los Angeles, wanted to introduce her at the Democratic state convention, where she was contending with Van de Kamp for the party nomination. Since the convention would be on his home turf and the Feinstein campaign appeared to be going after the Hispanic vote, Torres' offer was like the promise of a bishop's blessing. Because he was an outstanding Hispanic leader nationally, his support would have boosted her following not only in Los Angeles but throughout southern California.

Torres tendered his offer to Jim Gonzales, a San Francisco supervisor and a liaison for Feinstein with the Hispanic community. Gonzales replied, "I think we already have somebody, [but] we'll get back to you." Torres heard nothing further. The congressman had agreed to Gonzales' request that his name be used on Feinstein's letterhead stationery, but when Torres said he wanted to be included in the planning, the campaign ignored him. "Lend us your name," he was told, and what he heard was, "We don't want you to be on the campaign committee or do anything."

Finally, when Feinstein came to a fund-raising event in Wash-

---

*Texas Hispanics are also relatively well organized and forcefully led, and therefore more politically engaged than their counterparts in California. According to sociologist Chandler Davidson, who frequently serves as an expert witness in voting rights cases, Texas is twenty years ahead of California in such litigation, which is useful for the purposes of consciousness raising and often serves as a focus for political organizing.

ington, D.C., Torres raised the question directly: "I said I thought her people were not doing this right and she was probably not aware of it." She said, "Call Bill Carrick." So Torres called Carrick, who said, in Torres' words, "Yes, I understand; we're doing our best. We'll want to be calling on you." Nothing followed.

On a Friday in late September, there was a special event in Indio, near Palm Springs in southern California, that Torres wanted Feinstein to attend. It was a meeting of the National Hispanic Democrats, of which Torres was the co-chair, and in that area, as the congressman puts it, "there was a lot of support for getting Hispanics in the Democratic party to really participate." Here was a chance for the party's standard-bearer to tell these people they mattered.

When the Feinstein campaign worried about how the candidate would get to a scheduled event Saturday morning in Santa Ana, a two-hour drive away, the Indio organizers offered to reserve a hotel room in Indian Wells and drive her over the next morning—"or, if she wants to, we'll charter a small plane to get her there." For weeks, Torres was led to believe that Feinstein would put in an appearance so the organizers announced that she was coming and planned around her. Then, only a few days before, when they called to complete the arrangements, they were told, "Well, you know, we're not sure she can do this." Finally, Torres said, "they wouldn't even return our calls any more."

So Torres himself called Carrick. It is not customary for congressmen to intercede personally in such matters, and it is even less customary for the intercession to fail. Carrick put Torres off again. And Feinstein did not come. Since she kept close control over her own schedule, the decision cannot be written off as staff ineptness.*

---

*Torres and others took things personally that were generic to the Feinstein campaign, as they had been to the 1988 Gephardt campaign for the Democratic presidential nomination. In its retrospective, the St. Louis Post-Dispatch reported that campaign manager Carrick had been repeatedly accused of failing to return telephone calls: "Gephardt's inner circle became isolated from criticism and important details of the operation of the campaign. Gephardt's intimates found they often were unable to get through to Carrick, the campaign manager, when they needed him to nail down an endorsement or listen to a criticism." Some of Torres' problems, however, were endemic to politics in the 1990s. In an article the San Francisco Examiner published two months after the election, Darry Sragow told how the need to raise big money skewed priorities: "I had to constantly turn down invitations from real voters because of the fund-raising schedule . . . the $1,000 limit on contributions, which was in effect for most of the campaign . . . rewarded candidates who spent all their time at fund-raisers,

*   *   *

Asians made up roughly 9 percent of California's registered voters. Los Angeles City Councilman Michael Woo, whom Dianne Feinstein designated to head her efforts within the Asian community in southern California, had a clear and damaging view of the Democrats' problem: "Democrats have largely forfeited the new Latino and Asian voters because the Republicans put more work into it. While they focus on their traditional base, which has a low turnout, they fail to send campaign workers to put up voter-registration tables in the Vietnamese community in Orange County. Voters notice this. The Democrats have done a miserable job of explaining themselves to these people."

Feinstein herself had a better chance with Asian voters than many Democratic candidates, whom they perceived to be too liberal. Asians were inclined to look for candidates who were "not only pro-business, but pro-entrepreneur," and though Democrats "tend to mouth slogans about whatever the 1990s equivalent of Third World solidarity is—about how blacks, Latinos, and Asians ought to be working together"—that line often went over badly. By implying that everybody looks alike, it "ignores the cultural and economic differences between those groups."

Since Feinstein and Wilson were ideologically similar, the differences within the Asian community—between Japanese Americans, Chinese, Koreans, and Vietnamese, as well as between northern and southern California—had little bearing on the governor's race. But a general sense remained that the campaign was unfocused. As Woo put it, "A lot of voters don't believe the real issues facing the state—whether specific education issues, or environmental issues, or the cost of housing and transportation—are being addressed."

Other candidates were making determined pitches to Asians, and since Woo knew that as campaign pressures intensified, September and October would be impossible, he tried to get Feinstein into his communities in July or August. If he could get her to come early, her supporters could build on those appearances as election day

rather than meeting with just-folks voters." And because candidates had to spend 80 percent of their time with people who could write $1,000 checks—as Sragow phrases it, they had to put their energies into "chatting up rich folks by the pool"—they gradually began to screen out problems other than the capital gains tax, which their donors brought up constantly.

neared, "but nothing happened in the early weeks after her primary victory to take advantage of her triumph." Sometime during the summer, Asians had begun to lose interest: "They wondered where Dianne was."

Since Feinstein had sought Woo out to help her connect with the Asian community in southern California, he had every reason to think she might listen to him, but after the primary, she had not found the time. "The work would have been very labor-intensive," Woo said carefully. "She could have come to a banquet of eight hundred people, a large number of whom might have become contributors, or done a half-hour press conference on a subject like immigration, oriented to a large number of ethnic contributors." But she did not come, and consequently Woo, along with the other Asians who had hoped to help Feinstein become governor, had raised only "a small percentage of what I think we could have done" and had scaled back their efforts.

A Democratic candidate who abandons constituency politics is likely to be abandoned by those constituents in turn. This is far less likely to happen to Republicans. Since the GOP is better disciplined and funded, it does not run such a risk of defection. Especially in California, where the Republican party has been dominant histori-cally, its hold on the loyalty of its members is powerful.

Lynn Schenk, a stylish, articulate San Diego lawyer who served in Jerry Brown's cabinet and ran unsuccessfully for local office, learned this fact of political life the hard way. "Democrats are made up of a very diverse mix," she said, whereas "Republicans are much more homogeneous—like Japan or Sweden. In a homogeneous cul-ture, you don't have the problems or challenges you have in clashes between different opinions, values, life experiences, races, ethnicity." Close Republican friends told Schenk when she ran for office that they couldn't support her: "Lynn, you're the best person for the job. But you're a Democrat and she's a Republican."

Many Democrats in San Diego, however, committed themselves to Pete Wilson because he was a friend who had been a fine mayor. To a sizable number of Democrats, "friendship is more important than party," Schenk said, and their precarious loyalties might be expressed in other ways as well. "The big-money Democrats don't think they always have to support the party—they can come and go. If they feel burned out, they'll sit out [an election or two]; they'll feel free to take a pass."

In the beginning, Dianne Feinstein appeared to have a chance to change this dynamic. Since she is to the right of her party, and her political bent and temperament could appeal across party lines, it seemed that she might break the GOP's hold on the faithful by making a pitch to women. And sure enough, when she called on Californians to make history and elect the state's first woman governor, she excited a good many Republican women, some of whom even contributed to her campaign.

Feinstein's direct appeal to women, however, was much stronger in the Democratic primary than in the general election. Whether she thought she had made her point already or decided it was better to downplay her difference, "the euphoria of an historic moment" ran the risk of being dissipated and "Dianne [of becoming] merely a candidate," as Schenk put it. When Feinstein abandoned her special appeal to women, the result was predictable: "When the spotlight dims and you just see the two candidates of the two parties, you find the Republican women going home."

Since California women are not noticeably well organized, Feinstein had few mechanisms ready at hand to help her reach them. Beverly Thomas, who ran Kathleen Brown's campaign for treasurer, discovered that although the state could boast a good many women's networks—both professional and social—they had not, for the most part, had their political consciousness raised.

Prominent Democratic fund-raiser Suzanne Rosentsweig, for instance, was exasperated with women who refused to think of themselves as people who could give political money. With eyes rolling to the ceiling, she recalled "women with $200,000 hanging from their earlobes [who] have told me they don't have $50 to make a donation. It's astonishing: they think of themselves as people who give charitable money—but not political money."

Furthermore, Rosentsweig discovered that it was easier to get women to give to male candidates than to women. Beverly Thomas had also found that "women tend to put something else first—being a Jew, being a black—so to get women to unite behind a woman is really something." For Thomas, who, according to an observer, "busted her butt to do it," this meant that "we've kind of found the people and networks along the way. It took us a long time to find everybody," she added, "and I'm not sure we've maximized them."

To all this fuzziness and backsliding there was one major exception. The Supreme Court's *Webster* decision had galvanized women who had taken their reproductive rights for granted, so by far the best organized statewide women's network with an acutely sensitive political consciousness was the California Abortion Rights Action League. Its northern and southern branches both had crackerjack directors—Susan Kennedy in San Francisco and Robin Schneider in Santa Monica. In 1989 they had honed their skills by winning two special elections and getting a bill legalizing public funding of abortions through the legislature after a twelve-year fight. In 1990, CARAL was organizing a statewide Vote-Pro-Choice-by-Mail campaign.

Wilson and Feinstein each spent an hour making their respective cases for CARAL's endorsement to its Public Action Committee. Consultant Gina Glantz, who helped design the mail strategy, thought Wilson came into the room suspicious that he would not get it and consequently struck his audience as both patronizing and ill at ease. On the parental consent question, he said, "Look, it's simple: you just go to a judge."

Feinstein, however, came in "feeling uncertain but deserving" and fought to win it. According to Glantz, she said, "I'm going to make choice a part of my campaign, and if you don't endorse me, it will hurt my credibility." With five Republicans on its fifteen-member board, CARAL voted to endorse Feinstein.

Robin Schneider of CARAL South is a slight, engaging woman with masses of long, wavy brown hair and an open expression that belies the tough organizer she is, and the 1990 campaign was her first attempt to influence a gubernatorial election. "We're sending out hundreds of thousands of pieces of mail," she reported. "You have to fill out a form, stamp it, and mail it in. Then a ballot will come back to you, you fill it out, and send it back. You can vote in the privacy of your own home and take your time to figure out what you want. Your voting doesn't get derailed if your kid gets sick or you have to work overtime on election day—or something goes haywire!" Although CARAL was supporting all statewide candidates who were pro-choice, it concentrated on the races for governor, lieutenant governor, and attorney general. "It is *very* important to send a message that anti-choice candidates are not electable statewide."

CARAL's polling suggested that almost three-quarters of those likely to vote by mail believed that abortion should remain legal in California, but many did not take the threat to it seriously. Furthermore, a substantial number saw no difference in Feinstein's and Wilson's positions. "Both candidates say they endorse choice," Schneider said impatiently, and "the *LA Times takes that on face value!*— though one of their jump headlines said 'Wilson Opposes [Federal] Funding [for Abortions].' "

Insisting on a more nuanced understanding, Schneider argued that voting, as Wilson did, to confirm Supreme Court justices Bork, Kennedy, Scalia, and Souter was contrary to the interests of women. In her eyes, Wilson compromised his position further when he "highly trumpeted the fact that his vote [on the Civil Rights Restoration Act] broke the tie, killing the chance that women could get abortions as part of their health coverage."*

By early October, CARAL's telemarketing effort had identified two hundred thousand pro-choice voters to whom it sent its Vote-Pro-Choice-by-Mail material. Actress and CARAL board member Holly Hunter cut television and radio spots about voting that subtly reinforced the message that personal freedoms could not be taken for granted. And a week before the election, more than a thousand cheering students turned out for a CARAL rally at Santa Monica College's outdoor amphitheater to hear Dianne Feinstein rally the troops. "Because of Pete Wilson's vote, the 1990 Civil Rights Act is dead," she cried, "and the same civil rights protections that applied

---

*The original Republican on CARAL's board, Daralyn Reed, was convinced that choice was a crucial issue that both needed and deserved bipartisan support, and she had joined in February. Since two-thirds of the board members were Democrats, she was not surprised at the majority vote to endorse Feinstein. To her mind, however, Wilson's support for parental consent did not constitute an anti-choice position. Because she had been assured there would be no negative mailings against Wilson and told there would not be a mailing at all in the governor's race, Reed resigned in late October when a mailing went out implying that Pete Wilson was anti-choice.

today to people of color were not, by his vote, extended to women. I say a state that is 51 percent female can't afford Pete Wilson as governor!" The right to abortion was under siege throughout the country, Feinstein insisted, and she promised as governor to veto any legislation that would limit abortion rights.

Many outside the CARAL network were not persuaded. Calling the campaign "passionless," Margery Tabankin, executive director of the Hollywood Women's Political Committee, wondered how "invested" Feinstein's supporters were. "I think a lot of people who will vote for Dianne," she reflected, "are spending most of their time working for Harvey Gantt because he pulls at them better"*

On the other side of the political spectrum were the Republican women, and a principal reason they began to "go home" was that Pete Wilson had a solid record on most women's issues, including reproductive choice. Their own organizing did as much as anything to turn their support back to their own gubernatorial candidate.

Feinstein's initial appeal was obvious, for instance, to Barbara Stemple, a vice-president at the San Diego Chamber of Commerce and a woman so loyal to Pete Wilson that she not only worked for him for eleven years when he was mayor, but followed him to Washington to work for him there for almost four more. "Dianne is an extremely attractive woman and very smart," Stemple said, "and in the beginning she was the darling of the media." Since the *Webster* decision had made the abortion issue salient in ways it had not been earlier, women felt "a certain identity with a woman: they thought she'd understand." Indeed, even Republican women who were *not* pro-choice supported Feinstein initially.

So Stemple met with three other women over breakfast and made up a list of women who would knock themselves out working for Wilson. They staged at least three events in San Diego, one featuring women he had appointed to key municipal positions while he was mayor—six of whom took the opportunity to tell what they had managed to achieve after the start he had given them. Since Wilson's

---

*Gantt, the Democratic candidate for the United States Senate, was running against Jesse Helms in North Carolina.

strong pro-choice record put him directly in conflict with his party's official position on that issue, the women wanted to underscore his courage and tenacity.

Selecting among her former boss's virtues, Stemple noted that he was so progressive he initially offended the old guard: "He appointed a lot of blacks and browns, and at the time, Republican women were not as broad-minded as they are today. They were an older group. . . . Most of them had never worked."

The organization put together by Stemple and Julie Wright, the public relations director of TRW Inc., among others, was called Pro-Wilson '90, and it functioned as a part of the campaign. With about twenty-five women at its Los Angeles core and comparable numbers in other cities, it provided, as Wright put it, "a great deal of creative input and leadership, and definitive opinions on women's issues," and those involved went all over California proselytizing for Pete Wilson. Wright wrote a speech she both delivered herself and made widely available as background information—a speech that trumpeted Wilson's record on women's issues and picked Feinstein's apart.

Wright pointed out, for instance, that in 1983 Feinstein had refused to sign a resolution commemorating the anniversary of *Roe* v. *Wade*, "and the reason she most frequently gives is that she did not want to arouse controversy!"—an explanation Wright found less than compelling. In 1984, while supporting a judge's decision taking away maternal leave rights, Feinstein was quoted in the *New York Times* as saying that since women had a choice between careers and children, the workplace and the marketplace should not have to accommodate themselves to children. Wright pointed out that "1984 wasn't a lot different in terms of women's issues from 1990," and to a woman who worked for a corporation that paid attention to women's needs, Feinstein's position seemed insensitive at best. As mayor of San Francisco, furthermore, Feinstein had made 280-odd appointments but had increased the percentage of women in jobs at her disposal by only 1 percent. "Do you want to vote for rhetoric," Wright concluded, "or do you want to vote for a record?"

Pro-Wilson '90 not only championed its candidate effectively, it changed the way Republican women looked at themselves in relation to their party and each other. For the first time, they were working together all across California on a quasi-professional level. With a mailing list of thirty thousand names and a smaller, active core of twelve hundred, this new collaboration was both energizing and thrilling. "There has been no infighting," according to Wright. "We are very focused on our piece of the campaign."

The ultimate irony of Dianne Feinstein's campaign was that it raised the consciousness of Republican women whose next step would be to push more of their own number into high elective office. "It's been wonderful!" said Donna Damson, the San Diego co-chair of Pro-Wilson '90. "Now women are being identified by the occupations they hold, by how much they can influence other women, and by how much they can influence colleagues who are men—*not simply by how much money they can give*." As a result, "when it gets right down to it," Barbara Stemple said, echoing Lynn Schenk, "I think the Republican women will vote for Pete, [and] I like to think it's because he's getting his message across."

Within the Feinstein campaign, there was only one major project that reached out systematically to touch real people, and that was Jean O'Leary's Feinstein 1,000—an effort to hold a thousand house parties all around the state to raise money for Feinstein while showing people with modest means that if they organized, they could create political change as effectively as people who could write $1,000 checks. Its publicly stated goal was $1 million, or $1,000 for each house party—a figure O'Leary thought realistic had she been able to get under way in June.

A Van de Kamp supporter with impressive organizing credentials, she had worked for twenty years in national politics and had not only gone to every national Democratic convention during those two decades but had served as a whip at the last one. Her major organizing experience, however, had been as executive director of both the National Gay and Lesbian Task Force and the National Gay Rights Advocates.

After Feinstein "slaughtered" Van de Kamp, O'Leary had called Duane Garrett, the Feinstein campaign chair, to ask for a job, and he "advised her to do fund-raising," claiming that "the party was going to do the fieldwork." Garrett subsequently called Dick Blum to say, "She's outstanding, give her anything she wants," but even though O'Leary was "extremely persistent," because of the campaign's reorganization and Feinstein's two-week vacation, she was not on the staff until August.

The device that would combine fund-raising and political outreach had come to her in a flash: "House parties would be the only thing within the campaign that would look like a field operation." But the north/south problem that plagues California organizing insinuated itself into O'Leary's plans. During the primary, a program called the Feinstein 500 had been organized in San Francisco. Since O'Leary was in Los Angeles and supported Van de Kamp, she knew nothing about it. According to someone who worked closely with her, O'Leary called the San Francisco office the day before she was to be officially appointed, and the man at the other end said, "Who the fuck are you?"

O'Leary can be abrasive—as she herself put it, "People do get pissed off at me a lot!"—but this time she was caught off guard. A series of conference calls between O'Leary, Plaxco, and Blum ranged in and out of shouting matches and finally resolved the incipient territorial dispute in favor of O'Leary and the south.

The plan that O'Leary was able to implement involved working through the Democratic party structure to pull in volunteers who had a "natural affinity" for the campaign. Using the 1988 precinct captains' list, which included seventy-five hundred names, she called on elected officials and contributors as well, but many of the one thousand people who had signed up to be hosts dropped out after they found out they would have to work at it. "We'd given them explicit instructions about how to do it," O'Leary said, "but those didn't always work."

The house parties were casual receptions, several of which Feinstein attended in San Francisco on October 14, the first Sunday they were scheduled, and they continued until the election. O'Leary liked meeting the half-million-dollar target, and she was all the more pleased because her planning time had been telescoped. "The best thing was making a miracle happen," she confessed. "If we'd started in June, it wouldn't have been a miracle. It would have been an organizational feat. Starting in August, it was a miracle!"

Unfortunately for Feinstein, it would be one of the few.

CHAPTER 13

Feinstein says that Pete Wilson was absent from the Congress, which I'd think would weigh heavily in his favor. She even suggests that he usually votes under sedation, which would ensure the youth vote.

—MORT SAHL

Little more than a month after the June 5 primary, Pete Wilson hit Dianne Feinstein with an ad attacking her for advocating quotas. Using a *Los Angeles Times* headline, "Feinstein Vows Hiring Quotas by Race, Sex," a voice-over intoned, "Dianne Feinstein has promised as governor to fill state jobs on the basis of strict numerical quotas. Not experience, not qualifications, not ability . . . but quotas!"

"Quota"—a word Feinstein never used—was a code word, as "busing" had been in 1980, and it was used in the same way to trigger racial anxieties in the 80 percent of the California voting public that was Anglo. It was a scare word for Asians as well, who believed that quotas were keeping them out of prestigious universities like Berkeley. At a time when former Ku Klux Klan grand wizard David Duke was campaigning so effectively in Louisiana against United States Senator Bennett Johnson that even Republicans were frightened he might pull off an upset victory, Wilson's ad was a muted version of the same racist appeal.

It was by no means accidental that the quota ad evoked memories of Willie Horton, the escaped black convict whom George Bush had used so tellingly in 1988 against Michael Dukakis. Larry McCarthy, who designed the Horton ad, was now Wilson's media consultant, and in the ad attacking Feinstein, McCarthy once more demonstrated his skill at visual and verbal shorthand. Adding to his bag of tricks a flair for exploiting sexual as well as racial anxieties, McCarthy had declared, in Pete Wilson's name, that the dirty war was on.

But Dianne Feinstein had put the issue at the center of debate in the primary. Questioning the notion that John Van de Kamp was a better feminist than she, Feinstein had promised "gender balance" early on. She had later expanded that promise by pledging to make her appointments reflect the sexual and racial composition of the state—insisting all the while that those she appointed would have the experience, qualifications, and skills appropriate to the job.

In April, while speaking to the Mexican-American Political Association convention in San Jose, Feinstein had become more explicit, pledging that 25 percent of all judgeships and 25 percent of her appointments to boards and commissions would go to Hispanics. Since by the year 2000, California was expected to be majority minority, Feinstein took the position that it would be unfair for the existing state bureaucracy, which was largely white and male, to preside over a radically different population.

Wilson seized on the issue, and by mid-July, he had run three ads about quotas. One cited an *Asian Week* headline, "Feinstein Compares White Male Political Dominance to Apartheid." At the risk of confusing his own position, he ran another with a more interesting wrinkle, pitting Feinstein's promises against her nine-year record as mayor, when she had raised the ratio of women in jobs at her disposal by only 1 percent. (In an effort to preserve Feinstein's claim to lead and pave the way for professional women, press secretary Dee Dee Myers responded by pointing out that Feinstein had named the first woman treasurer and city attorney in San Francisco's history and appointed two women to the Board of Supervisors.)

In the Berkeley postmortem, campaign director Otto Bos admitted that Wilson was trying to goad Feinstein into responding: "Based on . . . her history, and based also on what we had seen in the primary, we felt that she would probably overrule counsel." The purpose was to deflate the balloon of Feinstein's exceptionalism as a woman and a superstar to make her seem like any other politician. The Hillside Strangler ad in the primary had struck many as both unfair and brutal. As pollster Dick Dressner put it, Wilson's staff wanted to provoke that kind of response again, so that "then we could fight back" against a woman. They were also maneuvering to "dictate the tempo of the campaign," forcing her to respond to them rather than the other way around. They succeeded.

In early August Feinstein hit back with ads that not only accused

Wilson of lying but of using quotas as mayor of San Diego. Her counthercharge proved to be a mistake, primarily for two reasons. First, since voters were not likely to believe that a Republican man would go out on a political limb for the sake of minorities, Feinstein inadvertently called attention to the fact that Pete Wilson's record on affirmative action was not bad. Second, it weakened her appeal to minorities and women who considered the issue specious in the first place.

In part because Feinstein's record as mayor had already called the value of her promises into question, these ads provoked a dispute that could not be resolved: they were the political equivalent of socking the tar baby. The dispute continued for six weeks with Feinstein and Wilson sniping back and forth about the difference between affirmative action, which many audiences grudgingly accept, and quotas, which they howl out of court.

It was hard to believe in the good faith of either side. Their exchanges showed how modern campaigns can take the most delicate problems a democracy faces and, by using code words, caricature, and name-calling, inflame latent passions that make resolution all the more difficult. Senator Jesse Helms of North Carolina, for instance, used the quota issue in the last days of his campaign to win 63 percent of the white vote and trounce his gifted black challenger, Harvey Gantt. As Gantt put it some months later, "We lost the election on a value issue—and that was race."*

Nor did the wrangling about values end with the quota issue. Citing Feinstein's pledge to appoint only pro-choice judges, Wilson next accused her of "seeking to politicize the courts"—a charge whose cynicism was apparent, given that a Republican president, Ronald Reagan, had taken the same position openly, although in reverse, during the eight years of his tenure and, using that standard, had appointed fully half the federal judiciary now sitting.

It was clear early on that no one, certainly not the public, would

---

*The quota issue was never central to the 1990 gubernatorial election in Texas, although Ann Richards said to virtually any audience not waving Confederate flags that her appointments would reflect the composition of the state's population. To anticipate objections, she could coolly point to her record at the treasury, where, by the end of her tenure, a staff that was 55 percent female, 27 percent Mexican American, and 14 percent black would have made $2 billion for Texas.

emerge from this prolonged dispute either wiser or better equipped
to decide on public policy, but it was equally clear that Feinstein was
the greater loser. Her own polls showed that Wilson had gained nine
points in three weeks, with the major defections coming from blue-
collar men and workers over age sixty. An *LA Times* headline described her as "defensive"—a stance a politician dreads like the onset
of boils or a stutter. And registering surprise that Feinstein had taken
so early to the air, the *Times* noted ominously that she had only
$645,000 in the bank as of June 30, while Wilson's campaign coffers
held $4 million.

The burgeoning television ad war followed hard on one the candidates had begun in June by means of faxes they shared generously
with the press. The subject of joint appearances had been batted back
and forth, and in the midst of the fax fury, Wilson had scored by
accusing Feinstein of lingering at her beach house in Marin County
during what the *Times* called "the continuing post-primary lull." (As
Jerry Roberts of the *San Francisco Chronicle* put it, "Pete Wilson
went looking for voters this week, while Dianne Feinstein went after
herons and loons.") She had countered by accusing Wilson of missing
important votes in the Senate, but once more the advantage seemed
to be with Wilson. "Feinstein's absence from public notice has raised
eyebrows among Democrats," Cathleen Decker wrote in the *LA
Times*, noting that aides explained that Feinstein was engaged in "the
private work of raising much-needed money."

All through the campaign and in the postmortems that followed,
Feinstein would be accused of failing to sustain the momentum from
her primary victory over Van de Kamp—a charge reminiscent of
Clint Reilly's year-old complaint that she was too lazy to be elected
governor. Unlike Ann Richards, who came out of a hard primary
weighted down with negatives that reached 55 percent and therefore
started the general election campaign far behind her opponent, Feinstein was three points ahead of Wilson in a June *LA Times* poll. But
while the press itself had trouble keeping up with Richards, the *Times*
called Feinstein's style of campaigning "laid back." This gave Wilson
a chance he fully exploited to reawaken the suspicions her own campaign manager had planted that she was too spoiled for the job.

Even if this accusation were true, however, it was not necessarily fatal to her candidacy, which depended on television. Manager Bill Carrick believed that winning the war of the TV ads meant winning the campaign. And now, since Feinstein's own polls showed her bleeding from the quota hit—she plunged from 45 to 38 percent in only three weeks, with Wilson rising to 49 percent, or eleven points ahead—Carrick thought she had to countercharge. On top of that, he knew the issue of Richard Blum's investments was smoldering, and he wanted to vent it sooner rather than later so that by November 6, the voting public might have forgotten.

In the second week of August, then, Feinstein went public with ads accusing Wilson of accepting more than $243,000 in contributions from savings and loan executives and implying that his Senate votes had harmed the public. Exploding with rancor and calling the attack "McCarthyite," Wilson demanded that Feinstein pull the ads, but they did much less damage than Carrick had expected.

Although Wilson had received more PAC contributions the year before than any other senator, Feinstein had already admitted that she had no evidence of his intervening improperly on behalf of the savings and loan associations. This disjuncture between cause and effect prompted the *Times* to call the attack "a risky strategic move"—risky not only because it allowed Wilson to compare himself favorably to Democratic Senator Alan Cranston, whose entanglements with the S&L business had proved not only clear but politically fatal, but because it squandered the little money Feinstein had left.

Newspapers had begun to publish critiques of candidates' ads, and the handful of voters who read them discovered that Wilson had even voted *against* the S&L industry in two crucial instances. The *Times* editorialized that neither of Feinstein's major charges was supported by the facts and took the occasion to accuse her of exploiting the public's anxiety in order to focus it on her opponent.

Not only was Feinstein dissipating the goodwill attached to the public perception that women are more honest than men, but her charges did not stick. By summer's end, her ads seemed to have had little effect on the voters of California, three-quarters of whom claimed not to know that a candidate for office had received large S&L contributions. A September *LA Times* poll even showed that 35 percent of the voting public thought *Feinstein* had been damaged by the S&L scandal, compared to Wilson's 19 percent.

*   *   *

The controversies that followed were as tedious as they were biting and personal. But if Carrick wanted the attack on Blum to surface, he got his way. Republican party leaders filed a lawsuit against the Feinstein campaign, charging that she and Blum had violated state election laws by loaning $3 million to the campaign. The fact that Richard Blum "happens to be married to the candidate," insisted one plaintiff, gave him no right "to buy the election." The novelty of Republicans charging Democrats with buying an election was for the most part lost on the public, though Attorney General John Van de Kamp jumped to the defense of his former antagonist by calling it a bogus issue.

Blum and Feinstein's bank records were subpoenaed and Wilson called on Blum to release his client list, which he did with extreme reluctance. (In early spring, Blum had rejected similar appeals from Van de Kamp.) For weeks the press focused on little else.

One set of headlines proclaimed apparent or potential conflicts of interest—"Blum's client list links Feinstein to Pier 39," one of the major tourist attractions in San Francisco—while another implied that Blum's dealings were suspect: "Feinstein's Husband Sold Stock Two Days before Value Plunged." Another suggested that Feinstein had a double standard: "Ads criticize thrift fiasco as husband profits from bailout."

Newspapers devoted so many hundreds of column inches to Blum's business dealings that he called a press conference in self-defense. Feinstein herself protested that he was "the most honest person I know," said she loved him very much, and stood up for her own reputation for integrity: "I've been a mayor without a hint of scandal. . . . There has never been raised [sic] any impropriety." Nor, she insisted, had any couple "in the history of American politics . . . made a more complete, forthright, and honest disclosure of everything."

Subsequently Blum complained that he and his wife were enduring the triathlon of politics: "No. 1, we get to see on a regular basis everything she's ever done and I've ever done distorted in the newspapers. No. 2, we get to share seventeen years of our tax returns on an intimate basis with 30 million people. And No. 3, I get to pay to watch all this happen!" The Securities and Exchange Commission

began investigating stock manipulation by an engineering firm in
which Blum was the dominant stockholder, and the gossip and hand-
wringing went on until the election.

Hadley Roff tried to be philosophical. "You have two vital and
engaging people here," he said, "one highly successful in business,
the other highly successful in politics. Both had well-established careers long before they married. They're involved in the vibrant life
of a complex city, and they can't be encapsulated from knowing
people. The mere fact that they know people doesn't mean that they'd
bring influence to bear." Roff, who had served as long in Feinstein's
administration as anyone, considered her "absolutely scrupulous."
But the process of scrutiny had become so severe and the standards
to which politicians were held so inflated that he worried lest all but
"lifeless or disengaged persons" be driven away.

Roff was right to worry about the long-term consequences, but
even in the short run, his candidate was in trouble. "Feinstein needed
the summer to gain visibility, to convey to voters that she is of a new
wave of politicians, that she has a vision for California," said San
Francisco pollster Mervin Field, measuring the damage. "Instead,
you had a wealthy man explaining why he makes so much money,
defending why he sold stocks when he did. It's hard for the average
voter to identify with that."

That spring, after the Democrats had spent upward of $6 million
on what Martin Smith of the *Sacramento Bee* called "a masterful, if
misleading campaign" to defeat two GOP-backed initiatives to reform the state's redistricting process, a prominent Republican had
consoled himself with an old John F. Kennedy quip: "At least we
suckered them into buying a landslide." Now, after a summer of
expensive controversy, Feinstein's own polls showed her four points
down, while the public polls showed her and Wilson approximately
where they had been before it started—they were still statistically
tied—with her party in far worse trouble financially.

The Democrats' two-to-one margin of victory in the spring referendum campaign was small consolation for the fact that by early
September, Feinstein's campaign was running on what Carrick called
gas fumes. The candidate put a stalwart face on it, claiming that she
was doing fine, given that Wilson was outspending her on television

by almost three to one, while running his fourth statewide race to her first. But an aide confessed that she was weary from the demands of fund-raising.

Feinstein had also lost her twelve-point lead among women. According to the *Los Angeles Times*, while Wilson maintained his lead among men, "the excitement of Feinstein's candidacy for women—especially women in the San Francisco Bay Area—has cooled significantly," and Feinstein's negatives had gone from 23 percent in June to 35 percent in late August.

The *Times* poll also found that, by a margin of four to three, voters now disagreed that it was time for California to have a woman governor and by a similar margin, five to four, opposed the idea that the governor should appoint women and minorities in proportion to their share of the population. California's desire to be different appeared to be on the wane, and after the two candidates together had spent more than $3 million attacking each other's integrity, the situation seemed a wash.

In California, neither the candidates nor the press went "a little crazy," as in Texas, but rationality did not enjoy its finest hour there in the 1990 electoral cycle. Although intelligent discussion seemed not only possible but expected, no one could be sure it mattered.

Both Dianne Feinstein and Pete Wilson were as reasonable and well informed as candidates are likely to be: if foreign policy had been on their agenda, they would have discussed missile throw-weights with the panache of experts, and the measure of their determined good sense was that neither pandered to voters' anxiety by declaring that he or she would not raise taxes. To be sure, Wilson accused Feinstein of being a "tax-and-spend" Democrat, but he did not grandstand on the tax issue.* On the other hand, rationality was debased by "spin doctors" trying to put the best or worst construction on matters, depending on the political needs of the moment.

In the remainder of the campaign, Wilson and Feinstein spent

---

*In the Berkeley postmortem, *Los Angeles Times* assistant poll director Susan Pinkus commented on Wilson and Feinstein's agreement that arguing over budget solutions would have been committing collective suicide: "I am frankly blown away that out of all the things you guys have chosen *not* to say that you would have no problem saying it's a suicidal move to talk about the state budget. That is an incredible admission on your part!"

millions arguing in numbing detail about who had lowered the crime
rate more significantly, whose plan to fight drugs was more realistic,
who as mayor had saved the citizens more money, who had raised
and who had lowered taxes, whose sewers had dumped more un-
treated crud into an unprotected bay. Only a fraction of the electorate
had either the time or inclination to follow them.

Polls had shown that California voters cared about crime, the
economy, the environment, health, the aging, and education. And if
voters did not respond to the details of the candidates' records, they
did respond to stereotypes—both about women and men and about
Democrats and Republicans—that were far more likely to influence
their choice between Dianne Feinstein and Pete Wilson than the most
admirably precise accounts of how much they had spent as mayors
on their sewage-treatment systems. Sam Dawson of the Steelworkers
put it concisely: "The education issue cuts for Democrats. The environment cuts for Democrats. Choice cuts for Democrats. Leave the
economy alone: nobody thinks we've got enough sense to balance
our own checkbooks. Every time we talk about it, we get votes for
somebody else."

The Republicans had key issues that cut for them. Wilson campaign manager George Gorton had known "that eventually we were
going to own crime [as an issue, and] we knew we'd end up owning
'tax and spend.' " Furthermore, as the months went by, the California
electorate, like voters all over the country, became less interested in
quality of life issues like the environment, where voters were more
likely to trust Democrats, and more focused on the economy and
fiscal management, where they were more likely to trust Republicans.

To be sure, Pete Wilson ran against stereotype, establishing his
claims in the fields of education and the environment. In 1989, after
campaign director Otto Bos "drove our policy people to come up
with a Pete Wilson platform," his staff had put together a far more
progressive set of proposals than voters typically associate with Republicans, including state programs to provide both prenatal care for
pregnant women and rehabilitation for pregnant addicts, and featuring ads that showed him holding tiny crack babies.

Nevertheless, the stereotypes—which is to say, fixed ideas
through which information is filtered—basically held. The environ-

ment worked for Feinstein as a Democratic woman, although Wilson had a good record on environmental issues. (When announcing the two-hundred-thousand-member Sierra Club's endorsement of Feinstein, political director Claudia Elliott said, "It was a choice between someone who is good and someone who is significantly better.") Crime worked for Wilson, though Feinstein had identified herself with law enforcement from the outset of her public career.

As Darry Sragow put it, "The fact that Dianne's a police groupie allows you, if you communicate it correctly, to take that issue off the table, but you're not going to win against Pete Wilson on crime." Her stand in favor of the death penalty, which meant being "tough on crime," plus her record in San Francisco, could at best nullify Wilson's strong advantage as a male Republican candidate.

Nor could a Democratic woman get away with arguing that she would manage money better during a time of recession, and Feinstein had a special problem. Although she bragged that she had balanced nine city budgets, Wilson undermined her, as Van de Kamp had done to less telling effect, with Agnos' charge that she had left San Francisco burdened with a $172 million deficit.

Like almost everything in California's 1990 electoral cycle, this was a fruitful source of irony because it was Feinstein's refusal to support Democrat Leo McCarthy against Pete Wilson that had alienated Agnos in the first place. And with Feinstein substituting "shortfall" every time Wilson used the word "deficit," Hadley Roff complained, in a typical understatement, that "the management issue . . . is difficult to explain in a thirty-second response."

So Wilson won on the management score, but Feinstein could nevertheless argue that she would do better at protecting people in a crisis. As Sragow put it: "A Democratic woman is going to look out for you. If the ship is sinking, the woman should argue that when the lifeboats get lowered, she'll make sure the average people are protected and the crew doesn't take over."

Feinstein got her highest marks from those who put caring first, who believed that what women have traditionally done is equally important for state governments to do. The last *LA Times* polls before the election showed that voters ranked Feinstein 29 percent better than Wilson on the environment, 32 percent better on health care, and 17 percent better on education.

Most people, however, did not consider those things nearly as important as keeping down costs and going after thugs and thieves. That is what state governments and men, particularly Republicans, were traditionally expected to do, and Wilson got high marks for doing them: in the same *Times* polls, he led Feinstein by 24 percent on the economy, 18 percent on crime, and 18 percent on taxes.

Unlike the other candidates, Wilson's standing in the polls never varied much, and the press was basically on his side. His image held, according to his pollster Dick Dressner, as a man who is "honest, stable, reliable, [and] trustworthy, in an environment where politicians are not really [considered to be] those things." Furthermore, as Boyarsky of the *Times* put it, Wilson did not make mistakes.

On September 25, six weeks before the election, U.S. District Judge Lawrence K. Karlton declared Proposition 73 unconstitutional, thereby lifting the $1,000 restrictions on individual giving and the $5,000 limit on groups. At the time of his decision, Feinstein had only $686,000 in her account, compared to Wilson's $3.3 million, but within a few days, she raised more then $750,000. At a fundraiser actor Chevy Chase handed her a personal check for $50,000. The California Highway Patrol officers gave her $150,000. And John Plaxco, her campaign finance director, said he expected now to raise an extra $2 million. The psychological boost was almost as crucial as the financial.

At this point, the *LA Times* ranked the gubernatorial contest a statistical dead heat, but the poll information was confusing. Three people out of every five thought that "it's time for a change to the Democratic party" in the governor's office. Voters most liked Feinstein's "political philosophy," which could mean nothing other than her party identification: as the *Times* put it, "Nothing else comes close." On the other hand, 64 percent found only "minor" differences in the candidates' positions, and regardless of whom they supported, two voters out of every three expected Pete Wilson to win.

Then, on October 7, in the first, and as it would prove, the only debate between the two, Wilson came out for Proposition 140, the more stringent term-limitation initiative. Some observers called the debate a draw and others gave it to Feinstein, but Wilson's bold move resonated with the electorate. As the *San Francisco Examiner* put it,

"Dianne Feinstein may have won the debate . . . but voters will determine on November 6 whether he won the war."

Again the Wilson strategy had triumphed. As Otto Bos had known, "no matter how good Pete Wilson would be in debate, the media had a preconceived notion that [Feinstein] was better on TV . . . they would always write that she had won. [So] we had to think out the post-debate spin for two or three days . . . [to] capture the momentum."

Term limits by now meant not only getting rid of Assembly Speaker Willie Brown but guaranteeing that there could be no more Willie Browns in California's future. When Feinstein refused to go along with Wilson and buck a man George Will called perhaps "America's last political boss," voters began to doubt her right to bill herself as the candidate of change.*

Wilson's bold move in support of term limits, of course, also resonated with Willie Brown and state senate president David Roberti, who became so wholly absorbed in their fight against the two propositions that Brown told a reporter the Democrats intended to spend $5 million in the final two weeks on mail, slate cards, and radio. (Three weeks earlier, Brown could have gotten Ronald Reagan to cut a commercial against term limits, but he had dismissed the possibility out of hand. "I'd spent so many years vilifying Reagan," Brown said with mock horror at his muffed opportunity, "that I'd have trouble explaining to my mother why she ought to be against term limits if Reagan was against them." Since Wilson had always been "a colleague—a regular, mainstream politician," Brown "hadn't a clue" that he, like Van de Kamp, might run against Sacramento.)

*Feinstein was personally bitter about term-limits legislation that had kept her from running for a third full term as mayor of San Francisco. And although voters in Colorado and Oklahoma also passed term-limits legislation in 1990, she had a powerful argument on substantive grounds. An amateur legislature is much more vulnerable to wealthy special interests and an entrenched and therefore more easily corruptible bureaucracy than a professional legislature with an expert staff. Still, legislative gridlock had so enraged the public that a Sacramento political junkie quipped that term limits were a bad idea whose time had come. A Los Angeles Times poll in mid-October revealed that 53 percent of California's voters believed that bribe-taking was common in Sacramento and, by a margin of two to one, they believed that "most legislators were for sale to fat cat contributors." The recent corruption convictions of former state senators Joseph B. Montoya and Paul Carpenter had only confirmed their suspicions.

His efforts against term limits, Brown insisted, would help Feinstein: "We're providing some of the only infrastructure she's got to
get out the votes." The people who voted against Propositions 131
and 140 were the closest she'd come to a "natural infrastructure."
But as much as $5 million in hard California Democratic currency
would be dedicated in the fall of 1990 to a fight that few people
other than the principals thought they could win.

By repeatedly attacking Wilson for votes he had missed—twenty-
six roll call votes since Labor Day, for the third worst attendance
record in the current Senate—Feinstein goaded him into returning
to Washington. But the political mileage she gained by calling attention to his indifferent performance as a high elected official was
subsequently offset by the spectacle of his enjoying the prestige and
exercising the power of a United States senator.

It was further undermined when Feinstein went back on a promise
to suspend her own campaign if he returned—a reversal she tried to
explain on the "MacNeil/Lehrer Newshour" by saying that since
"the offer I made was well more than a week before he took me up
on a second offer," she had "said at the time, *at least to myself*, all
bets are off then." The explanation fell short of its promise. The *LA
Times* poll showed that more than one voter in five would be less
likely to choose Feinstein because she had broken her promise and
that her negatives had risen to 37 percent—7 percent higher than
Wilson's. John Jacobs of the *San Francisco Examiner* would go so
far as to call the time when Wilson went back to Washington the
turning point in the election.

Then, in a peculiarly tacky ad, Feinstein quoted a teasing remark
about Wilson by Senate Majority Leader Bob Dole as though it were
serious—he said Wilson did better under sedation—embarrassing
more than a few supporters. Dole called the ad "character assassination," while Wilson said it was "the ugliest and most mean-spirited
commercial of 1990." Nicknamed the "gurney ad" because it showed
Wilson being wheeled into the Senate on a gurney after an emergency
appendectomy to cast a tie-breaking vote in 1985 against Social
Security cost-of-living allowances, its effect was remarkably different
from what Carrick and Morris intended. Media guru Bob Squier said
they must have been the only people in the country who didn't un-

derstand that the picture of a man doing his duty from a stretcher would inspire sympathy. Mort Sahl had his usual droll comments: "Feinstein says that Pete Wilson was absent from the Congress, which I'd think would weigh heavily in his favor. She even suggests that he usually votes under sedation, which would ensure the youth vote."

But Wilson gave Feinstein another golden opportunity when he voted against the 1990 civil rights bill, characterizing it as a "quota bill." After the Senate vote on President Bush's veto fell one short of the necessary two-thirds to override, the bill's most distinguished sponsor, Senator Edward Kennedy, flew to Los Angeles to help Feinstein in Hispanic neighborhoods where Kennedys can pull 120 percent of the electorate. Lashing Wilson for his nay vote, Kennedy rang out: "Quota, schmota! All we were doing was returning to what the law was for seventeen years. He made sure he was there to vote no!" Charging that Wilson's vote was decisive, Feinstein lambasted him too: "Should a man be governor of the state of California that says 'no' to equal opportunity, that says 'no' to civil rights?"

It wasn't enough. By now, Feinstein had made so many mistakes that Bill Carrick spoke of her as Lucille Ball and Ronald Reagan rolled into one. Sometimes the Teflon had worked and sometimes it hadn't. "She can say something it takes us a day to get free of," said one of her top aides, "and then she can say something she just gets away with." In an interview on the "MacNeil/Lehrer Newshour," she repeatedly called MacNeil "Bob" rather than "Robin," and too often she confused the names of local reporters.

But the problem was more serious than a few verbal gaffes. Demonstrating that she understood the power of bold image, she had run against form by supporting the death penalty and billing herself as "tough and caring." But by keeping a convulsive grip on mundane campaign details and burrowing in minutiae, she had too often lost sight of the "big picture." This could be devastating to her staff, as a former aide testified when he commented wryly that she hired good people and then drove them nuts.

The hard truth was that Dianne Feinstein had an erratic sense of her audience, so that her political instincts too often failed her. Vicky Rideout, who had moved from Van de Kamp's campaign to be Feinstein's issues director and speech writer, discovered that "often

Dianne wants to do detailed policy stuff on what I consider minor issues." She joked weakly that in the last few days of the campaign, Feinstein would "be dying to do something on the wetlands policy."

A candidate whose issues director thinks she is focusing too narrowly on issues is in bad trouble politically. "I've tried to get her to give speeches that are more rhetorical than substantive," Rideout said, but "she wants to say, 'Here's my growth policy.' . . . 'Here are the four things I think we should do for seniors' housing.' " Rideout argued to Feinstein that she should hammer away, insisting that Californians "won't support a guy who votes for tax cuts for the rich and Social Security cuts for the elderly!" She needed to make *strategic* points.

As a speech writer and domestic policy adviser to Michael Dukakis for two years, Rideout had been here, politically speaking, before. "We tried to get Dukakis to do a populist message," Rideout remembered, "and he didn't do it until the very end," when it was too late to do much good. After being reluctant in her daily campaigning "to use free media to drive home negative messages," in the last ten days before the election, Feinstein "suddenly unloaded with all of it."

The time and place, however, were at odds. During the final days of the campaign, Celinda Lake, who polled for Kathleen Brown, the Democratic candidate for treasurer, noticed that while Feinstein was trying to push a populist message, she was also spending a lot of time in the Central Valley. Early on, however, Lake's polls had "found that the Central Valley was very unsupportive of women candidates, and of Browns, and also of candidates they perceived to be liberal." San Francisco tinted Feinstein liberal in the eyes of the Valley, so that while Brown was spending her last days in San Diego and the Los Angeles suburbs among the swing voters who proved critical to her victory, Feinstein was in the Central Valley working "the traditional strategy of picking up moderate and conservative Democrats who were never going to be there for women candidates."

In the Berkeley postmortem, Otto Bos confessed that the Wilson people had been "confused about the change of messages in the Feinstein campaign: it didn't seem to us until maybe the last weekend or so that they finally had a defining message of what the Feinstein candidacy was about." Once more, he was correct.

*   *   *

Some things were still working for Feinstein: *women for:*, the influential newsletter that had supported Van de Kamp in the primary, now came out for her, albeit reluctantly, "since a 'No Recommendation' would be, in essence, a vote for Wilson." Perhaps the most telling of Feinstein's endorsements, however, came from the *Sacramento Bee*, which had written so slightingly of her while endorsing John Van de Kamp in the primary. She had done her homework, and now the *Bee* could write that she had "worked successfully to overcome her unfamiliarity with state government and to sharpen her analysis of state issues." She had also developed an agenda "as sensible as the problems are severe, and she has shown increasing passion for getting to it."

But the Republicans were simply outclassing and outworking the Democrats. Having discovered that 80 percent of the people the Republican party registered between June and the close of registration in October were likely to vote—and to vote Republican—they had been pouring money into registration since June to get 250,000 new Republicans on the rolls, and they were clearly coming close to target. (In the Berkeley postmortem, one Republican operative put it bluntly: "We gained something like three hundred thousand registrations on the Democrats because so many of their people fell off the rolls and they never went out to replenish them.") The GOP outspent the Democrats by four to one on Get-Out-the-Vote strategies, putting $5 million into getting absentee ballot applications to every registered Republican. Furthermore, former President Ronald Reagan, Vice-President Dan Quayle, First Lady Barbara Bush, and former First Lady Betty Ford were merely the most illustrious Republicans who beat the political bushes with Wilson, while Kennedy was the only Democrat of comparable stature who stumped for Feinstein.

The operative word was "weary." Less than a week before the election, the *New York Times* ran a half-page article dissecting a political ad with a negative message and proclaiming that "swaying voters is less an orchestrated symphony of manipulation than a last-minute improvisation of sounds and symbols." So much for the vaunted expertise of media consultants. Eight people out of ten in an *LA Times* poll said they did not believe ads anyway.

In a final assault on anyone who took politics with a solemn face, comedian Mort Sahl wrote a takeoff on Prop 128: "This is the one they call Big Green. Republicans are not as afraid of malathion as they are of Tom Hayden becoming environment czar. This comes as a relief. I thought he wanted Willie Brown's job. The proposition got its name from the color Hayden turns when he sees Brown in action."

Despite Feinstein's claims that Wilson was dramatically outspending her, Cathleen Decker of the *LA Times* reported that the two candidates had raised and spent almost the same amount of money. But as Sherry Bebitch Jeffe of the Claremont Graduate School observed, Feinstein had not ignited the public enthusiasm in the general election that she had in the primary, and a few days before the election, Jeffe gave the edge to Wilson: "I have not seen her give people a strong enough reason to vote for her."

At the beginning of November, the newspapers were describing Wilson as "suddenly buoyant . . . his testiness gone." Setting up their own operations in key counties to supplement the Republican party networks already in place, his campaign organization, together with the party, had sent out 7.5 million pieces of absentee ballot mail and made an estimated 18 million contacts with voters. Although the Wilson tracking polls showed the race a dead heat three days before the election, newspaper headlines proclaimed that Wilson's campaign was surging, while Feinstein belatedly tried her populist assault.

On the Sunday before the election, the *Los Angeles Times* published predictions from nine experts, every one of whom came down for Wilson. One wrote, "DiFi lost much of her outsider status" and blamed "the excessive particularism of her attacks on Wilson," which made them easy to refute. Another said she "came across as the money candidate, saddled with husband Richard Blum." Yet another claimed that her "positive 'star quality' image faded fast over the summer when her negative TV ads matched Wilson's." Still another observed, presciently, that "white women feel too threatened to ally themselves with minority groups generally."

Only 62 percent of eligible Californians were registered to vote in the fall of 1990—the lowest percentage for a governor's race in history and lower by some 835,000 than in 1988. On election day Democratic registration was down by 30,000 from where it had been in January, while Republican registration had gone up 50,000. After the candidates had spent a total of $45 million on their campaign for governor, November 6 saw the lowest turnout in California history—one out of three eligible voters—the previous low being for the primary in June.

Pete Wilson won the precinct vote on election day by 19,000 and the absentee vote by 247,000. More than a third of the electorate turned out to have made up their minds during the last two weeks, and their anger at Sacramento proved to be potent: not only did over 80 percent of the voters disapprove of the way the legislature was doing its job, but more than 60 percent of those who voted for Proposition 140 and term limits also voted for Wilson.

Sherry Jeffe wrote that the results revealed "voter schizophrenia from the word go," and John Jacobs in the *San Francisco Examiner* claimed that in the end the better team had won, "but barely." Except for Feinstein, however, who lost by less than 270,000 votes, and Arlo Smith, the Democratic candidate for attorney general, who lost by less than 29,000—or 0.39 percent of the total—the other Democratic candidates for statewide offices won their races. The Democrats proved to have a team after all.

Campaign manager Bill Carrick speculated that in the spring Californians had voted their hopes and in the fall, their fears. But in the end, Feinstein's bright red splash against a sea of battleship gray had proved superficial. Her experience as a woman had given her no more spacious or compelling a vision than Wilson's, and the thirst Darry Sragow had discovered in four years of focus groups would not be slaked in this gubernatorial campaign.

Or perhaps it was simply that neither the candidates nor the campaign professionals they hired had ever learned how to talk about much of anything in a way that moved the electorate. As the *San Francisco Examiner* would say about their one debate, "Most of the time, both candidates spoke an insider-ish jargon that made them seem like they have spent the last year in a hermetically sealed space capsule talking only to political junkies, rather than campaigning up and down the state listening to the concerns of real people."

Except for the "grabber ad," the one that began with the shot of Feinstein on the steps of City Hall and the voice-over that rang out "Forged from tragedy!," her ads for the most part did not work. As consultant Pacy Markman put it, her "advertising [was] mediocre. There was a way to take the fact that Pete Wilson took more money from the S&L people than any other senator and make a powerful argument, but they just did a bad job of it. They took a good idea and blew it." According to the *LA Times* poll, a fraction more voters thought Feinstein's ads ineffective than otherwise (46 percent to 45 percent), while 48 percent thought Pete Wilson's did the job they set out to do—8 percent more than those who turned thumbs down.

Though her ads made the point that Dianne Feinstein was competent and forceful, they showed her in so many different hairstyles and clothes that her image was muddled. Her own campaign staff referred to her preachy demeanor in two ads as Church Lady I and Church Lady II, and as A. G. Block of the *California Journal* put it, "She can be pretty smarmy: she can come off as the aunt who folds her hands and smiles while she tells you bad news because she knows what's best for you."

In the Berkeley postmortem, a Wilson aide observed that, ultimately, the media blitz may have made no difference: "What we did didn't move our numbers very much, what you did didn't move our numbers very much, and your numbers kept going up and down and up and down." Bill Carrick lamented that "the real lesson of this campaign" was "that the paid media didn't matter." For consultants who would leave a campaign with almost $2.7 million for a year's work, not counting whatever cut they got off the top of the media buys, this may have been less discouraging than for their boss.*

The strategic thinking that issues director Vicky Rideout had missed in Dianne Feinstein depends on vision, and in the end, although she was a manager of exemplary toughness and skill, Feinstein could not convince people that she had it. Neither did Pete Wilson, but as a man and a Republican in a state that tended to go Republican in big-ticket races, he had the voters' presumption in his favor.

In the minds of many, Feinstein was not perceived to be a real Democrat, any more than she was perceived by segments of the

---

*According to financial reports filed with the secretary of state, Feinstein paid Carrick and Morris $2,698,445 for "professional management and consulting" between July 1, 1989, and the end of 1990. She paid them $6,898,445 for "broadcast and advertising," of which $145,000 was refunded.

women's movement to be a real feminist. Since Feinstein and Wilson
were not only friends but saw things in much the same way, her
attacks on him had the flavor of a game she knew she had to play—
not the reflection of a cluster of beliefs and principles on which
people's lives and well-being depended. Although Rideout found
Feinstein "more committed to fundamental changes than I thought,"
she saw nevertheless that the campaign "didn't have a clear message
working."

And whether a populist message might have played in California,
as many people believed it would at a time of impending recession,
Feinstein was ill-equipped to deliver it. A woman whose income in
1989 was reported to be in excess of $7 million and whose husband
invested hundreds of millions for a dozen corporate clients, including
Bank America, is not ideally suited to rally the troops against the
excesses of the rich.

Nevertheless, Dianne Feinstein had run a remarkably close race
against the most formidable candidate the California Republicans
could offer. With a final donor list of sixty-six thousand, she had
proved that she could raise record-breaking amounts of money and
convince many interest groups to make an investment in her career
that they would be reluctant to write off. According to campaign
chair Duane Garrett, by the end of the campaign she had learned so
much "she really was running as almost the optimal candidate."
When the shouting and hoopla wafted away, then, it remained possible that if Feinstein could learn the lessons of her loss, she had a
shot at an impressive political future.

CHAPTER 14

> *You bet your boots I think it's significant that a woman, a Hispanic, and a black were elected to statewide office! This is sociological change, not just governmental change. It means the doors are going to be open to everyone.*
>
> —ANN RICHARDS, November 7, 1990

Ann Richards' election as governor of Texas reawakened the public's flagging hopes for what women can do in the public world. Liz Carpenter was speaking for hundreds of thousands of women when she said, "Ann is one of us, and we are part of her. We would have crawled to the polls on ground glass if necessary."

Nor was the hope Richards awakened confined to Texas. The day after the election, Kay Mills, an editor in the Opinion section of the *Los Angeles Times*, was listening to the radio while driving to work from Santa Monica, when she heard her say, "Come January, we're going to gather at the Congress Avenue Bridge, and we're going to link arms, and we're gonna take back the Capitol for the People of Texas!" And Kay Mills got goose bumps. People all over the country identified with Ann Richards and saw in her election a promise that their own future might be more spacious and their nation's more sane.

It was Richards' power to arouse and then embody the hopes of those who have been left out that her consultants didn't fully appreciate because they were white men in a society that white men have ruled for millennia. No matter how poor they might have been when they were young—no matter how ugly, thwarted, or despised— they didn't know what dispossession meant because they grew up in a world that people like them had made.

Women did not grow up in that kind of world, nor did black people or brown. They grew up in a world that stuffed them into boxes too narrow to contain their spirits, their talents, and their dreams, and they were told that unless they wanted to be even worse off, they needed to please the men who had designed the boxes. The Texas election was about prying those boxes open.

Dianne Feinstein's race, ultimately, was politics as usual. For all her political shrewdness and impeccable sense of timing, Ann Richards' was not. Women in the years to come will win with Feinstein's politics. The historical momentum, however, is behind Richards: in a country rhetorically committed to equality, the bills eventually fall due, and those most likely to lead the way to a more egalitarian society are the ones who have been left out. The 1990 general election vote reflected the biggest gender gap in history because it was a referendum on a world that white men had made, and the women's vote went against them.

Anyone bemused by the power of the fixed ideas or stereotypes that played so large a role in the 1990 gubernatorial elections would do well to take a lesson from American history. Because they undermined key stereotypes in Western culture, the potent emotions that fueled Richards' historic triumph and helped take Feinstein so near to victory had had to build for well over a century and a half.

For that long, two powerful ideas had been in conflict. One was explicitly stated in that cornerstone of American democracy, the Declaration of Independence: all men are created equal. The other was embedded in the cultures, religions, and folkways Europeans had brought to the newly discovered continent: the belief, sometimes explicitly stated but more often merely assumed, that men are superior to women, that whites are superior to people of color.

In its bearing on the relations between men and women, the conflict between these two sets of ideas was first aired publicly in 1827, when a Scotswoman named Frances Wright began to insist in print and on platforms from New Orleans to Boston that women are men's equals. She also argued that women should act and be treated like equals in all the business of public life. But the position that men could not "protect" women from anything that mattered was heresy in nineteenth-century America: women had a "place," and people found it terrifying that Fanny Wright should want them out of it.

Although she said nothing theoretically at odds with Jefferson's Declaration of Independence, the more insistently Wright pointed out that women and black people should be included in its great promise, the quicker she became the most notorious woman in Jacksonian America. Before it was over, her name was used to frighten even the brave.

Fanny Wright's notoriety derived in part from her refusal to remain a closet theoretician. Not only did she point out the fundamental conflict between two ideas central to American culture, but she was probably the first white woman to make an alliance with people of color, as Ann Richards and Dianne Feinstein would do 150 years later. In 1825, she established a commune she called Nashoba outside Memphis, Tennessee, and became the first woman in this country to act publicly to oppose slavery.

Since that time, the politics of the American women's movements have been entwined with the politics of race, so that in their attraction to the cause of civil rights, Richards and Feinstein were joining a long and vital tradition. Their gubernatorial races finally brought the alliance between white women and people of color into the mainstream of American electoral politics.

For a century and a half, and in the proverbial mode of two steps forward and one back, two movements had been at work stubbornly undermining the cultural forces hostile to them. One was the revolutionary power of a truly great idea—the idea of equality that Jefferson took from the eighteenth-century rationalists. The other was the organizing power of women. Sometimes the two worked in tandem and sometimes they did not.

Following Fanny Wright in her crusade against slavery, for instance, abolitionists like Lucretia Mott, Sarah and Angelina Grimké, and Elizabeth Cady Stanton left their crewel work and tea cozies behind and discovered in that crusade a galvanizing insight into their own deprivation. Fighting for the freedom of the slaves taught them how easily they were dismissed as mere women. But the struggle provided, at the same time, a vehicle by which they liberated themselves from the stultifying constraints on Victorian ladies.

As in Western society for all of recorded history, the economy, along with fixed ideas about women's place, dictated that most women in nineteenth-century America should marry young and that those who could afford to should stay home to bring up their children and shape an environment in which the gentler virtues could flourish.

The gentler virtues were assumed to be characteristic of women and alien to men, whose role was to rule over the world, the state, and the family—preferably, though not necessarily, in that order. Women were the nurturers, to be protected in this necessary if secondary role by men, who acted in their interests even when they seemed to be undermining or even violating them. To question these arrangements—to point out the conflict between ideas fundamental to American culture—was to let oneself in for a great deal of trouble.

Fanny Wright began questioning these arrangements in 1827 and scandalized the country by warning that if women were kept in a state of mental and political bondage, the republic would fall far short of its promise: "Let women stand where they may in the scale of improvement, their position decides that of the race." Not long before she died in 1857, Wright argued that justice would come only when "the two persons in human kind—man and woman—shall exert equal influences in a state of equal independence."

Fanny Wright was thought to be so radical, however, that only people with the courage and strength of Quakers were willing to make common cause with her, and women like the Grimkés and Elizabeth Cady Stanton were very little less so. Their identification with the causes of women and black people took them out of mainstream American society altogether and made them prophets, visionaries, or lunatics, depending on one's perspective.

Ann Richards and Dianne Feinstein are none of those things. They are mainstream politicians, but when they came of age, although many things had changed for women, true equality, or justice in Fanny Wright's sense, remained a chimera. For every inch women had won, they had had to struggle with almost mindless tenacity, and over the course of many years. For generations, for instance, women had worked to gain the most elementary political rights. From 1870 to 1910—a period of forty years—they had conducted 480 campaigns in thirty-three states to get the issue of female suffrage before the voters. Of these campaigns, only seventeen resulted in actual referendum votes, and of those, only two succeeded. By the time the Nineteenth Amendment passed in 1920, American women had been working for the vote for seventy-two years.

The vote had done less for women than many who gave their lives for it had hoped: by the time Richards and Feinstein ran for governor of their respective states, women were still nowhere near the "state of equal independence" that Fanny Wright had posited as the fundamental condition of a just society. But economic and social change had by now undermined the informing idea about woman's place that had shaped the women of Richards and Feinstein's generation as it had their ancestors for millennia.

That story can be told by statistics. More than half of all marriages now end in divorce, which leaves women who have spent years as homemakers and tenders of children at a radical professional and financial disadvantage. According to Lenore J. Weitzman's *The Divorce Revolution* (1985), a Michigan study that included five thousand families across the nation discovered that men's economic position improved 17 percent in the seven years following divorce, while women's declined by 29 percent.

In part because of their disadvantage after divorce, women are much poorer than men in every racial or ethnic category. In 1989, black men made 75 percent of what white men made; white women made 68 percent; Hispanic men, 66 percent; black women, 62 percent; and Hispanic women, 56 pecent. A male high school graduate who worked year-round and full time earned, on average, more than a woman with comparable work experience who had graduated from college. The same male high school graduate earned 52 percent more than his female counterpart. While 10 percent of all families are poor, almost a third of those headed by women are poor. While 15.5 percent of all families with children are poor, nearly 43 percent of those headed by women are poor.

Most working women were clustered in a few low-status occupations dominated by women. But 1990 Labor Department statistics confirmed that even a woman who has the same job as a man gets less money: a woman department head averaged $458 a week to a man's $698; a woman assembly worker, $236 to a man's $366; and even a female nurse made $564 to a male nurse's $629.

Never before in American history had women's disadvantage been spelled out so clearly, and their burden was further illuminated by statistics about rape: more than 100,000 women in the United States in 1990 reported being raped, which meant that the rate of sexual assaults, according to a Senate Judiciary Committee study, was increasing four times faster than the overall crime rate. And the states that led the nation in rapes were California, with 12,413, and Texas, with 8,427.

Statistics like these explain why so many women no longer trust men and why they cast a disproportionate number of their votes for women, who they think are more likely to understand their problems and address them. Although Ann Richards was identified with the women's movement and Dianne Feinstein was not, according to the exit polls, Feinstein got almost the same percentage of the women's vote—58 percent to Richards' 59 percent.

Women expect a woman in power to do what she can to improve the lot of women and children because she is more likely to know from personal experience that it is not true that people get ahead because they work harder and better. As Mayor Carrie Saxon Perry of Hartford, Connecticut, puts it: "Women don't subscribe to the bootstrap theory. Everybody who's made it had subsidies. The government gives them to Chrysler, to the farmers, to the S&Ls, to Saddam Hussein. . . . But when you're talking about the poor, [subsidy] becomes a bad word." A world in which Hispanic women average little more than half what white men make is a world that is skewed, and not by the weaker group in the equation. Women want power because they want control over their own lives.

So Ann Richards and Dianne Feinstein are part of a bridge generation of women, rooted in ancient expectations and extending into the twenty-first century, when technology and economics are likely to have transformed patterns of mating, child rearing, and professional development even further. Meanwhile, men still call most shots in the world of work, and old habits and ideas about what men and women properly do still dictate that a woman who marries and has a family shoulders an overwhelming portion of the responsibility for her home and children. All this means that heterosexual women who want to live full lives—who want to love men and give birth and do work they can be proud of—have far less power over their own lives than men who want no more. Their frustration at this structural injustice fuels the votes that women give to other women.

CHAPTER 15

I want to teach people how they can take their private pain, their private hopes, their private aspirations, and translate those into public issues which can qualitatively improve their lives and the lives of their children.
—ERNESTO CORTES to Bill Moyers

If the first woman God ever made could turn the world upside down all alone, these women together ought to be able to get it rightside up again!
—SOJOURNER TRUTH

On November 7, 1990, Dianne Feinstein told her husband, "The good news is we raised the money; the bad news is we lost." At about the same time, in Austin, Texas, Liz Carpenter complained to a reporter: "I hope Ann will move into campaign reform right away! It is obscene that this race should take $48 million. It's obscene that it should be this hard and this battering."

The 1990 Texas and California governor's races broke even their own states' records for high-spending campaigns, Texas at just over and California at just under $50 million. Pete Wilson spent $23.9 million and Dianne Feinstein $19.5 million, which the *Los Angeles Times* put at approximately $5.60 per vote. This far outdistanced the Bradley/Deukmejian race in 1985–86, which costed out at $3.04 per vote. Adding John Van de Kamp's $5 million, the figure is higher still. In Texas, each general election vote cost $12.85.

According to census figures from 1989, $1,416 would raise a person out of poverty, so the $100 million that the gubernatorial races in Texas and California cost could have brought 70,621 people to a level where they could live adequately and therefore with dignity.

After the 1990 elections, in which women had proved that they could raise as much money as men, observers began to talk more seriously about reforming the system. In Texas nothing had been done to reform campaign finance since 1962, when an ashen Don Yarborough, the liberal Democratic candidate for governor, emerged from a meeting with Houston oil men and told a reporter, "Anybody who can get elected governor of this state doesn't deserve it."

Only time could tell whether Ann Richards had given away the store in order to raise enough money to win her chance to live in the Mansion. But reform would mean that the people willing to engage in politics would not have to spend virtually all their time, as Darry Sragow put it, "chatting up rich folks by the pool." In early January 1991, the *San Francisco Examiner* published an article he wrote with John Jacobs, arguing that "in the marketplace of California politics, the price of office—and access—is out of control. . . . Wholesale change is the only hope for our bankrupt democracy."

Ann Richards won by fewer than one hundred thousand votes, and Dianne Feinstein lost by fewer than three hundred thousand in a much larger field. Since there was a Libertarian candidate in Texas who polled a small but sufficient fraction of the vote, Richards got less than 50 percent, as did Pete Wilson.

These were therefore close and costly elections that a slightly different allocation of funds, a handful of telephone calls, a freak accident, or a sensational TV ad could have sent the other way, and therefore, sweeping statements about what won or what lost them would be out of place. Neither Richards' nor Feinstein's campaign will go down in history as a model for the young or innocent. Both have been bitterly criticized, even by their partisans, and Richards came from so far behind to win by so little that Republicans could console themselves that they were the victims of a miracle.

Still, Kirk Adams, who put together the Richards field operation, finds the virtue of her narrow victory in the fact that everyone could know that his or her bit counted. Even though her opponent *did* shoot off the lower half of his body, without the hard work and persistence of a long list of people, Ann Richards would not have won. As Richards herself puts it, Democrats will always lose the game of competing dollar for dollar with Republicans, "and so we have got to maximize what our strength is, and that's people." The knowledge so many Texans have that they mattered to Ann Richards' victory makes their investment in politics deeper and their continuing interest all the more likely.

Since Feinstein's campaign spent most of its $20 million on media, the California equivalent of Kirk Adams' list is not only very much shorter but heavily weighted toward the wealthy: according to Sragow, Feinstein averaged twenty-five fund-raisers a week and spent roughly 80 percent of her time attending them. What she lost by not involving large numbers of people in a field operation can be suggested not only by what Richards did in Texas but by Paul Wellstone's insurgent campaign for the United States Senate from Minnesota—a state, to be sure, a mere fraction of California's size.

The Wellstone example is germane, however, because he first engaged the voters of Minnesota through a truly imaginative ad campaign. Wanting to "get people smiling about politics," he found an agency called Northwoods Advertising that donated its creative skills to design his television spots. After captivating the electorate with some of the most delightful ads ever shown in an American political campaign, Wellstone volunteers called seven hundred thousand voters in only four days to get them to the polls. Because he had galvanized people into believing that ordinary folks could do something about politics and convinced them that he as their agent was warm and trustworthy, on election day, Wellstone defeated an incumbent senator who outspent him seven to one. The California Democrats' coordinated campaign, Victory '90, by contrast, called no more than two hundred thousand voters, and the Feinstein campaign called none at all.

According to the Election Data Service, approximately 62 percent of the voting-age population in both Texas and California was registered to vote in November 1990, but the turnout in California was somewhat higher: 36 percent of California's voting-age population actually went to the polls, or 58 percent of the registered voters. The comparable numbers in Texas were 31.3 and 50.5 percent. Miserably low in themselves, these figures are embarrassing when compared with almost any other industrial democracy.*

*The Texas figures, nevertheless, are significantly higher than in gubernatorial elections between 1974 and 1986 that did not coincide with presidential elections: average turnout in

Still, the exit polls tell a fascinating tale. The California electorate
was much more prosperous than its Texas counterpart—40 percent
made $50,000 or over, compared to 28 percent in Texas—and it
was significantly more liberal. Only 29 percent of California's voters
called themselves conservatives, compared to 42 percent in Texas,
and 23 percent called themselves liberals, compared to 14 percent in
Texas. California's electorate, furthermore, included almost twice as
many feminists and more than two and a half times the number of
union members. Texans were slightly more likely to be married and
employed and Californians significantly more likely to be retired (21
percent to 16 percent). In California 80 percent of the electorate was
white, compared to 76 percent in Texas. There were 6 percent more
Catholics in California (28 percent) and 10 percent more white Prot-
estants in Texas (56 percent).

Given the wealth of California voters, Feinstein's middle-of-the-
road position had a wide appeal, and she got a slightly larger proportion of the voters who made over $50,000 than Richards (47
percent to 45 percent). Richards got 17 percent more of the union
vote, 5 percent more of the feminist vote, and 7 percent more of
those over age sixty than Feinstein. Richards also got more than
twice the number of new voters, with 65 percent compared to Feinstein's 30 percent. It is not only a telling irony that the more liberal
woman was elected governor in the more conservative state, but a
comment on the skill with which the Richards campaign appealed
to voters.

In California, 54 percent of the voters thought abortion should
always be legal, compared to 32 percent in Texas. Among Feinstein's
voters, abortion ranked third in order of importance, while among
Richards' it ranked ninth, and though 13 percent of Feinstein's voters
named abortion as one reason for their vote, only 8 percent of Richards' voters listed it. Since Richards' opponent, however, was anti-
choice, she won 18 percent of the GOP vote, compared to Feinstein's
13 percent, and many of those switch-over voters are likely to have
been pro-choice women.

those elections was 26 percent. According to sociologist Chandler Davidson, never in the
twentieth century has a majority of Texas' voting-age population gone to the polls in a single
election.

These figures can underestimate the power of the abortion issue. Among other things, they fail to suggest the political energy, sophistication, and commitment of the pro-choice movement. Both the Texas Abortion Rights Action League and the California Abortion Rights Action League worked hard and effectively to get sympathetic voters to the polls, and the National Abortion Rights Action League contributed to both campaigns. The women who staff these organizations know how to put the right combinations of people together, and benefits come from their connivings that cannot be measured with numbers.

For the foreseeable future, abortion rights will play a significant role in American politics—and particularly in women's races. Joan Finney, the anti-choice Democratic woman who was elected governor of Kansas in 1990, is likely to prove the exception to the rule that Democratic women running statewide who have a real chance of being elected will typically be pro-choice. Since most organized anti-choice women have gone into the Republican party, to the dismay of many old-line Republican women, Democratic activists are for the most part strongly pro-choice. EMILY's List, the highly successful national women's PAC that gave over $400,000 to Richards, will not endorse a woman who is anti-choice, and neither will a number of other women's PACs and organizations. The Supreme Court decision in *Roe* v. *Wade* will go on being a cornerstone of the women's movement because it gave women more control over their lives, and that is the direction toward which we move, albeit slowly.

The three most important issues that worked for Ann Richards were experience, education, and ethics, in that order. For Feinstein, the three most important were the environment, the need for change in government, and abortion.

Richards believed her principal advantage over Feinstein was that she had already run two statewide races and knew almost exactly what to expect. A woman who has been seriously considered as a vice-presidential nominee, however, learns to aim high, and Feinstein never considered running for a lesser office than governor.

Richards' success in using the state treasurer's office to demonstrate that she was fiscally conservative and knew how to manage money contrasted to Feinstein's disadvantage, when her opponents raised the question of San Francisco's finances when she stepped down as mayor. Richards' strategy has already inspired other women. Mary Landrieu, whose father was mayor of New Orleans, is now treasurer of Louisiana, and Kathleen Brown, whose father and brother were both governor of California, was elected state treasurer in 1990. Women—and particularly Democratic women—will be problematic as top-of-the-ticket candidates until they demonstrate their financial acumen beyond any question, but if Brown and Landrieu succeed in doing that as treasurers of their respective states, their political futures can be spun gold.

The minority vote has played a large role in Democratic victories since the days of Franklin Roosevelt, but Republicans have begun to court it. In Texas, blacks made up 13 percent of the electorate, and Richards won 90 percent of their vote. In California, blacks were 9 percent of the electorate, and Feinstein won 86 percent of their vote. In Texas, blacks voted maybe 1 percent less than their share of the population, while California blacks are so well organized and politically astute that their percentage of the vote was 2 percent higher than their percentage of the population. Since exit polling is somewhat less than scientific, it is fair to say that Richards and Feinstein did about as well as they could in the black community, and since a majority of blacks are liberal on economic and social issues, they are likely to cast the bulk of their votes for Democrats in the foreseeable future.

This is not true among Hispanics. In both states Hispanics make up roughly 25 percent of the population, although since many are children and some are illegal, they are a smaller portion of the eligible voters. The *Los Angeles Times*, for instance, puts the Hispanic share of the voting-age population in California at 13 percent, and fewer still are registered. In Texas, the Hispanic share of the 1990 general election vote was 9 percent and Richards got 71 percent of it. In California, the Hispanic share of the vote was 5 percent, and Feinstein got only 53 percent of it.*

---

*The Southwest Voter Research Institute did exit polls in both states that gave higher figures than the network exit polls for the Democratic gubernatorial candidates' share of the vote, with Richards at 77 percent and Feinstein at 65 percent.

Both women were running against men who worked hard to get the Hispanic vote, and in California both the Republican party and the Wilson campaign did "special outreach" and hard-nosed registration in the Hispanic and Asian communities. Wilson pollster Dick Dressner knew that the Hispanic vote was crucial to his candidate: in the Berkeley postmortem, he said, "If our vote was reduced from 50 percent to 20 or 25 percent among Hispanics, Pete Wilson loses." Wilson had gone to the trouble of trying to learn Spanish, and as mayor, assemblyman, and United States senator had come through time and again for his Hispanic constituents. Clayton Williams spoke ebullient Spanish and spent a good deal of money in south Texas.

Since Republicans are more conservative than Democrats, and since Hispanics are more likely to be conservative on social issues, especially abortion, Republicans are bound to get a higher percentage of the Hispanic vote. Hispanic men also pose a problem for Democratic women elected officials, and vice versa, and the macho factor is an element of political life that women will be obliged to work into their calculations.

As Congresswoman Maxine Waters points out, however, Gloria Molina, among others, has made an impressive career in Los Angeles politics, demonstrating that the right appeal can be effective. And Ann Richards and Unity '90 went after the Hispanic community with far more determination and skill than Dianne Feinstein and Victory '90 did. Without their vote, Richards would not have won. If California Hispanics had voted in the percentage that Texas Hispanics did, and Feinstein had gotten Richards' percentage of their vote, she would have come much closer to beating Pete Wilson.

The major question in constituency politics, of course, is how to reach and mobilize various groups. Although blacks reach their constituency primarily through the church, no institution in the Hispanic community is so nearly the focus and center of its partisan political activity. According to Speaker Willie Brown, 90 percent of California blacks belong to a church, and "in the real black churches in California, they just tell you up front how to vote. The minister publishes a slate card, the politician [running for office] speaks from the pulpit, and the ushers will show you how the minister voted." The strong-arm approach may scandalize a good many people, and black politicians such as Maxine Waters may have contempt for that brand of politics. The plain fact, nonetheless, is that politicians who can deliver votes have a lot more clout than those who cannot.

Anglo and black politicians tend to blame Hispanics and Hispanics tend to blame Anglo and black politicians both for their low rates of voter registration and their low turnout. Whatever the merit of the respective arguments, the Texas Hispanic community is clearly more adept at the game of electoral politics than its counterpart in California.

Los Angeles–based Richard Martinez of Southwest Voter, however, points out that a Democratic candidate at the top of the ticket can win in California with 75 percent plus of the Hispanic vote, as Senator Alan Cranston proved in 1986. When voter registration drives like the ones conducted that year target Hispanic communities, and when candidates like Cranston give Hispanics something worth voting for, both sides end up relatively satisfied. (Cranston ultimately drew 120,000 newly registered voters to the polls—a decisive margin since he defeated his challenger by less than 105,000 votes.)

In 1990, however, Antonia Hernandez, president and general counsel of California's Mexican American Legal Defense and Educational Fund, said, "We're going out there and telling the community to vote, and they say, 'What for? They're not talking to me!'" Like Congressman Esteban Torres, neither Martinez nor Hernandez could see that Feinstein was doing or saying anything that engaged the Hispanic community. Although Tony Zamora, a Los Angeles lawyer who represented her among Hispanics, believed that Feinstein wanted to reach his community, the decision was made to divert the available resources to media.

Ann Richards, by contrast, sought Henry Cisneros' endorsement and used it effectively. She chose Lena Guerrero to be her political director in the primary, and when Guerrero moved to co-chair Unity '90 in the general election, she took Richards' interests with her. Mary Beth Rogers, Richards' campaign manager in the general election, had a well-known commitment to Ernesto Cortes, whose influence extended to parts of the Hispanic community that even Cisneros could not touch and whose networks reached deep into the black community as well.

Unlike Richards, Feinstein directed none of her TV ads to Hispanics, nor did she run anything comparable to the Richards ads celebrating the endorsements of Barbara Jordan and Henry Cisneros. Not only did she forfeit her chance to have Esteban Torres appeal on her behalf to the Democratic convention and the Hispanic community, but according to both Torres and Martinez, she pursued a strategy that slighted Hispanics in areas of the state like the Central Valley and the coast, failed to put Hispanics in key positions in her campaign, and made a minimal investment of finance and staff in the Hispanic community.

Writer Juan Sepulveda complained that Richards went mainly to upscale places in Hispanic San Antonio, rather than into the heart of the barrios, yet Feinstein scarcely went at all. Although Nancy Clack noted that south Texas had the lowest turnout of any region in the state—39.3 percent, compared to 58.8 percent in 1988—and concluded that Richards' margin of victory would have been more substantial had turnout there been higher, Richards still got over 60 percent of the south Texas vote. Her margin of victory among urban Hispanics was clearly higher.

The Asian community was more significant in California than in Texas, and while the Wilson campaign and the Republican party targeted that community, Feinstein responded to it much as she did to Hispanics. Los Angeles City Councilman Michael Woo lamented Feinstein's failure to court Asians who not only would have backed but contributed to her. As a key Feinstein staff member explained, there is a time-consuming protocol a candidate must observe if she wants to raise money in the Asian community, and he admitted that his boss was not willing to spend the time. Since, as Councilman Woo bemoaned, Feinstein and the Democratic party did no serious voter registration among Asians and little to make Democrats attractive to them, she won their vote by a bare 52 percent majority.

Minority voters and women in Texas believed that Ann Richards' campaign was about opening doors. Dianne Feinstein convinced only women and blacks. Although Feinstein pledged proportional representation, she did not persuade most minorities that she understood exclusion and was passionately committed to ending it. In light of the scant attention she paid to other minority groups, Feinstein's extraordinary rapport with blacks came to seem a mere temperamental attraction. After the election, she told Dan Walters of the

Sacramento Bee that the "party can't depend on minority votes to pull it through a general election." Since Feinstein had done relatively little to win those votes, Richard Martinez of Southwest Voter was only one of many observers who were skeptical about her electoral prospects in the future.

Other lessons can be learned from the 1990 Texas and California elections and from the experiences of the two women who ran for governor. One has to do with shaping the message. The central problem in a modern campaign in such big states is how to communicate with so disparate an audience, and both Richards and Feinstein were anxious for voters to perceive them as knowing enough about state government to hold the top job.

They needed to convince the editorial boards of newspapers, as well as the voters at large, of their competence, but these they would address in traditional ways: each encounter would be something like an oral examination for a doctoral degree. Although it was an experience unlikely to be pleasant, the ground rules were nonetheless familiar and clear. Demonstrating competence to a huge public through television sound bites, however, was a relatively new problem, and no one was certain how to do it most effectively.

The stump speech presented a challenge that lay somewhere between addressing these two kinds of audiences but was more nearly linked to the thirty-second ad. In this category, Richards is at the head of any class: with her, political oratory is performance art. And since she considers it her job to communicate with people, if they do not understand what she is trying to say, she considers that her fault. In the last six weeks of the campaign, she was invariably at her best on the stump.

During the 1990 electoral cycle, Feinstein was sometimes on and sometimes off, and when she was off, it was frequently because she believed she had to prove her expertise to her audience. Since the polls showed that the public, by a wide margin, held her to be the least knowledgeable candidate, she thought that to convince voters she knew her stuff, she had to bring up her wetlands policy or spell out her proposals for seniors. That was a mistake.

Politicians from other, albeit smaller, states can prove excellent models. Senator Tom Harkin of Iowa, for instance, is the first Democrat ever to be reelected to the U.S. Senate from that state, and his success comes in part from knowing how important it is to express ideas in clear, vivid, and therefore memorable ways. Convinced, like pollster Harrison Hickman, that "people vote for people," not for platforms, Harkin insists that they vote "with their hearts, and only, as a distant second, with their minds." This does not mean that ideas are unimportant, but rather that political discourse during elections is not primarily about the abstract elaboration of ideas. It is about finding ways to convey ideas and convictions all at once.

An outspoken liberal in a conservative state, Harkin wins because "it's not how you vote, it's how you *translate* your vote into values people understand." An example of his style is the succinct maxim: "It's hard for a poor kid to pull himself up by the bootstraps when some rich kid's stolen his boots." Harkin insists, furthermore, that confidence is also crucial: "*Never* defend yourself: *always* attack. Always define *them*."

Suzanne Coleman, who has written speeches for Ann Richards for years, was asked how she managed to convey the clarity and verve of the Richards style—how Richards convinced the state association of school superintendents, for instance, that she knew what she was talking about without losing herself in detail and boring her audience. (Like ballet, the work cannot show, but if it isn't there, the performance will not come off.)

"You don't have to do a litany of detail about the issues," Coleman answered, "a few simply chosen declarative sentences indicate that [mastery] nicely. I think people look to political leaders to reduce complex issues to memorable terms. . . . But as cynical as we've become about politics, I think people want to give their leaders the benefit of the doubt. They're perfectly willing to believe you know a great deal about what you're talking about or you wouldn't be standing up there. You don't have to prove it."

Coleman was always looking for the perfect line that gets its point across in a few simple words, like Richards' frequently repeated "If they do the crime, they'll do the time." Humor is particularly effective. During the Christmas season a few weeks after her election, for instance, Richards made a contribution to the art of political humor, if not to strengthening the First Amendment. Approached by civil libertarians worried about the crèche under the capitol dome,

Richards said: "Oh, y'all, let's not make a big fuss about this. It's probably the closest three wise men are ever gonna get to the capitol, so what say we just leave them be?"

Although the election confirmed many observers' belief that Richards' ads were more effective than Feinstein's, neither did their subject full justice, and neither solved the problem of showing a woman candidate to be tough enough for the office she sought without alienating voters who thought her too hard. As Bill Carrick said in the Berkeley postmortem: "We got beaten up as much as I've ever been beaten up in public life for some of the commercials we did during the course of the summer. It turned a lot of our base [voters] off . . . our women's support was fugitive during that period . . . because they didn't like the way the campaign was being run." He added wistfully that if a woman seems less tough than her opponent, however, she "will fall off the edge of the [political] globe."

But male media consultants may have an image of toughness that is inappropriate for women candidates. Although Harrison Hickman's polls and focus groups showed that Richards' positives went up in response to her positive television spots, for instance, he never managed to persuade Bob Squier to do ads connecting Richards to that Barbara Stanwyck no-nonsense frontier woman. A month after she was sworn in as governor, Richards still had high negatives, and this was in part because her television campaign had not fully capitalized on her strengths.

In her best-selling book, *You Just Don't Understand*, Deborah Tannen shows that men and women do not speak quite the same language. Thus it is tantalizing to imagine that women consultants might be able to design ads that capture and communicate women's political strengths better than men have done. There is no more mystery or genius necessarily involved in political communication than there is in anything else in politics, and it is a field wide open to women. That Wellstone's ads were designed at cost by people without big-time experience in political advertising, and that Richards and Feinstein paid consultants millions for theirs, suggests that the consultants' expertise may be overrated.

*　　*　　*

From Richards' experience, other women who go into politics with unconventional résumés can find tips on how to persuade their audience that they are prepared for the job they are seeking. Although Jim Mattox, for example, insisted contemptuously that Ann Richards was little more than a media creation, that she had done nothing that qualified her for office, the truth was that her credentials, like many women's, were simply different from his. For a long time to come, women will be fighting the quota battle, with the combatants on one side clinging to a narrow standard of merit and those on the other insisting that several criteria should be brought to bear. (As the distinguished Harvard sociologist David Riesman has pointed out, if SAT rankings had been important at the time, Franklin Delano Roosevelt and many other outstanding Americans would never have been admitted to Harvard.)

In 1984, Richards talked to *Austin American-Statesman* reporter Dave McNeely about what she had learned as a homemaker and mother that she took into the world of paid work to help her create a spirit at the treasury that inspired people to do their best. "We [as housewives] are trained in detail," she said, "and we are expected to juggle a lot of balls at once. . . . I think most of us believed all the expectations of the supposedly great American woman: all that junk about being a nurse, a chauffeur, a chef, a lover, and a perfect everything. We really tried to do all that. And most of us still do, even when we know that we're just cheap help."

When she took over a drab state office, she took down the somber pictures of her predecessors and hung paintings from Laguna Gloria, a local art museum, and the place began to look dramatically different. She actually listened to her employees and asked them to call her "Ann," which in itself was enough to make the nearby Balcones Fault shift. She sent flowers to bankers with warm notes of thanks. If employees did a particularly good job, she would reward them with an odd toy or a funny sticker, and at Christmas the staff were invited to decorate their doors and compete for prizes. As one man said, "That created a kind of camaraderie that I don't think existed much before then."

Richards had also learned that you don't get "quality performances" from people by intimidating or frightening them. "I've done a lot of things because I was afraid," she told McNeely, "but I didn't do them over and over again—I tried to avoid them. So I think bosses and managers who instill that fear in the long run are not very good." In part because Richards was fair, she got what Suzanne Coleman calls "an incredible level of loyalty from her staff, even though she works them hard enough to kill them." Their loyalty, Coleman concludes, "demonstrates that she is very good with people. You can't teach somebody that."

It is tempting to imagine that women politicians in the future will emulate Feinstein's life rather than Richards', establishing a career early and pursuing it single-mindedly. But two crucial incalculables make prediction risky. One has to do with children, the other with husbands.

Many women will want to bring up their own children, and many will want to have more than one. And for all the professed willingness of a new generation of husbands and fathers to share more responsibility for child rearing, women will go on doing most of the work. Anyone who doubts this should read *The Second Shift* by Berkeley sociologist Arlie Hochschild. As Ann Richards put it in her autobiography: "Keeping a household fairly clean and attractive and decorated, putting good food on the table, getting children delivered to the various places they need to be; fighting the battle of the PTA or the school board, being involved peripherally in political races, volunteering at school, being room mother—I mean, you have here a tossed salad that's bigger than most bowls." On paper, bringing up children looks far more manageable—and perhaps less rewarding—than it often turns out to be. No doubt that is why so many women in the past decade have left promising careers to stay home while their children are young.

But politics is something women at home with children can do more readily than, say, law. A serious campaign involves scores of jobs—among them fund-raising—that can be done outside an office and in the company of children. A woman who proves herself as a volunteer, who works in one campaign after another and learns how to do the many tasks that must be done, and done well, in a winning race will have laid the foundation for a career in electoral politics.

Young women who decide in the future to spend some time at home raising their children will be more self-conscious than Ann

Richards and the women of her generation about where their political involvements may lead and how to get there most expeditiously. But they will still face the intractable problem that Richards described about the days when David would come home and she would find herself at a loss for something gripping to tell him: "Of course, I didn't have anything stimulating and interesting to say, because all I'd done was either chase a pet mouse that had gotten loose in the house or a crushed lizard, or the plumber didn't come, or the kids set fire to the oven and the firemen had to. . . ." So the actual time between their initial volunteer efforts and their professional involvements may well be telescoped. But they will not be doing things that are radically different.

Technology has changed politics irrevocably, and envelope-stuffing parties will be less common in large urban areas. Professional consultants run more of the show. But neither machines nor experts will ever eliminate ordinary people: campaigns will always need them to make telephone calls, distribute leaflets and yard signs, and get voters to the polls. Ann Richards will not be the last to prove that from such inconspicuous beginnings, dramatically successful careers can grow.

If bringing up children will inevitably make a woman's career pattern more eccentric than a man's, an even more intractable problem for political women will be men. Many American men seem to have egos too fragile to accept, much less enjoy, a conspicuously successful wife. One graceful exception to the rule is Garry Trudeau, the creator of the comic strip "Doonesbury." His wife, Jane Pauley, is probably better known to the public at large than he, although he is at the top of his own field and has a following that amounts to a cult. Another is James Schroeder, who left his law practice in Colorado when his wife, Patricia, was elected to Congress and who became a successful Washington lawyer. One of Pat Schroeder's most trusted advisers, he is a man who seems at ease with himself, and by all accounts, their marriage is solid.

But a political career will always be hard on marriage. Beyond the question of male ego in a culture that has conditioned men to expect far more deference than is good even for them, much less for the women who do the deferring, politics is like a vacuum with a diesel engine that sucks up every millisecond of available time. One of the worst things about it—and the reason most healthy, normal people will not go into it—is that it decimates private life. Politicians have so many people to placate, if not to please, that the higher their office, the less free time they have.

On the most obvious level, there are voting constituencies they lose touch with at their peril: the politician who does not go to prayer breakfasts, Rotary lunches, and backyard clambakes or barbecues, depending on the region and season, has a seat as enviably secure as Congressman Henry Waxman's in Los Angeles or Charles Rangel's in Harlem. Most politicians who want to keep their jobs show up at graduations, bar—and now bas—mitzvahs, christenings, weddings, funerals, and festivals of ancient saints and long-dead heroes.

If technological changes mean that most politicians today have less direct contact with voters than their predecessors, they have far more contact with contributors. In these days of multi-million-dollar races, a candidate running for a statewide office almost has to have big donors. Former Senator Lawton Chiles's successful campaign to become governor of Florida—a campaign that limited contributions to $100 each—proves the rule by its very uniqueness.

As Hadley Roff puts it, it takes as much time and money to process $25 and $50 checks as it does to process $1,000 checks. This puts a premium on large contributors, many of whom expect to share at least an occasional lunch or dinner with the candidate or intrude in one way or another on what passes for her leisure. (Their more substantial expectations are another matter.)

Finally, politicians have colleagues who can sail their programs through or bury them in committee, and the higher the office, the larger the number of people whose goodwill matters. It takes a big staff to run a governor's office, and after securing their loyalty, if not their affection, the governor will need to court her lieutenant governor, attorney general, and secretary of state, along with legislators and many hundreds of members of boards and commissions.

Recognizing the existence of all these people, much less cultivating their goodwill, takes time that extends far beyond the hours of nine to five. A high-ranking assistant to Kathryn Whitmire, former mayor of Houston, called this process frog-kissing. American women have been brought up to kiss frogs. American men have not. And the prospect that they would enjoy sharing their wives with frogs is meager.

If a high-stakes political woman has a marriage that self-destructs, and if no congenial man appears who is willing to put up with the special hazards of marriage to a politician, on top of the hazards of marriage generally, she should expect to be called a lesbian. The insinuations about Ann Richards made most of the rounds, and there is no way to calculate the damage: Richards *did* win the election, though at the last minute. Still, it would be a mistake to underestimate either the psychological scars that vicious charges leave behind, or their potential for decimating the ranks of voters.

Middle-aged women who are seriously involved in politics and who lose their spouses are even more likely than their peers to spend the rest of their lives without sexual companionship. They will not be alone—politicians are never alone unless they fight to be. But no woman who has had a happy marriage will honestly give up the possibility of touching and holding, much less sexuality, without an abiding sense of loss, and the prospect of destroying her marriage by plunging into politics may well turn many a woman away.

Although politics at the highest levels is very, very hard, there is nothing strange or mystical about it, and the lessons are there for women to learn as they gradually take their places in equal numbers in the legislatures and statehouses of the United States of America.

The toughest lesson is at once the simplest: first, they need to separate their own sense of self from the flattened and caricatured image that politics invariably creates. As Ann Richards learned, "It is very important for those of us in the public eye to develop what I call the inner light. Your identity has to be inside you: it cannot be external."

Until those who go into politics can make that separation, they will be wracked with pain, anger, and impotence at being criticized and misrepresented, and their emotions will make them liable to mistakes like Dianne Feinstein's in the ads that earned the sobriquet Church Lady I and II. According to her pollster, Ed Reilly, Feinstein did the latter, which accused Pete Wilson of lying, "because she felt so strongly about it," and Wilson campaign director Otto Bos admitted that they had goaded her. Highly charged emotion, as Bos knew, seldom lends itself to good judgment.

After that, the rest is simple, although it will never be easy. Women now have the chance to take "their private pain, their private hopes, their private aspirations" as outsiders in a world that men created and, as Ernesto Cortes taught, "translate those into public issues which can qualitatively improve their lives and the lives of their children."

Almost a year after the 1990 elections, many women found their status as outsiders made abundantly clear as they watched the surprising last stage of the Senate Judiciary Committee hearings on the nomination of Clarence Thomas to the U.S. Supreme Court. Two days before the scheduled final vote, the public learned that Thomas had been accused by University of Oklahoma law professor Anita Hill of sexually harassing her ten years earlier when she was his assistant in the Education Department and then at the Equal Employment Opportunity Commission. Women also learned that members of the Judiciary Committee, all of whom were white men, had known of the charges for some time and had apparently dismissed them. Senate switchboards were jammed by protests against what seemed a callous disregard for a reputable woman, and seven female members of Congress charged across to the Senate to insist that their colleagues take these accusations seriously.

During the three days that the nation sat transfixed by the televised hearings, more than one male columnist would be offended by Hill's treatment at the hands of the Republicans on the committee. "She had to be destroyed by suggestion," Russell Baker wrote: "The burden of these [damaging speculations] was that she might be mentally or emotionally disturbed . . . a woman driven to horrible acts by poisonous imbalances of hormones and mental juices."

Baker's disgust was nothing compared to the outrage many women felt, and leaders of women's groups vowed to defeat the senators they considered abusive to Hill. The National Women's Political Caucus took out a full-page ad in *The New York Times* with a drawing of seven women sitting in the Judiciary Committee chairs looking down on Thomas. The caption read "What If?" Above a membership application were the words: "Turn your anger into action. Join us."

Theirs was a modest version of the great hope that the former slave Sojourner Truth expressed a century and a half ago: "If the first woman God ever made could turn the world upside down all alone, these women together ought to be able to get it rightside up again!"

SOURCES

The interviews on which this book is based were done in 1990 unless otherwise indicated.

INTERVIEWS REGARDING ANN RICHARDS:

Kirk Adams (12/8); Bob Armstrong (9/25); Libba Barnes (9/12); Alan Bernstein (9/18); Sissy Bravo (9/11); Bob Brischetto (9/11, 12/27, 4/10/91); George Bristol (9/14); John Bryant (11/8); Mickey Buchan (9/19); Julie Burton (12/7); Alma Butler (9/16); Liz Carpenter (9/20, 9/23, 11/7); Billie Carr (9/8–9); George Christian (9/25); Nancy Clack (9/22, 11/28); Suzanne Coleman (1/24/91); Bill Cryer (9/1, 9/24); Joe Cutbirth (9/9, 3/20/91); Chandler Davidson (9/16, 1/19/91); Leslie Dawson (12/29); Sam Dawson (9/10, 11/5, 12/29); Phyllis Dunham (12/14); Al Edwards (9/18); Rodney Ellis (9/18); Jane Ely (9/17, 9/27); Frances "Sissy" Farenthold (9/17); Tim Fleck (9/17); Martin Frost (11/8); Ernestine Glossbrenner (9/27); Larry Goodwyn (9/8); Harriet Griffin (9/20); Hollis Grizzard (9/23); Susan Gross (9/4); Lena Guerrero (3/14/91); Jane Hickie (9/15, 12/17); Harrison Hickman (12/5); Jim Hightower (9/13); Bill Hobby (9/17); Joe Holley (9/21, 3/19/91); Jan Jarboe (9/20); Franklin Jones (9/15); Margaret Justus (12/13); Cinny Kennard (12/14); Carole Kneeland (11/4, 1/20/91); Sheila Jackson Lee (9/18); Gary Lipe (9/13); Jack Martin (9/26); Jim Mattox (12/27); Janelle McArthur (9/12); David G. McComb (11/20); John J. McDermott (9/19); Mark McKinnon (12/11); Dave McNeely (9/7, 11/4); Darla Morgan (9/9); Judith Moyers (9/23, 1/16/91); Richard Murray (9/4, 10/23); Kaye Northcott (9/12); Ginger Purdy (9/9); Janie Reyes (9/18); Ann Richards (9/24, 1/7/91, 3/14/91); Cecile Richards (9/21); Dan Richards (12/15); David Richards (9/21); Robert Riggs (12/12); Geoffrey Rips (9/15); Mary Beth Rogers (9/15, 12/26); Judd Rose (12/17); Anne Schwartz (12/7); Juan Sepulveda (9/26, 11/5); Wendy Sherman (8/21); George Shipley (9/25, 12/27, 3/18/91); Dee Simpson (9/25, 10/17, 1/7/91); Maizie Simpson (9/9); Martha Smiley (9/23); Glenn Smith (9/26); Bob Squier (12/11, 12/20); Mimi Swartz (9/18); Linda Chavez Thompson (9/20); Saralee Tiede (9/19); Paul Tully (12/16); Janie Velasquez (9/12); Kathleen Voigt (9/12, 9/23); John Edward Weems (9/22); Michael Whitehurst (9/13); Virginia Whitten (11/7, 3/14/91); Harriett Woods (1/26/91); Carol Yontz (11/27)

INTERVIEWS REGARDING DIANNE FEINSTEIN:

A. G. Block (10/9); Bill Boyarsky (10/22, 3/9/91); Martha Bredon (10/15); Edmund G. (Pat) Brown (10/23); Willie Brown (10/14); Bill Carrick (10/25); Donna Damson (11/1); Lee Dembart (10/11); Peter Donahue (1/16/91); Troy Duster (10/13); Thomas B. Edsall (1/6/91); Dianne Feinstein (1/10/91); Herb Fredman (10/31); Henri Galina-Rosin (10/25); Elaine Gallinson (10/31); Rotea Gilford (10/14); Gina Glantz (10/15); Herbert Gold (10/16); Joe Holley (9/21, 3/19/91); John Jacobs (5/10/91); Sherry Bebitch Jeffe (10/18); Janice Kamenir-Reznick (11/3); Connie Koenen (10/1, 10/27); Celinda Lake (12/19, 1/26/91); Bob Lawson (10/30); Pacy Markman (10/2); Richard Martinez (1/24/91); Jay Mathews (10/5); George Metrovich (10/31);

Bobbie Metzger (10/9); Kay Mills (10/3, 10/19); Lynn Montgomery (10/9); Hank Morris (10/25); Jean O'Leary (11/2, 3/23/91); Rick Orlov (10/28); John Plaxco (10/25); Tony Quinn (10/10); Joyce Ream (10/8, 10/15); Daralyn Reed (3/6/91); Ed Reilly (1/31/91); Vicky Rideout (11/2); Hadley Roff (10/30, 2/11/91); Suzanne Rosentsweig (10/19, 10/24); Bob Schelen (10/10); Lynn Schenk (10/31); Michael Schneider (10/15); Robin Schneider (10/3); Peter Schrag (10/10); Derek Shearer (10/24); Stanley Sheinbaum (10/17); Jim Shoendig (10/4); Martin Smith (10/10); Darry Sragow (10/22, 12/11, 3/3/91); Mark Stein (10/17); Barbara Stemple (11/1); John Sullivan (10/4); Margery Tabankin (10/23); Beverly Thomas (10/20, 10/22); Esteban Torres (1/26/91); Beegie Truesdale (10/25); Hope Warschaw (10/24); Maxine Waters (4/12/91); Diane E. Watson (10/24); Jane Wellman (10/10); Cecil Williams (10/16); Jan Williams (10/16); Michael Woo (10/22); Julie Wright (11/26, 2/20/91); Susan Yoachum (10/16, 1/18/91); Tony Zamora (1/16/91); Richard Zeiger (10/9); Bill Zimmerman (10/3, 10/26)

Additional commentary about Dianne Feinstein's campaign comes from official transcripts of the Berkeley conference on the 1990 California gubernatorial race, held Jan. 18–19, 1991.

Unless otherwise indicated, the biographical material about Ann Richards comes from her autobiography, *Straight from the Heart: My Life in Politics and Other Places* (Simon and Schuster, 1989), which she wrote with Peter Knobler. The following articles have also been useful: Vicki Haddock, "The Wit and Wisdom of Ann Richards," *San Francisco Examiner*, Jan. 27, 1991; J. Michael Kennedy, "The Cowboy and the Good Ol' Girl," *Los Angeles Times Magazine*, Oct. 21, 1990; Dave McNeely, "A Lone Star," *D Magazine*, Sept. 1984; Sara Sanborn, "Ann Richards's Success Story," *Ms.*, June 1984; Mimi Swartz, "Ann Richards: How Perfection Led to Failure," *Texas Monthly*, Oct. 1990.

Unless otherwise indicated, the biographical material about Dianne Feinstein comes from the following articles: Sidney Blumenthal, "A Woman of Independent Means," *New Republic*, Aug. 13, 1990; Cynthia Gorney, "Dianne Feinstein in the Corridors of Power . . . ," Style section, *Washington Post*, June 25, 1984; Keith Love, "Will Dianne Feinstein Play in Pacoima?" *Los Angeles Times Magazine*, Feb. 25, 1990; George Raine, "Tough Love," *San Francisco Examiner*, Oct. 28, 1990; J. D. Reed and Dianna Waggoner, "Dianne Feinstein," *People*, Oct. 8, 1990; Robin Toner, "California Showdown," *New York Times Magazine*, Sept. 30, 1990; Garry Wills, "Guv Lite!" *California*, Nov. 1990; Susan Yoachum, "Smiling Through," *San Jose Mercury News*, Jan. 14, 1990.

ADDITIONAL MAGAZINE ARTICLES:

John Balzar, "John Van de Kamp Pleads His Own Case," *Los Angeles Times Magazine*, Jan. 14, 1990

Ronald Brownstein, "Robopol," *Los Angeles Times Magazine*, May 13, 1990

Jan Jarboe, "Onward to the Past," *Texas Monthly*, Oct. 1990

Richard Jonathon Rapaport, "Those Bad, Bad Burton Boys and the Postmodern Liberal Blues," *California*, April 1988

William Schneider and Patrick Reddy, "Altered States," *American Enterprise*, July–
    August 1990
Mike Shropshire, "Texas Crude," *D Magazine*, Sept. 1990
Darry Sragow with John Jacobs, "Democracy Inc.," Image section, *San Francisco
    Examiner*, Jan. 6, 1991

NEWSPAPER ESSAYS:

Bill Lambrecht, William H. Freivogel, and Margaret Wolf Freivogel, *St. Louis Post-
    Dispatch*, 4/17–20: four-part postmortem on Richard Gephardt's campaign for
    the Democratic presidential nomination
Mark Tatge, "Williams' image, business history differ," *Dallas Morning News*, Aug.
    5, 1990

BOOKS:

Robert Caro, *The Path to Power* (New York: Alfred A. Knopf, 1982)
Chandler Davidson, *Race and Class in Texas Politics* (Princeton: Princeton Uni-
    versity Press, 1990)
Celia Morris Eckhardt, *Fanny Wright: Rebel in America* (Cambridge, Mass.: Har-
    vard University Press, 1984; Champaign: University of Illinois Press, 1992)
Arlie Hochschild, *The Second Shift* (New York: Viking, 1989)
Larry L. King, *Confessions of a White Racist* (New York: Viking, 1971)
Willie Morris, *North Toward Home* (Boston: Houghton Mifflin, 1967)
Kevin Phillips, *The Politics of Rich and Poor* (New York: Random House, 1990)
Mary Beth Rogers, *Cold Anger* (Denton: University of North Texas Press, 1990)
Deborah Tannen, *You Just Don't Understand* (New York: Morrow, 1990)

FILM:

Ernesto Cortes interview with Bill Moyers, "A World of Ideas," PBS, Nov. 18, 1990
Dianne Feinstein interview on the "MacNeil/Lehrer News Hour," Oct. 9, 1990
"Give Them Wings," celebrating the life of Helen Farabee, produced by Electronic
    Data Systems for the Texas Foundation for Human Services
Judd Rose, "Texas Crude," on ABC's "Prime Time," Aug. 16, 1990
Lesley Stahl, "Face the Nation," April 8, 1990

REPORTS:

Celinda Lake, "Campaigning in a Different Voice" (EMILY's List, 1989) and "Chal-
    lenging the Credibility Gap" (EMILY's List, 1991)
Bob Lawson and Larry Tramutola, "A Report on the Field Operation of California
    Campaign '88," Dec. 19, 1988

CONFERENCES:

"Campaign '90: A Look Back at the California Governor's Race," Institute of
    Governmental Studies, University of California at Berkeley, Jan. 18–19, 1991
    (participants included key political operatives from the Feinstein, Van de Kamp,
    and Wilson campaigns)
"Conference on the Future of the Democratic Party," sponsored by the Coalition
    for Democratic Values, Jan. 26, 1991 (participants included Harvey Gantt, Sen-
    ator Tom Harkin, Senator Paul Wellstone)

"Women and Texas History," panel on "Texas Women and Politics," Oct. 4, 1990
(participants included Liz Carpenter, Hazel Falke-Obey, Frances ["Sissy"] Farenthold, Elizabeth Fox-Genovese, Kathryn J. Whitmire. Tape available at the
Barker Texas History Center, University of Texas at Austin)

STATISTICS:

Children's Defense Fund; Election Data Service; United States Department of Labor;
Women's Research and Education Institute of the Congressional Caucus for Wom-
en's Issues

INDEX

Ely, Jane, 79, 99, 141, 162
EMILY's List, 46, 98–99, 291
Environmental issues: in California, 208–210, 224–225 and n., 226, 241 and n.–242n., 269, 270, 277; in Texas, 116, 123, 158
Eppstein, Bryan, 160
Equal Rights Amendment (ERA), 44, 45
Evans, Rowland, 162

"Face the Nation" (TV show), 94, 101–102
Falke-Obey, Hazel, 62
Farabee, Helen, 67, 120
Farenthold, Frances (Sissy), 23, 44, 95–96, 97, 99–100 and n., 118, 166
Faulkner, Danny, 90
Federal budget debacle, of 1990, 8–9, 165, 167
Federal Bureau of Investigation (FBI), 22, 158
Feinstein, Bertram, 19, 25, 181, 186
Feinstein, Dianne, 4–6, 72n., 169, 178–304; on abortion, 14, 229, 231, 255–258, 263, 290–291; on AIDS medications, 233; antivice campaign of, 192, 195; assessment of her 1990 campaign, 282–304; background of, 6–7, 18–20, 178, 182–186; campaign problems of, 216, 220, 227, 242, 261–280; on capital punishment, 6, 8, 226–227, 229, 233, 238, 270, 274; on civil rights, 14, 195, 256–257, 274; considered for 1984 Democratic vice-presidential nomination, 5–6, 25, 179, 203, 291; Coro fellowship of, 18–19 and n., 186; on crime, 195–196, 269, 270;

decision to run for governor, 179, 183, 202–213, 214–215; on economic and social issues, 193–197; education of, 18–19, 185–186; on environmental issues, 224–225 and n., 269–270; and female support for, 183, 185, 196, 217–218, 227, 230–233, 236, 249, 254, 255–259, 262, 268, 279–280, 290; first marriage of, 19, 186; fund-raising and spending of, 25, 145, 208, 215, 216–224, 229, 248, 249, 251n., 254, 260, 264, 266, 267–268, 271, 277, 279 and n., 280, 287–289; on gay rights, 196–197; and grass-roots effort, 243–245, 247–249, 260; on gun control, 195–196; house parties of, 260; hysterectomy of, 216, 217; income of, 8, 280; and initiative process, 208–210, 216; and labor support for, 187, 196, 218, 227, 236; last weeks of gubernatorial campaign, 271–277; losing vote of, 278, 287, 288, 290; as mayor of San Francisco, 9, 20, 181–184, 187, 193–197, 205, 221, 222, 231, 234, 235, 258, 263, 270, 272n., 292; media campaign of, 204, 218–220, 228–236, 242–243, 247–248, 261–279 and n., 289, 294, 298, 303; and minority support for, 188–192, 232–233, 236, 249–253, 256–257, 261–264, 292–295; and murder of George Moscone, 180–181, 193, 228–229; and negative campaigning, 27–28, 234–236, 261–268 and n., 273–274, 277–279, 303; newspaper endorsements of, 276–277;